Instructor's Resource Manual

to accompany

Psychology of Success

Finding Meaning in Work and Life

Fourth Edition

Denis Waitley, Ph.D.

Boston   Burr Ridge, IL   Dubuque, IA   Madison, WI   New York   San Francisco   St. Louis
Bangkok   Bogotá   Caracas   Kuala Lumpur   Lisbon   London   Madrid   Mexico City
Milan   Montreal   New Delhi   Santiago   Seoul   Singapore   Sydney   Taipei   Toronto

Mc Graw Hill Higher Education

Instructor's Resource Manual to accompany
PSYCHOLOGY OF SUCCESS: FINDING MEANING IN WORK AND LIFE

2 3 4 5 6 7 8 9   QPD/QPD   07 06 05 04

ISBN 0-07-829977-2

www.mhhe.com

TABLE OF CONTENTS

PART 1
INSTRUCTOR RESOURCES

INTRODUCTION

Welcome to the *Psychology of Success Instructor's Resource Manual*. This manual is designed to facilitate effective teaching. It gives suggestions for organizing your course, handling common classroom issues, presenting material, and leading activities.

Goals of the Book

Psychology of Success is a valuable teaching tool for courses designed to help students prepare for success in school, work, and life. It equips students with the skills and personal qualities they will need to set, pursue, and attain their goals.

Psychology of Success sets the following objectives for its student users. By reading the text and completing the activities, students will:

- understand the basic principles of psychology
- develop a clear vision of what success means to them
- gain self-awareness and emotional awareness
- pinpoint their personality traits, values, skills, interests, and career preferences
- set specific, achievable short- and long-term goals
- learn strategies for coping with stress, anger, and other negative emotions
- improve their self-image and self-esteem
- break negative thought patterns and learn positive new ones
- harness self-discipline to control impulses, break bad habits, and make positive life changes
- develop critical thinking and decision-making skills
- examine what motivates them and why
- overcome fear of failure and fear of success
- manage their time and money effectively
- become effective speakers and active listeners
- appreciate diversity and reject stereotypes and prejudice
- build skills necessary for fulfilling, healthy relationships

Themes of the Book

Several themes are emphasized throughout the text. You may wish to discuss these themes on the first day of class in order to preview the course content.

- **Goals are crucial for success.** Self-direction, the ability to set well-defined goals and work toward them, is crucial for success. Goals give our lives direction and help us organize our time, energy, and effort around the things that matter the most to us. Goals motivate us and help us take charge of our lives. Goals are stepping stones to our dreams. Goals provide standards by which we can measure our progress, and they give us a sense of achievement. Setting and achieving a series of goals is an effective way to boost self-esteem, overcome fears, and build skills.
- **Success is personal.** There is no one "correct" definition of success. Each of us must examine what we want from life and from ourselves and clarify our personal vision of success. Other people's skills, qualities, possessions, and achievements can inspire us, but we should measure our progress by our standards, not others'.

- **Self-awareness is essential for a meaningful life.** Before anyone can answer the question, "Where do I want to go in life?" he or she must be able to answer the question, "Who am I?" Self-awareness, the ability to pay attention to oneself, is the prerequisite for making the choices that are right for us. Self-awareness helps us set goals, overcome obstacles, and feel comfortable with ourselves.
- **Self-esteem is a right.** Self-esteem is more than simply a feel-good concept. Every person is unique and valuable, and every person has the right to enjoy self-esteem—confidence in and respect for him- or herself. People with low self-esteem anticipate failure and think they are unworthy of success. They therefore have difficulty setting and achieving goals, taking risks, making changes, and building relationships. Low self-esteem can also cause a great deal of emotional pain.
- **Success is a choice.** What sets successful people apart from unsuccessful people is their willingness to take charge of their lives, to pursue opportunities, and to make their goals happen. Each of us, no matter what our life circumstances, can make a conscious choice to become more self-aware and self-confident, to work hard, to build self-discipline and self-motivation, and to persist until we achieve our goals.

New and Expanded Topics

The fourth edition of *Psychology of Success* has been extensively updated and expanded to respond to your needs and the needs of your students. The new edition contains extensive new pedagogical features. The chapter introduction, chapter objectives, and summary by learning objectives help students preview and review chapter content, while the key terms and section self-checks help students focus on important concepts as they read. Each Real-Life Success Story has been revised to better reflect the choices facing today's diverse students. Follow-up activities to each Real-Life Success Story call on students to complete the vignettes in a satisfying way. The new *Psychology of Success* also includes new and expanded coverage of these important topics:

- goals of psychology
- cognition and emotion
- identity and the self
- values, personality traits, skills, intelligences, and interests
- stress and anger management
- self-acceptance and self-esteem
- body image and the media
- healthy lifestyles
- cognitive distortions and irrational beliefs
- critical thinking standards
- the decision-making process
- motivation
- time and money management
- the communication process
- effective speaking and active listening
- relationship skills and conflict management

These expanded topics are accompanied by completely revised and expanded in-chapter Exercises and Personal Journals, as well as critical thinking questions and Application and Internet activities.

ORGANIZATION AND CONTENT

The Student Edition

The student edition of *Psychology of Success: Finding Meaning in Work and Life* contains nine chapters that ideally should be taught in sequence. Each chapter offers a variety of features and pedagogical tools to encourage student interest and involvement.

Real-Life Success Story

Begin each chapter by reading the Real-Life Success Story, a vignette about an ordinary person struggling with the problems and challenges addressed in the chapter. Use the question following the story to have students put themselves in that person's shoes and to assess how much they already know about the topic of the coming chapter. At the end of the chapter, use the follow-up activity for the Real-Life Success Story to reinforce key concepts and provide a satisfying resolution to the character's problem.

Chapter Introduction and Objectives

Every chapter has an introduction and a list of objectives that preview the chapter's subject matter and set expectations. Suggest to students that they read the introduction and objectives before they begin the chapter, then review them afterwards. You can also use the chapter objectives to assess whether students have understood the main points of the chapter.

Opening Quote

Each chapter features an opening quote that sets the tone of the chapter and prompts students to think about the subject. Ask students whether they consider the quote to be thoughtful, intriguing, or interesting. Suggest that they bring in additional quotes, cartoons, or stories that relate to the chapter's subject matter.

Key Terms

Each section begins with a list of bolded key terms that will be discussed in the chapter. Definitions of each key term appear in the margin at the point in the text where they are discussed. Suggest to students that they skim the key terms in order to familiarize themselves with the coming section. Key terms, along with italicized terms, are defined in the Glossary beginning on page 393.

Keys to Success

The Key to Success feature appears in the margins of each chapter to help students remember main lessons and action points of the chapter. Lists of Keys to Success for each chapter are provided as reproducible masters in Part 4 of this Instructor's Resource Manual. They can be used to preview and review the chapter, as well as to call students' attention to important principles of success that they can use in their daily lives.

Exercises

Each chapter has five to seven Exercises that are an integral part of the material. These Exercises allow students to apply newly learned concepts to their own lives through self-assessment, real-world observation, and critical thinking. Exercises are generally two pages in length, although some extend to three or more pages. (For suggestions on grading Exercise responses, see the grading suggestions on page 43.)

Personal Journals

Each chapter also has several Personal Journals, short notebook-style activities that let students pause to offer personal reflections on the material. You may wish to use these as ungraded (credit/no credit) homework assignments or as in-class activities.

Internet Action

Appearing once per chapter, this technology feature discusses how to use computers, the Internet, and e-mail effectively. It also illustrates the link between technology and psychology in areas such as artificial intelligence and online learning.

Applying Psychology

This feature links one or more chapter topics to cutting-edge issues in psychology. It focuses on thought-provoking issues such as memory, personality testing, and the psychology of aging. Use the critical thinking question at the end of the Applying Psychology feature to spark class discussion and to link the material in *Psychology of Success* to the study of general psychology.

Professional Development

Professional development is the continuous process of building knowledge and skills in order to grow as a person and a professional. The Professional Development feature makes chapter concepts relevant to the world of work, providing information on topics such as job stress, multitasking, and résumé writing. This feature also provides an opportunity to stress to students that all workers, whatever their fields and educational backgrounds, need to continue to learn throughout their careers.

Chapter Review and Activities

The three pages of chapter review and activities give students an opportunity to expand their understanding of chapter concepts and to apply what they've learned to real-world situations. This section has seven parts:

- **Key Term Review** lists the chapter's key terms and references
- **Summary by Learning Objectives** summarizes the chapter's main themes to help students check their progress
- **Review Questions** test students' recall and understanding of chapter concepts
- **Critical Thinking** questions encourage students to think deeply and creatively about the material
- **Application** activities help students see the relevance of chapter concepts in real-world settings
- **Internet Activities** ask students to use relevant, up-to-date Internet resources to explore chapter topics and conduct independent research
- **Real-Life Success Story** follow-up activity brings the chapter full circle, asking students to use what they have learned to resolve the situation described at the beginning of the chapter

Supplementary Critical Thinking questions and Application and Internet activities for each chapter are provided in this *Psychology of Success Instructor's Resource Manual*.

Consult all the available activities before deciding which to assign as homework and which to use in class.

Further Reading

The books listed on pages 391–392 are suggested further reading for students. These titles have been selected not only for their subject matter but also for their readability, engaging style, and positive tone. Encourage students to use critical thinking to explore these authors' ideas. You may wish to ask each student to select a book to review and share with the rest of the class. You may also suggest that students consult the further reading list before they begin a research project for the class.

Glossary

The Glossary, which begins on page 393, provides definitions for all key terms in the text as well as for all terms that appear in italics. Italicized terms represent concepts with which students may not be familiar. Point out to students that they should look up all unfamiliar italicized terms as they read.

The Instructor's Resource Manual

The *Psychology of Success Instructor's Resource Manual* is divided into four parts:

Part 1 • Instructor Resources
Part 2 • Chapter Notes and Answers
Part 3 • Tests and Answer Keys
Part 4 • Reproducible Masters

Part 1 • Instructor Resources

Materials in the Instructor Resources section are intended to help you use *Psychology of Success* in an effective student success course. This part of the IRM includes:

- organization and content of the student text and the IRM
- goals and themes of *Psychology of Success*
- suggestions for planning a successful course, including suggestions for day-one and day-two activities
- overview of cooperative and experiential learning
- strategies for helping students with special needs
- suggestions for handling common classroom problems

Part 2 • Chapter Notes and Answers

The second part of this IRM contains chapter-by-chapter notes and answers. For each chapter in the student edition, it provides:

- chapter overview and objectives
- list of chapter topics, Exercises, Personal Journals, and features
- strategies and tips for introducing each major chapter topic
- additional activities
- answer keys for Exercises, Personal Journals, figure and feature caption questions, and end-of-chapter review and activities
- sample answers
- tips for further exploration of chapter topics and activities

- culminating activity
- suggestions for implementing the Personal Success Portfolio project
- book and periodical references, including the titles listed in the further reading list in the student edition as well as academic and research-oriented titles that you may wish to explore or assign to more advanced students

Part 3 • Tests and Answer Keys

This section includes reproducible assessment materials. A reproducible one-page quiz and three-page test are provided for each of the nine chapters in *Psychology of Success*. Each quiz contains ten vocabulary questions and one brief-answer question. Each test contains ten completion questions, ten multiple-choice questions, and two short-answer questions. A midterm exam follows the Chapter 5 test, and a final exam follows the Chapter 9 test. The midterm and final exams, which are exclusively short-answer-based, ask students to make connections across chapters, to apply concepts to real-world situations, and to back up their ideas with critical thinking and evidence. Answer keys for all quizzes, tests, and exams begin on page 215.

Part 4 • Reproducible Masters

Part 4 contains a chapter-by-chapter collection of visual resources that can be used to make handouts or transparencies. In this section you will find:

- Personal Success Portfolio worksheets
- opening quotes from each chapter, along with a selection of further thought-provoking quotes relevant to the chapter content
- Keys to Success from each chapter
- figures from each chapter
- supplementary figures
- worksheets and figures for use with additional activities

COURSE PLANNING

Course Goals

Thorough planning is the foundation of a successful course. When you sit down to plan your course, first review the philosophy, goals, and themes of the book. Write the course purpose in your own words. Make sure you have a clear vision of what you want students to gain from this class.

Write down your goals for the course. Review your purpose for each class period. Writing down your goals helps you clarify your methods, communicate expectations to students, and evaluate your success. It is often helpful for students to see the class objective(s) written on the board for each class period.

Course Relevance

Student success courses can be extremely rewarding for both students and instructors. Some students, however, see this kind of course as irrelevant to their studies and career. To overcome this attitude, make a continuous effort to highlight the link between school and job success and to point out real-world applications of the material.

Highlight the usefulness of and insight to be gained by applying the strategies described in *Psychology of Success* in the working world. Use the Real-Life Success Stories, the Professional Development feature, and the Application activities to guide the discussion to how success in school, work, and personal life are related. Explain the importance of the Exercises and Personal Journals as tools for developing self-awareness and critical thinking skills. Encourage students to make connections between their experiences and the situations discussed in the text. Point out that students can also use their experiences to help them understand what they are reading. Encourage them to ask themselves questions such as, "What would I do in this situation?" "How does this apply to my life?" "How could I use this strategy to …?"

Personal Success Portfolio

The Personal Success Portfolio, presented as a series of reproducible masters on pages 231–239, is a supplementary project that allows students to recap the main points of each chapter. By completing the nine worksheets in the Portfolio and collecting them in a folder or notebook, students build a tangible record of their progress. The Portfolio reflects not only what each student has learned throughout the course but also what he or she plans to do in the future to implement this learning. For example, the Personal Success Portfolio worksheet for Chapter 1 asks students to select four positive qualities that he or she intends to develop.

The Personal Success Portfolio is also designed to be expanded to suit the needs of your students and the goals of your course. For each chapter you may wish to have students complete a short research project, writing assignment, journal entry, or other creative project for inclusion in their Portfolio. You may also ask students to include an example of their best work from each chapter, such as a well-reasoned answer to a critical thinking question.

Other projects that you may wish to ask students to complete for their Personal Success Portfolios include:

- job-search-related documents, such as a chronological or skills résumé, a cover letter, and a list of references
- career-related self-assessments, either self-administered (such as the O*NET Interest Profile or the O*NET Work Values Indicator) or professionally administered (such as the Strong Interest Survey or the Myers-Briggs Type Indicator)
- a personal mission statement in which the student describes his or her purpose and how this purpose relates to his or her values and goals
- a weekly log of a semester-long project, such as a community service (service learning) project, a new extracurricular activity, or a new job

There are several ways to use the worksheets in the Personal Success Portfolio. Here are some suggestions:

- Distribute copies of the relevant chapter worksheet and assign this page as individual homework. In class, discuss students' responses. (To test students' recall and to reinforce the material, you may wish to collect the worksheets before beginning the discussion.)
- Make handouts or a transparency of the relevant worksheet and have students discuss their responses in small groups, allowing them five minutes or so at the end of the discussion to write down their responses.

- Make handouts of the relevant chapter worksheet and ask students to work in pairs, interviewing one another to elicit answers to each worksheet question. Reunite the class and have pairs share one another's answers with the rest of the class. (Ask student pairs to agree upon which items may be shared with the class and which they prefer to keep private.)
- Distribute copies of the relevant chapter worksheet and assign the page as individual homework. Begin the next class period with ten minutes of spontaneous writing on the back of the worksheet about the topic, "One thing I will remember about [chapter title] and why," or "One thing I will remember about this week of the course, and why." Ask students to share their responses, if desired.

Managing the Portfolio Process

Before implementing the Personal Career Portfolio project, think through the management of the process. Will students keep their portfolios in three-ring binders, large envelopes, folders, or something else? Where will these materials be stored, and how will you provide access to them? One method that works well is to provide a plastic packing crate with a hanging file for each student. Each hanging file should accommodate several file folders, which can be used to house the different types of documents students choose for their portfolios. If you think students will want to include oversize documents, such as art boards for showing a mock advertising campaign, consider legal size hanging files. Make sure students understand that they are responsible for the care and maintenance of their portfolios.

Including the Personal Success Portfolio in your course will require some extra class time, as well as extra time for organization and assessment. Make sure to allow time to explain the project to students, explain the assessment criteria, help students compile portfolio documents, and assess portfolio contents.

Syllabi

A syllabus adds order and organization to your course. Students want to know what to expect from you, so it is important to have a detailed written guide for them to follow and refer to throughout the semester. The syllabus should include:

- your name (and teaching assistants' or peer facilitators' names, if applicable)
- your office phone number, location, and office hours
- your e-mail address
- textbook requirements
- course purpose and objectives
- learning climate or teaching method
- course requirements
- course outline
- evaluation methods

The sample syllabus on the next two pages has been structured to follow the textbook. This syllabus emphasizes cooperative and experiential learning and puts emphasis on participation and critical thinking. You can adapt this syllabus or any of its parts to the specific needs of your class. Tell students that the syllabus is a guide and that you may change the order of topics, exercises, and guest speakers when appropriate.

Sample Syllabus for Student Success 100

Instructor: Joan Smith
Office: Jones Hall 113
Office Hours: MWF 10:00–12:00
Phone: (213) 555-0111
E-mail: smith@university.edu

Required Textbook

Psychology of Success: Finding Meaning in Work and Life, fourth edition, by Denis Waitley, McGraw-Hill © 2004.

Course Description

Student Success 100 is a freshman course designed to increase your success in school, at work, and in your personal life. The course will help you increase your self-awareness, set and pursue meaningful goals, and develop positive personal qualities such as self-esteem, a positive attitude, self-discipline, and self-motivation. This course will also help you adjust to transitions such as progressing from high school to college, returning to college, and making the leap from college to the world of work. By participating in class activities and discussions and by completing the activities in your text, you will build a valuable record of your dreams, goals, skills, interests, values, and more.

Course Objectives

This course will help you to:

- understand the basic principles of psychology
- develop a clear vision of what success means to you
- gain self-awareness and emotional awareness
- pinpoint your personality traits, values, skills, interests, and career preferences
- set specific, achievable short- and long-term goals
- learn strategies for coping with stress, anger, and other negative emotions
- improve your self-image and self-esteem
- break negative thought patterns and learn positive new ones
- harness self-discipline to control impulses, break bad habits, and make positive life changes
- develop critical thinking and decision-making skills
- examine what motivates you and why
- overcome fear of failure and fear of success
- manage your time and money effectively
- become an effective speaker and an active listener
- appreciate diversity and reject stereotypes and prejudice
- build skills necessary for fulfilling, healthy relationships

Learning Climate

This class is not a lecture course. It is structured around cooperative and experiential learning, which are based on two key concepts:

- **Cooperation**—You are actively responsible for your learning and for helping each other. I will guide and assist your learning, but I will not provide you with the one "right" answer.

- **Experience**—You gain the most from a course when you actively engage with the material. This means that you are expected to reflect on and analyze the material, to participate in class, to complete the exercises, and to apply the concepts to your own experiences.

Requirements and Expectations

- **Attendance**—You are expected to attend each class and to be on time. Much of the class progress depends on the involvement and participation of every student. Come to class prepared and ready to learn.
- **Critical Thinking**—You are expected to use critical thinking to complete exercises and to apply the concepts you are learning to your school, job, and life experiences. You are expected and encouraged to develop independent opinions and to back them up with logical reasoning and specific examples. Bring questions and comments to class.
- **Make Connections**—You are expected to make connections between success at school, success on the job, and success in your personal life. Reflect on your ideas and experiences in written assignments and class discussions, and be open to your classmates' ideas and experiences as well.

Evaluation

Evaluations will be based on attendance, participation, assignments, and chapter tests. Quizzes may also be given throughout the course.

Grading will be as follows:

Class Participation	30%
Homework	30%
Chapter Tests	20%
Midterm	10%
Final	10%
TOTAL	100%

A = 90 to 100 points
B = 80 to 89 points
C = 70 to 79 points
D = 60 to 69 points
F = less than 60 points

Suggestions for Day One

On the first day of class, write the class name, number, and section (if applicable) on the board along with your name, office number/address, and e-mail address. Hand out note cards to students as they walk in the door and ask them to fill them out with some or all of the following information, which you can also list on the board:

- name
- telephone number
- e-mail address
- year in school and major
- main interests and hobbies
- career objective
- major work experience
- what they most want to learn from this course
- grade they expect to earn

Give students a few minutes to read the syllabus as you collect the note cards. Introduce yourself and welcome the students, then do the ice-breaker exercise that follows.

Day One Ice-Breaker Exercise

The purpose of this ice-breaker exercise is to help students relax, get acquainted, and understand expectations. Ask students to work in pairs, but request them not to pair up with people they already know.

Explain that one student will speak to his or her partner for two minutes, describing his or her major, interests, job experience, career goals, hometown, and one experience or trait that makes him or her unique. The other student will then do the same for two minutes. Tell students they will be timed. While students are conducting this first part of the ice-breaker exercise, review their completed note cards (see above) and group students into small, diverse discussion groups of five or six people.

At the end of the four minutes, gather together as a class and have each person briefly introduce his or her partner, taking no more than twenty or thirty seconds each.

Now ask students to assemble into the small discussion groups you selected. Have each group choose a leader responsible for keeping the discussion going and recording questions and comments. Instruct students to reintroduce themselves briefly and to spend five minutes sharing their ideas on the following two topics:

1. Expectations—What would you like to learn in this course? What topics are most important? What would you like to see emphasized?

2. Questions—What questions do you have for the instructor? (These may include personal questions such as: What made you decide to go into college teaching? Where did you get your degrees? What are your hobbies and interests? What do students do that irritates you? What should we call you?)

After the five minutes are over, have the leader of each team ask you one question. Go from team to team as time permits. Use this opportunity to clarify expectations and stress topics that are especially important to you. For example, you might respond to the question, "What do students do that makes you mad?" in this fashion: "I am irritated when students miss class, come in late, leave early, or don't get involved. Most annoying are students who interrupt other students or act disrespectfully. I want this class to be a supportive and safe haven for everyone to grow and learn."

Of course, before you conduct this exercise, you will want to be honest with yourself about how comfortable you will be answering questions. Tell students that they may ask you any question they want, but that you will feel free to let them know if you think any question is too personal. Being able to answer students' concerns or questions honestly is important for conducting an open class. If you do not feel comfortable with personal questions, have students write their questions or concerns on cards, and you can then choose to discuss those you feel are most relevant.

Day One Homework
Ask students to generate a list of five goals for the course. These goals can be anything—how to deal with a specific personal problem, how to handle time more efficiently, or even just to get a good grade.

Suggestions for Day Two
You may have new students at the second class meeting who have added the class to their schedules late. Briefly review the purpose and theme of the class. Explain that the major goal of this class is to help students learn skills and personal qualities for school, job, and life success. You may also want to talk about your philosophy of education.

Next, ask students to share the goals they wrote down for the first homework assignment. Ask them to name the subjects they would like to see emphasized in the course. (Make clear, however, that this is not a request for them to design the course.) What you want is a statement of the types of subjects that students think would best meet their needs. This exercise will help clarify expectations, interests, and concerns.

Goals Exercise
The purpose of this exercise is to prompt students to explore their motives for attending school, to review the value of continuing their education, and to assess their long-term goals. Ask students to fill out the questionnaire on page 15. As preparation, you may want to ask students to write down the answers to these four questions:
1. Why did you enroll in school?
2. How committed are you to completing your education?
3. What do you want to accomplish while you are in school?
4. How do you see the connection between success in school and success in life?

Students should not write their names on the cards. After a few minutes, collect the cards and read some of the answers aloud, or break students into small groups and have them discuss their answers for ten minutes or so. Then discuss with the entire class the advantages of continuing one's education. These advantages are many, including self-improvement, career advancement, exploration of interests and ideas, and the experience of meeting new people and making new friends.

After students have discussed their reasons for furthering their educations, explain how this course can help them reach their educational goals. If students are attending school to prepare for a satisfying career, for example, you could point out that career success requires not only job-specific skills but also "soft" (transferable) skills such as self-awareness, self-discipline, self-motivation, and good interpersonal skills, all of which they will learn about in *Psychology of Success*.

Why Are You Continuing Your Education?

Reflect on why you want to continue your education. Put a check mark next to each statement that is true for you.

I am continuing my education...

1. To please my parents. _____
2. To get a better job when I graduate. _____
3. Because I don't know what else to do. _____
4. Because I can't find a job. _____
5. To find a life partner. _____
6. Because I really want to learn and expand my skills. _____
7. To learn to take full responsibility for my life. _____
8. To become an educated person. _____
9. Because my friends are going. _____
10. To please my boss, partner, or friends. _____
11. To earn more money. _____
12. To gain prestige and respect. _____
13. To prove that I can. _____
14. Because my job is at a dead end. _____
15. To learn interesting work. _____
16. Because I love to study and learn. _____
17. For the parties. _____
18. For the challenge. _____
19. Because I have always known I would. _____
20. Because it is expected of me. _____
21. (Other—specify):

_____

_____

_____

_____

_____

Summary of Expectations

End the second class by emphasizing the importance of participation and teamwork. Part of being successful in school, at work, and in life is learning to work with others, to respect differences, and to accomplish goals through teamwork.

Students often underestimate the value of their contributions or see little connection between their learning and that of their peers. Emphasize that each student's experiences and ideas contribute to the learning of the others. Emphasize the importance of respecting others' opinions as well. You may wish to lay down ground rules for discussions, such as raising hands before speaking, paying full attention to the person who is speaking, and so on. Encourage students to bring questions to class, to get involved in class discussions, and to form independent opinions about the material.

Most of your students will probably be used to passive learning (lectures, recall-based testing, etc.). They may therefore feel uncomfortable with the idea of active participation. Point out that participation helps them learn the material and makes it more fun. Help students see that participation is an opportunity, not a burden.

Guest Speakers

As you plan your course, make sure to allow time for guest speaker presentations. Guest speakers not only add variety and real-world relevance to the class, but also serve as valuable sources of information for you in helping students develop the skills to succeed in the competitive workplace. Presentations by guest speakers are most successful when the guest speakers receive key information from you in writing in advance, particularly:

- the purpose of the course and the presentation
- a description of the students and their level of sophistication
- the purpose of the presentation, and how the presentation fits in with the material being covered
- specific topic(s) you would like to see covered
- level of formality of the presentation and appropriate amount of time to talk
- time, place, and directions to the classroom

Before the presentation, ask the speaker for a brief description of his or her background and how he or she would like to be introduced. Also ask the speaker if he or she has questions for the students to answer so that you can be prepared to facilitate. After the class, remember to send a thank-you note and comments from students.

For a student success course, the list of possible speakers is almost endless. Considering inviting some of the following people to your class:

- career center staff member
- time management expert
- president of the college
- administrator
- mayor
- city council member
- health, fitness, or nutrition expert
- alcohol or drug counselor
- alumnus or alumna

- financial planner
- financial aid officer
- motivational speaker
- business leader
- student exchange or activity coordinator
- sport psychologist
- career counselor
- personal counselor or therapist
- research psychologist
- psychology instructor

You may wish to evaluate guest speakers for your records by using copies of the form below.

Guest Speaker Form

Guest Speaker: _____

Date: _____

Topic: _____

Students' reaction: _____

_____

_____

_____

My assessment: _____

_____

_____

Other possible guest speakers in this area: _____

_____

CREATING A LEARNING-CENTERED ENVIRONMENT

Making Learning Personal

The conventional model of the instructor lecturing to passive, inexperienced students is inadequate for today's complex and diverse world and is ill suited to *Psychology of Success*. Students need to learn how to think, not how to memorize data. They must be actively involved in order to question their assumptions and make meaningful connections among their various courses and between school, work, and life.

Students need to be encouraged to focus on developing and demonstrating self-awareness and positive personal qualities rather than on simply memorizing the material. Each chapter of *Psychology of Success* contains Personal Journals, Exercises, and end-of-chapter activities designed to help students clarify their goals and reflect on their lives as they review key concepts. Point out to students that the thoughtfulness of their answers is more important than the specific opinions, ideas, or examples they use in their answers. Encourage them to develop their own ideas and to back them up with critical thinking and examples from their life experiences.

Using Journaling

Depending on the focus of your course and the time available, it can be extremely productive to have students make entries in a separate journal or notebook. This approach is particularly fruitful for writing-intensive courses, for English language learners, and for students who need additional composition practice. In addition, journaling helps all students:

- set aside time for self-reflection
- build self-awareness
- hone critical thinking skills
- gain practice articulating their thoughts
- make connections between classroom learning and real-life situations
- create a record of their decisions and decision-making style
- make plans and set goals

Journal entries can touch on nearly any course-related topic. For example, they can be used to answer follow-up questions in Personal Journals or to expand on topics covered in Personal Journals, Exercises, features, or figures. Journals can also be used as a tool for students to record their thoughts and feelings about the course and their college and work experiences. Journal or notebook entries differ from Personal Journal activities in *Psychology of Success* because they are free-form, allowing students to make new associations and explore concepts of their own choosing.

Educating the Whole Student

Educating the whole student means fostering students' intellectual, emotional, social, spiritual, and physical growth. It goes beyond transmitting knowledge and skills to helping students develop ethics, social responsibility, self-awareness, coping skills, strength of character, and the ability to make healthy life choices.

A student success course is an optimal place to begin educating the whole student. Stress the importance of self-awareness, effort, and positive personal qualities throughout the course. Ethics, discussed in Chapter 2, can be woven into the course content by asking students to share ethical questions they have encountered in their jobs and personal lives. Help students become aware of their world by referencing current events and bringing in articles from newspapers to spark discussions.

Stress that attitude has an enormous effect on students' learning. Learning is increased when students communicate openly with one another in a positive, noncompetitive environment, work on experiential exercises, and complete group projects. Students learn best by being actively involved in the learning process.

Increasing Students' Motivation: The ARCS Model

Students of all ages are most motivated to learn in an environment that fulfills their psychological needs—in an environment that helps them feel good about themselves, experience a sense of belongingness, build competence, and guide their own learning.

The key to motivating students is to create an environment that encourages their natural curiosity and engagement. The *ARCS model of motivation*, created by education researcher John Keller, is a useful approach to understanding student motivation. The ARCS model represents the four most important factors affecting student motivation: Attention (A), Relevance (R), Confidence (C), and Satisfaction (S).

A—Attention

Focused attention is the prerequisite for learning. Two key ways to elicit students' attention are to activate background knowledge and to encourage discussion and critical thinking.

Learning is most effective and lasting when students integrate new knowledge into their preexisting network of associations. To understand, retain, and engage actively with the material, students must be able to make connections between new information and the information they already possess. Before beginning a new topic, therefore, it is important to activate students' background knowledge. This also helps you, the instructor, present the material at the right pace and level of sophistication.

You can focus students' attention and activate their background knowledge in several ways. One strategy is to lead a brainstorming session on the new topic, writing all the information solicited from the students on the board or a transparency. A second strategy is to ask students to solve a problem or role-play a scenario related to the topic. The Real-Life Success Story at the beginning of each chapter can serve as a springboard for all of these activities. A third strategy is to ask either specific or general questions about the topic, such as, "What do you think _____ means?" "What comes to mind when you hear the word _____?" "Have you ever experienced _____?" Other ways to elicit attention include:

- using specific examples, ideally with accompanying visual stimuli
- introducing a provocative point of view
- using a variety of media, instructional techniques, and activities
- having students get actively involved through games, role-plays, small-group activities, or hands-on projects
- giving students creative problems to solve

R—Relevance

To be highly motivated to learn, students need to understand why a course is relevant to their lives. In other words, they should be able to answer the question, "What's in it for me?" To make subjects more relevant to your students, challenge them to generate concrete, real-world examples and to relate the subject matter to their individual dreams, goals, values, and interests. Ask them to think of ways that the information they are learning could benefit them in their academic pursuits, career, or personal life. How is this course helping them reach their educational or career goals?

Ask students to think of times when they have experienced the situations and challenges described in the text. Pose thought-provoking questions that help students relate the material to their lives. Use open questions, which allow for a broad range of responses, rather than closed questions, which elicit only one- or two-word answers. Make sure to pose critical thinking questions that do not have a "correct" answer. Also call on students to generate their own questions. Encourage them to disagree—respectfully—with statements made in the textbook, with the opinions of their fellow students, and with you. Emphasize that all opinions and ideas are welcomed, but call on students to back up their opinions with critical thinking and specific examples.

C—Confidence

Low confidence in a subject or in a classroom situation can dampen the enthusiasm of any student. All students should be encouraged to participate and should be given clear, positive expectations of success. All students have greater motivation when they see that their instructors believe in them.

Give students learning goals that are challenging enough to encourage effort, but realistic enough to be achievable. Students gain confidence by succeeding at tasks that are challenging—neither too easy to help build new skills nor too difficult to do with their existing skills. One way to find the right level is to begin with relatively easy questions, adding difficulty until you see that students are engaged but not stumped.

Students also gain confidence when they know exactly what they need to do in order to succeed. Make your expectations clear from the beginning of the course. What do students need to do to master the material? What do they need to do to earn a good grade in the course? Make sure students have realistic time estimates for homework, exercises, test preparation, and so on. Students should understand that there is a correlation between the amount of energy they put into a learning experience and the amount of skill and knowledge they will gain from that experience. Using a Gantt chart or some other graphical planner to demonstrate the amount of time needed or given to complete a task will give the learner a clear picture of what to expect.

Students should feel some degree of control over their learning and assessment. They should feel that they are, for the most part, in control of their outcomes and that their success is a direct result of the amount of effort they have invested. Encourage students to "backwards-plan" their efforts. This process will help them to determine the amount of time that they will need to spend on each task.

S—Satisfaction

Students' motivation to learn is heightened when they know that they are gaining something of value in a course. This might be job skills, intellectual satisfaction, or progress toward a valued educational or life goal. Give students this satisfaction by providing opportunities for students to use their newly acquired knowledge or skills in a real or simulated (role-play) settings.

Peer teaching is another satisfying activity. In several studies, students who learned new material with the explicit goal of teaching it to others retained much more than students who learned the same material with the goal of getting a good grade on a test. Thinking about how to explain material and make it relevant to others helps students develop self-esteem and derive greater satisfaction from the course.

Cooperative Learning

Cooperative learning is an educational approach in which students work together to achieve a common learning goal. In traditional educational settings, students usually work alone and compete with one another. In the cooperative learning environment, students work in teams and contribute to each other's learning. Each member of the group benefits from the efforts, experiences, and insights of the other members. To be effective, cooperative learning must take place in a supportive, student-centered, and noncompetitive climate.

Cooperative learning supplements, rather than replaces, traditional educational approaches, including lectures. It can invigorate the classroom dynamic, increase respect for diversity, and help students develop skills in effective speaking, active listening, leadership, critical thinking, decision making, and conflict resolution. Cooperative learning requires students to:

- have mutual goals
- be supportive of one another's learning
- have structured tasks to which each team member contributes
- practice social skills
- rotate interdependent roles (leader, recorder, observer, listener, speaker)
- ensure equal participation by all
- show individual responsibility

Part of the student's role in a cooperative learning environment is to contribute to his or her team. Team members rely on each other for input and support, so it is essential that each team member come prepared to participate in team and class discussions. Students are quick to realize that it is difficult to contribute to their team and to the class in general if they do not complete their assignments and readings. Because students know their peers will review their work, they tend to make a more concerted effort to complete assignments.

Experiential Learning

Experiential learning is essentially learning by doing. It occurs when students think, reflect upon, and learn from a real-life situation or a simulated real-life situation, such as a role-play exercise. When cooperative learning is combined with experiential exercises, learning is greatly enhanced.

Psychology of Success is well suited to the experiential learning approach. Experiential learning is built into Application and Internet activities, Exercises, Personal Journals, role-plays, and small group discussions. Exercises and Personal Journals in *Psychology of Success* call on students to reflect on topics' relevance to their lives. Critical thinking questions help students explore the real-world relevance of theoretical concepts.

The Real-Life Success Stories and personalized examples in the text also help to make the concepts relevant and personal.

Short presentations, rather than long and detailed lectures, work best for experiential learning. As the instructor, you are not a lecturer but rather a facilitator, resource, discussion leader, coach, and role model. To play these roles requires the ability to communicate clearly, remain nonjudgmental, pose engaging questions, use interesting stories and examples, and relate main points and strategies to actual student experiences. Keep in mind that your attitude at the beginning of class is a major factor in the course's success. Monitor your attitude as the course progresses. As an instructor, you can make a difference.

The rewards for teaching an experiential class are many. You will notice increased student interest and involvement, feel that you are creating real learning and understanding (rather than just feeding students rote information), and gain a better understanding of your students. You will also learn from your students, which increases your own sense of involvement and motivation.

Encouraging Student Involvement

Students derive maximum benefit from *Psychology of Success* when they are encouraged to become active learners, to work together, and to make connections between school, work, and life.

Promote Attendance

Explain to students that regular attendance is vital to success in the course. Poor attendance or tardiness results in confusion, reduced motivation, and resentment from students who attend and are well-prepared and punctual. Take attendance at each class period and meet with students who miss two or more sessions. Explain to students that discussion and the sharing of ideas are important for learning and building self-awareness. When students are often absent, the group becomes less cohesive and students are less likely to be open with one another. Frequent absences also make it impossible to have students work in consistent teams or pairs.

Also make sure students understand the importance of coming to class on time. If students miss five or ten minutes, they miss the introduction and review, causing them to fall behind and to interrupt with questions.

Encourage Participation and Preparation

In many classrooms, relatively few students participate actively. However, one of the goals of cooperative learning and of this course is to get all members of the class to share ideas, express opinions, and participate in group exercises. Emphasize the value of inclusive participation and the responsibility of outspoken members to encourage less talkative members to express their views. Stress the importance of listening and taking turns to talk.

Also stress that full participation includes preparation as well as speaking up in class. Ask students to come to class prepared with reading assignments and homework. Students should bring their books and other assigned material to each class unless otherwise instructed. If students are not prepared, they are less likely to participate and less likely to grasp concepts. Underscore the importance of completing assignments and coming to class prepared to discuss them.

It if does not seem that students are really sharing their personal ideas and feelings, consider setting aside a time when any topic is allowed, perhaps at the end of the class or once a week during an extended break. This can help students get acquainted, gain an understanding of one another's views, increase their motivation, and practice their speaking skills. Make certain you have an agreement that what is said during this time is confidential.

Preview and Review

Previewing activates background knowledge and helps students relate what they will be learning to what they have just finished learning. To help them make these connections, review and discuss the previous chapter before previewing the next. Also, preview assignments with students to clarify your expectations.

Tell students that at the top of every class session hour you will call on one of them to give a concise summary of the main points and important strategies covered in the last class meeting. This will not only encourage students to participate and be prepared, but will also help them build their public speaking skills. Beginning each class with a quick review also helps students build associations among topics.

Create a Positive Atmosphere

Your attitude plays a major role in student learning. Respond seriously to students' questions and concerns. Be enthusiastic and positive and show that you enjoy teaching this class. Be on time for class and be available during office hours and breaks to meet with students. Do not claim to have all the answers. Suggest to students that your role as a facilitator is to present strategies that have worked for many students, but remind them that they must find their own answers.

Students will be more enthusiastic about class and homework activities if they see that you are enthusiastic and interested and that you value the assignments. Walk around the class while students are doing in-class activities to check how they are doing, but do not join teams. Give students abundant examples to reinforce the material, ask them to share their opinions in discussions or in writing, and introduce variety to the class through lectures, films, guest speakers, and field trips.

Stress Confidentiality

Students do not need to give names of friends, partners, family members, instructors, supervisors, or coworkers in the Exercises, Personal Journals, and other activities that call for examples to be taken from their personal lives. Remind them that what is said in the classroom is confidential and should not be shared outside of the class with others. Tell them that no one will see their work but you, unless they elect otherwise. Students should never feel pressure to share personal details of their lives or discuss any topic with which they feel uncomfortable.

Incorporate Peer Teaching

Peer teaching refers to one or more students teaching other students in a particular subject area. It can take many forms, from a single student leading a class lesson to a pair of students peer-teaching one another. Peer teaching is effective because students are able to relate to and encourage one another. It also gives students a chance to practice articulating concepts in their own words. Peer teachers need not be the students with the best grades. Average students, as well as struggling students, can choose a topic and explain it effectively to others. Try to do one peer-teaching exercise every class period and to incorporate peer teaching throughout the course.

Encourage Critical Thinking

Students need to learn how to make decisions, solve problems, and think through issues rationally. Critical thinking skills are an enormous asset to students academically, personally, and professionally. Help students use critical thinking skills during class discussions. Always ask students to be sure to back up their beliefs with clear reasoning and specific examples. Through questioning, help students to examine whether their opinions are based on false information or illogical thinking. Critical thinking questions in chapter figures, features, and activities present an opportunity for students to think independently, to question their assumptions, and to accept that there is no "right" answer to many questions concerning success and human behavior. Encourage students to bring in articles from the newspaper and to talk about life or work situations that highlight the importance of critical thinking.

Encourage Service Learning and Contribution

Encourage students to become involved in campus and community activities. Many colleges have service learning projects in which students perform community service, often for credit. Service learning and campus involvement provide leadership experiences and opportunities for networking. Students feel real satisfaction when they know they are contributing to their campus and to their community.

Establish Heterogeneous Groups

Establishing heterogeneous student groups is important because it helps students develop self-awareness, respect for diversity, and interpersonal skills. Many instructors like to have permanent teams throughout the course to add continuity, increase teamwork skills, and encourage friendships and social development. You can create heterogeneous class teams by combining students with different characteristics in:

- learning ability
- age
- experience (such as full-time students, part-time students, students with full-time jobs, students with part-time jobs, traditional students, and returning students)
- gender
- culture
- ethnicity

Ideally, all groups should have the same number of students. When determining group size, you need to take into account both the number of students in the class and the number of students that can comfortably work together in an individual team. Groups of four to five usually work well in a postsecondary setting. In groups with six or more members, one or two students may feel left out or begin to trail behind.

Designate Group Work Areas

The configuration of your classroom plays a role in the success of in-class groups. Ideally, chairs and tables will be movable to allow students to form small circles where they can work comfortably. If desks are affixed to the floor, you might ask each group to pick a secretary to be in charge of writing down the group's ideas. If space allows, you can also ask groups to work at the board or even on the floor. Also rotate the location of teams so that students who usually sit in the back of the classroom are encouraged to come to the front of the classroom.

Designate Group Roles and Responsibilities

Designating specific responsibilities to different group members ensures that every student has a productive role to play in his or her group. Designate a number of interdependent roles such as discussion leader, recorder/secretary, and group spokesperson (for full-class discussions). You can also assign roles for a group role-play. For example, in a lesson on communication skills, you might ask students to take turns playing the role of speaker, active listener, and ineffective (poor) listener.

It is also important to make sure that groups are not dominated by any one or two students in particular. Set up a leader-selection process, which can be random (such as whomever guesses closest to a certain number between one and ten) or based on specific criteria. The leadership role can also rotate from student to student each week or each class meeting. Rotating the role of leader encourages shy students to participate and learn leadership skills.

Provide Clear Instructions

Vague instructions make it difficult for students, whether singly or in groups, to get started and focus on their task. Instead of asking groups to simply discuss a certain idea or answer a certain question, for example, you might specify that each group member take one minute to share his or her opinion with the others, and that each member then give a response to each of the other members' statements. You can also set up a debate situation in which each member is assigned to advance and defend a certain point of view.

Also make sure that students understand the overall purpose of every activity. Read the chapter objectives at the beginning of each class so that students know the class expectations. Review the instructions for the Exercises and Personal Journals out loud as students follow in their books so that everyone is on the same track, questions can be clarified, and everyone is ready to start on time.

Minimize Exchanges of Information Between Groups

There is often a temptation for members of different groups to talk amongst themselves, especially if groups can overhear one another as they work. Help students resist this temptation by spacing groups apart as far as possible from one another, by circulating around the room to offer guidance, and by stressing that group work is a noncompetitive activity.

Encourage Group Cohesiveness

Encourage students to learn more about one another, to be open and share experiences, and to become part of a team. Also encourage students to think of their group as a unit rather than to be concerned with competing for points. At the beginning of the term, groups will look to you, the instructor, for feedback on how well they are doing. Praise groups that are able to answer their own questions and resolve their own internal disputes. You and the members of each team should assess the team's effectiveness and reflect on learning processes and outcomes. Is the team effective? Does everyone contribute? How can the team be more effective?

Conflict can occur among group members due to personality differences, clashes of opinion, and so on. Stress that group work is about sharing ideas, not about changing other people's minds or coming to one single "correct" conclusion. Provide clear directions and stress that it is the leader's role to make sure that discussions flow smoothly and that differences are respected. Consider distributing a handout that describes the respectful conduct expected of every group member.

Accommodate Different Learning Styles

You can improve your teaching effectiveness by understanding the different ways in which students learn and by tailoring your instruction accordingly. Students can also benefit from understanding how they learn best. Vary the ways in which you present material so that you are appealing to the three primary learning styles: visual, auditory, and kinesthetic. The three types of learners are:

- **Visual learners**—Visual learners prefer to see and read. They learn well by using pictures, graphs, illustrations, diagrams, timelines, photos, pie charts, and other visuals. They like to contemplate concepts, reflect, and summarize information in writing. Visual learners tend to remember what they see better than what they hear, and they prefer to receive written directions for assignments.
- **Auditory learners**—Auditory learners rely on hearing to learn. They like recorded words and music and usually enjoy working in study teams and participating in class discussions. Auditory learners tend to remember what they hear better than what they see, and they prefer to receive spoken directions for assignments.
- **Kinesthetic learners**—Kinesthetic learners are usually well coordinated and like to touch things, and they learn best by doing. They like to collect samples, write out information, spend time outdoors, and connect abstract material to something concrete in nature. Kinesthetic learners tend to like hands-on activities, such as playing computer games, drawing, collecting objects, and building things.

You may wish to ask students to complete the Learning Style Inventory provided on pages 27–28. Being aware of of their preferred learning style(s) helps students choose the most effective note-taking and study techniques.

You can use the results of students' inventories to plan the most effective activities and ways of presenting information. To appeal to visual learners, use visual aids, such as PowerPoint presentations, a chalkboard or dry-erase board, and transparencies. To appeal to auditory learners, present lectures, use small group discussions, and repeat important material. To appeal to kinesthetic learners, use field trips, student presentations, objects, case studies, and activities such as role-plays that involve physical movement.

Learning Style Inventory

A. Complete each sentence below by circling the letter (a, b, or c) of the statement that most accurately describes you.

1. I learn best when I
   a. see information.
   b. hear information.
   c. have hands-on experience.

2. I like
   a. pictures and illustrations.
   b. tapes and listening to stories.
   c. working with people and going on field trips.

3. For pleasure and relaxation, I love to
   a. read.
   b. listen to music and tapes.
   c. garden or play sports.

4. I tend to be
   a. contemplative.
   b. talkative.
   c. a doer.

5. To remember a ZIP code, I like to
   a. write it down several times.
   b. say it out loud several times.
   c. doodle and draw it on any available paper.

6. In a classroom, I learn best when
   a. I have a good textbook, visual aids, and written information.
   b. the instructor is interesting and clear.
   c. I am involved in doing activities.

7. When I study for a test, I
   a. read my notes and write a summary.
   b. review my notes aloud and talk to others.
   c. like to study in a group and use models and charts.

8. I have
   a. strong fashion sense and pay attention to visual details.
   b. fun telling stories and jokes.
   c. a great time building things and being active.

9. I plan the upcoming week by
   a. making a list and keeping a detailed calendar.
   b. talking it through with someone.
   c. creating a computer calendar or using a project board.

10. When preparing for a math test, I like to
   a. write formulas on note cards or use pictures.
   b. memorize formulas or talk aloud.
   c. make charts and graphs or use three-dimensional models.

11. I often
   a. remember faces but not names.
   b. remember names but not faces.
   c. remember events but not names or faces.

12. I remember best
   a. when I read instructions and use visual images to remember.
   b. when I listen to instructions and use rhyming words to remember.
   c. with hands-on activities and trial and error.

13. When I give directions, I might say
   a. "Turn right at the yellow house and left when you see the large oak tree. Do you see what I mean?"
   b. "Turn right. Go three blocks. Turn left onto Buttermilk Lane. OK? Got that? Do you hear what I'm saying?"
   c. "Follow me" after giving directions by using gestures.

14. When driving in a new city, I prefer to
   a. get a map and find my own way.
   b. stop and get directions from someone.
   c. drive around and figure it out by myself.

B. **Scoring:** Add up the number of times you checked **a**, **b**, and **c**.

Total number of a's _____ *(Visual Learning Style)*

Total number of b's _____ *(Auditory Learning Style)*

Total number of c's _____ *(Kinesthetic Learning Style)*

Your highest total indicates your dominant learning style.

Working With a Diverse Student Population

The number of nontraditional students is growing, and you are likely to encounter students with a wide range of backgrounds. For example, your class may contain returning students, older students, and international students. By taking the needs of a diverse student population into account, you can create a supportive classroom climate and ensure that all students have an equal opportunity to benefit from the course.

Multicultural Students

Part of the value of a college education is the opportunity to work with fellow students from other social and ethnic groups and to understand and value diversity. College is also the ideal time for a student to become aware of his or her conscious and unconscious stereotypes and prejudices and to change these thinking patterns.

According to the 2000 U.S. Census, one-third of the population of the United States consists of racial minorities. Make certain that your student discussion groups reflect the diversity of class members. Invite guest speakers and students to discuss diversity and special concerns. Include information about campus and community resources for students of different ethnic and cultural groups. Explore the available resources in the school and community that support diversity. Post lists of noted speakers, events, and opportunities promoting increased awareness and understanding. Encourage students from different cultures to participate and assume leadership roles.

The material in *Psychology of Success* lends itself well to an exchange of information about cultural influences on self-image, self-esteem, values, decision making, relationships, and other important issues. Psychology of Success takes the approach that there are no right or wrong answers to questions of success and happiness. Each student is encouraged to explore his or her own behavior in a nonjudgmental way, and to look at the underlying thoughts, feelings, and motivations behind that behavior. If you have students from varied cultures and ethnic groups, you have a wonderful opportunity to discuss issues of cultural and family influence versus personal choice. How much of what we think, feel, and do is influenced by our society, culture, and family? How do other cultures define important concepts such as success, happiness, intelligence, and self-discipline?

Many important topics covered in the book, such as values, personality traits, personal and collective identity, gender roles, body image, communication strategies, and relationships, are interpreted differently in different cultures. The presence of students from other cultures in your classroom provides an excellent opportunity to discuss personal and cultural differences. Make it a matter of course to ask English language learners to comment on likenesses and differences between their home cultures and this new one. Also make clear to the rest of the class that students from different cultures have much to offer them. Point out how these students can enrich their understanding of psychology by discussing norms in other cultures. Bringing culture, language, and society into the discussion can also serve to break down stereotypes.

Try these general strategies in multicultural classes as well:

- **Create diverse groups.** Promote an appreciation of diversity by creating diverse groups. Encourage each student to act as group leader. Rotating the leadership position builds confidence and helps students feel a sense of belonging.

- **Be welcoming.** Make your classroom and office inviting; get to know students and welcome them to your office. Ask questions about how they are adjusting and show that you are interested.
- **Invite diversity into the classroom.** Invite guest speakers, as well as teaching assistants or tutors, from different cultural backgrounds.
- **Encourage cultural exploration.** Investigate resources on campus and in the community. Have students attend different cultural events or take field trips as part of the class experience. Have lists of resources available for various cultural groups.
- **Promote critical thinking.** Encourage students to examine their perceptions and attitudes. Point out that understanding and respecting differences is the foundation for building common bonds.
- **Stress the skill of adapting.** Being able to relate to diverse people is a crucial personal and career skill.
- **Celebrate diversity.** Help students celebrate their unique identity. Ask them to bring in examples and discuss situations in which they felt different because they were younger, older, of a different religion or culture, a college student, or a minority of some other type.

Returning or Older Students

More and more students are returning to school after being in the working world for a few years or more. Many people are also deciding to start college at a later age. According to the U.S. Department of Education, 41 percent of all college students are twenty-five years old or older, and 56 percent are twenty-two years old or older. The average age of students in career schools and community colleges is higher still. Here are a few tips for teaching older or returning students:

- **Connect college with job and life success.** Older students are often more practical-minded than younger students and want to see the immediate relevance of what they are studying. Stress how they can use course ideas in their jobs and everyday lives. Use practical applications and case studies and request personal examples from the class. Make the course practical and relevant.
- **Value students' experiences.** Older students have a wealth of life and work experience. Have them link course concepts with their experiences. Discuss their viewpoints and encourage classroom discussions.
- **Create diverse teams.** Younger students can learn from older students who offer different perspectives. Older students can also help younger students stay on task in team discussions and projects. Though students often want to sit with friends or with students who are the same age, gender, race, and so on, diverse groups can foster understanding and respect for differences.
- **Encourage openness.** Encourage students to consider new perspectives. Some older students may demonstrate set attitudes and values. Discuss the benefits of examining questions from a new perspective.
- **Show concern.** Be aware of other demands on students' time. Many older students have jobs, spouses, children, and community obligations that demand their time. Offer understanding, but also discuss the necessity of making a commitment to school. Encourage students to discuss their many roles and concerns.

- **Encourage support groups.** Older students need support from other students, instructors, advisors, and sometimes academic support groups. Encourage them to create informal support groups as well. For example, single or working parents may want to join a group whose members can help each other with child care, carpooling, or forming study teams. Point out that learning time management techniques can help students in their careers. Discuss with them the value of gaining the support of spouses, children, coworkers, and supervisors for returning to school. Encourage students to form study groups during the first week of class. Call students' attention to the chapter on time management (Chapter 8) early in the term.
- **Hold flexible office hours.** Since older students have other obligations, assure them that you will meet them at times convenient for you and them. You might explore offering evening or weekend classes or office hours.
- **Encourage responsibility.** Stress that students are responsible for participating in class, looking for innovative solutions to obstacles, and being aware of academic expectations. They must read the school catalog, become aware of deadlines and procedures, and understand how the system works.
- **Look for the positive.** Focus on the advantages of being an older student. Discuss how older students' life experiences have given them direction. Acknowledge how much wisdom they bring to a class.
- **Find resources.** Discuss school and community resources that can help older, returning students, such as child care facilities, carpooling, job sharing, and support groups.
- **Make lessons relevant to all ages.** Make certain that your examples are relevant to older as well as younger students and that you ask them for examples that illustrate concepts. Use group discussions, varied teaching methods, and guest speakers that are relevant to all students—young and old.

Some returning or older students may have recently transferred to your school or be preparing to transfer to another school (such as a larger college or university). These students are often concerned with which credits are transferable and which courses will satisfy major and general education requirements. It is critical that transfer students see their advisors to plan their educational programs as soon as possible. Stress that every campus is different and that students should not assume that procedures are the same from school to school, even if schools are part of the same university system.

International Students

At many North American colleges and universities, the number of international students is increasing dramatically. International students face an often difficult adjustment to a new culture, language, and climate. Try these general strategies to help international students:

- **Stress the importance of getting involved.** Encourage students to form supportive relationships with various people—friends, advisors, instructors, fellow students, relatives who may be nearby, and so on.
- **Explore resources.** Learn what resources are available both on and off campus for international students.
- **Encourage mentoring.** Many campuses have a mentoring program. Connect international students with students who have been on campus for at least a year.

- **Speak clearly.** If a student's primary language is not English, make certain that you speak clearly, avoid slang, and explain what is meant by common expressions and phrases, and that you enunciate and speak slowly. Clarify and check for understanding. Take care not to come across as condescending or patronizing.
- **Write down important information.** Make certain to put important information in writing so that students can review it at their own pace.
- **Accommodate different learning styles.** Like all other students, international students benefit from activities that allow them to see, hear, touch, and do.
- **Learn about other cultures.** Cultural differences can be great in areas such as nonverbal communication, self-esteem, relationships, and attitudes toward time and money. Ask questions and be respectful.
- **Encourage students to talk.** Encourage international students to share their views and experiences. Have them talk about their customs, country, and background.

STRATEGIES FOR TEACHING STUDENTS WITH SPECIAL NEEDS

Understanding Special Needs

The term *special needs* is used to describe students who face specific physical or behavioral challenges. However, it can also be used in a wider sense to describe students who have greater difficulty learning than the majority of their fellow students.

Every teacher has a wide range of learners in his or her classroom. Using strategies targeted to students with special needs will help you teach *Psychology of Success* more effectively and ensure that all your students derive the most from the course.

Early in the term, it is a good idea to break the class into groups and have students discuss their needs, problems, fears, and goals. This will help students to be more sensitive to one another's needs and challenges. Stress that we can all learn from one another by being open and sharing different views, values, ideas, and goals. Encourage all students to get to know people from different races, cultures, backgrounds, and religions. Strive to demonstrate sensitivity to the needs and views of all students. Examine your own prejudices and assumptions, too. Avoid generalizations, and ask students to let you know if you appear insensitive. Be a model for tolerance, understanding, and change.

English Language Learners

Students learning English as a second or foreign language will come to your classroom with varying degrees of skill in English. In addition to linguistic barriers, social and cultural differences can affect these students' comfort and academic performance. The content of *Psychology of Success* offers a unique opportunity to help these students become more comfortable with themselves and their identity. Try these general strategies:

- **Be respectful.** Remember that students' ability to speak English does not reflect their academic ability. Avoid raising your voice or talking too quickly to students still acquiring English proficiency.

- **Consider a bilingual aide.** Bilingual aides can be very helpful, especially in cases where all the English language learners in the class speak the same first language. However, if a number of different languages or dialects are represented in your classroom, an aid is of limited value.
- **Learn about ESL and EFL.** Consult teachers of English as a Second Language (ESL) and English as Foreign Language (EFL) for specific strategies that you could use in your class.
- **Supply outlines.** Provide outlines of planned class content to English language learners in advance so that they can look up new vocabulary and preview material at their own pace.
- **Use visuals.** Use graphic organizers and other visual tools wherever appropriate.
- **Don't rush discussions.** Allow adequate thinking time between your questions or comments and students' responses. Make sure that class discussions don't resemble a game show, where only the few students who are good at quickly shouting out responses can be winners. All students—but especially English language learners—benefit from being given enough time to process information before answering.
- **Pair students.** Pair students who are fluent in English with English language learners as appropriate for class activities.
- **Write down important information.** Write numerals and key terms on the board as you say them. Use gestures and visuals whenever possible to illustrate both ideas and examples.

Students With Vision Impairments

Vision impairments range from moderately impaired vision to total blindness. Vision impairment can, but does not always, affect cognitive, motor, and social skills. To successfully include students with vision impairments in your class and to offer them the necessary individual guidance, try these strategies:

- **Speak clearly.** Unless a student with vision impairment also has hearing loss, do not shout or speak in an unnaturally loud voice.
- **Use precise language.** Be specific in your instructions and references. Describe what you are doing as you do it. Use specific references such as "on the table near the door" or "in the bookcase in the back of the room" as opposed to "up here" or "over there."
- **Pair students.** Have sighted students work with students with vision impairments, giving spoken descriptions of illustrations and other visuals in the textbook or in the classroom.
- **Arrange optimal seating.** Seat students with vision impairments near the front of the classroom. Avoid standing between partially sighted students and light sources such as windows. Ask the students what seating works best for them.
- **Provide recordings.** Build a classroom library of audiotaped readings of the chapters in the text and other related materials. (Tapes will also prove helpful for English language learners and for those who are working on their reading skills.)
- **Use Braille.** Determine whether your students with vision impairments use Braille; if so, locate sources for materials in Braille and secure any materials related to the class.

- **Find resources.** Look for community resources such as schools, charitable organizations, and special education departments at local colleges devoted to working with the blind and partially sighted. Help students connect with any suitable services, and check out any assistance these sources might offer you as an educator.
- **Seek guidance.** Check for guidance offered online by colleges, government agencies, and other organizations devoted to the education of persons with visual impairments. A search using the keywords *teaching* and *visually impaired* will yield a large listing of Web sites on this topic.

Throughout *Psychology of Success*, graphics are used to present key information. Pair a sighted student with a student with a vision impairment to read and talk about information presented in figures and other visuals. Both will benefit from this close examination of key concepts.

Encourage students to work in pairs or small groups to explore the electronic aids available to students with vision impairments. Students can research software and hardware that enlarge images and type and that turn written commands into spoken words. Students might borrow these programs from distributors for a class demonstration, and students with vision impairments can offer their evaluations. Setting the task for the whole class encourages all students to work together.

Students With Hearing Impairments

Students with hearing impairments have partial to total loss of hearing. These students may communicate through sign language or speech. They may read lips, use a hearing aid or a cochlear implant (a surgically implanted device operated through a box worn around the waist), come to class with an interpreter, or use a combination of these strategies. The ability range of hearing impaired students is similar to that of hearing students; but, as is the case with other special needs, hearing loss may affect cognitive, motor, social, and speech skills. Try these general strategies:

- **Assist the student.** Determine the means each student uses to communicate and individually discuss how you can create a classroom that aids, rather than detracts from, these efforts. For example, you might determine the best seating arrangements, minimize background noise, and make sure you and other students face students with hearing impairments when speaking.
- **Watch for misunderstandings.** A teacher was once put off by what he read as an enraged facial expression of a deaf student. When he addressed his concern to her interpreter, he commented that he found her obvious anger almost frightening. The interpreter explained that the look was not one of rage but of fierce concentration as the girl struggled in the early stages of learning to read lips.
- **Write down important information.** Write out instructions on paper or on the board. Consider using an overhead projector, which allows you to maintain eye contact as you write.
- **Supply word lists.** Unfamiliar words can be difficult to lip-read or sign. If materials for a lesson involve new vocabulary, supply word lists in advance to students and their interpreters.
- **Pair students.** Pair hearing-impaired students with hearing partners. Hearing students will gain knowledge about how students with hearing impairments meet this challenge. They can also help their partners by repeating the words of others;

monitoring the level of environmental noise in the classroom; and repeating public addresses and other announcements.

- **Introduce ASL.** Hand out a copy of the alphabet for American Sign Language and practice using this means of communication as a class.
- **Explain closed captioning.** Explain what closed captioning is and how it works.
- **Check Internet resources.** Colleges, organizations for people with hearing impairments, and family/school support groups all offer information and services.

As you explore the topic of career choice, have students with hearing impairments share how the tools and communication skills necessary for the jobs they research can be modified to open the fields to hearing-impaired workers. If students demonstrate little knowledge of this, encourage research on the topic. Students might work in groups and then present their findings to the class.

Students With Behavior Disorders

Students with behavior disorders deviate, usually to a marked degree, from expectations of acceptable classroom behavior. Such students impair not only their own functioning but also that of their other students. Students with behavior disorders range from gifted through severely learning impaired. Try these general strategies:

- **Have positive expectations.** Be prepared, but don't prejudge. Students with behavior disorders will often be made known to you before class begins. You may have met with counselors, deans, school psychologists, and other personnel; and you may have heard informal comments by former teachers. However, approaching the class with the expectation that everybody in it will live up to behavioral norms can be the first step in breaking unwanted behavior patterns.
- **Make rules.** Clearly define rules for behavior. When deviations from these rules occur, intervene at once.
- **Communicate expectations.** Clearly define goals and expectations for the course at the beginning.
- **Get to know the student.** At the start of the term, you will probably have information about the student with behavior disorders from everyone *except* the student. The self-awareness activities in Chapter 2 of the student text can provide you with valuable insight into the student's values, personality traits, and interests. Determine the student's interests and ways of learning, and make use of this information when forming groups and preparing assignments.
- **Aim for long-term improvement.** Don't be discouraged if you do not have immediate success; work toward long-term improvement.
- **Check Internet resources.** A search using the key words *teaching students with behavior disorders* will yield sources ranging from guidelines issued by boards of education to student-targeted sites that offer tips for building self-esteem and coping skills. Be aware that many of these sites lump all special needs together, from physical impairments to behavior disorders. Therefore, preview sites before recommending them to a student.

Students With Learning Impairments

Students with learning impairments have problems in one or more areas, such as academics, language development, perception, social/emotional adjustment, memory, or the ability to pay attention. They often require additional support and structure in a classroom setting. However, like their peers who come to class without these problems, most students with learning impairments benefit from instruction that incorporates a variety of visual, auditory, and kinesthetic approaches. Try the following:

- **Communicate expectations.** Clearly define the guidelines for classroom behavior, preparation of assignments, and other student responsibilities. Explain that students with learning impairments are expected to adhere to the same standards as all the other students.
- **Monitor progress.** Break complex tasks into steps and make periodic informal checks to see that students with learning impairments understand the purpose of the work and are not falling behind.
- **Supply outlines.** Distribute outlines of material to be presented in class; this can help students with learning impairments preview and review content as necessary.
- **Pair students.** When possible, have a student with learning impairments work with a partner who is not learning impaired. Encourage the sharing and comparing of class notes, homework assignments, and preparations for class projects. Pairing dissimilar students helps them develop social skills and encourages an atmosphere of collaboration.
- **Provide recordings.** Create a library of audiotaped readings of the chapters in the text and of any other related print materials. Encourage students with learning impairments to use these resources to stay current with course content and to improve their reading comprehension skills.

Students With Physical Impairments

Students with physical impairments can be broadly classified into two groups: those with severely restricted use of one or more limbs, and those with other health impairments such as uncontrollable body movements or inability to breathe without assistance from a respirator. Some students with physical impairments use wheelchairs, while others make use of crutches, leg braces, or other such aids. Students in wheelchairs may or may not have use of their arms.

Students should investigate the resources available on campus. Most colleges have a disabled student support services office. Public campuses provide accessibility to classrooms, labs, and the library. In your classroom, try these general strategies:

- **Encourage responsibility.** Encourage students to think about what they need to be successful and to take responsibility for their learning. Students are responsible for documenting an impairment and requesting accommodations and assistance. Help students locate needed resources on campus and in the community.
- **Be informed.** Learn about the Americans with Disabilities Act (ADA). Meet with the staff in the disability support services office to gather advice and find out what further resources are available.
- **See the whole student.** Do not allow impairments to create a faulty perception of students' talents, efforts, and abilities.

- **Accommodate different learning styles.** Use visual, auditory, and kinesthetic techniques by incorporating visual arts, music, and tactile activities into the curriculum. Encourage students to discover how they process information and relate to others.
- **Encourage planning.** Encourage students to meet with each of their instructors and advisors individually at the outset of the term. Students should review course expectations, plan a course of study, and seek feedback.
- **Communicate with the student.** Talk one-on-one with students with physical impairments about what they perceive to be the stronger and weaker points of the classroom setting and your instructional approach given their particular physical impairments. Decide together how these issues can be addressed.
- **Respect students' needs.** Before classes begin, determine the needs of students with physical impairments and make sure the basic layout of your classroom allows them the necessary access.
- **Plan for emergencies.** Make plans for emergency evacuation of the classroom and building and go over these with the entire class.
- **Check community resources.** Look for organizations that offer services to people with physical impairments. If there is a need, work to connect the families of students with physical impairments with these organizations.

Above all, help all students see that having a physical impairment does not prevent a person from having a fulfilling career and social and family life. As students explore different areas of interest and specific careers throughout the course, encourage them to research how people with physical impairments can pursue particular careers and life goals. Plan a regularly occurring discussion on this topic. Setting the task for the whole class encourages all students to work together.

Students With Speech Impairments

Students with speech impairments may have problems with articulation or voice strength, may have impairments such as stuttering, chronic hoarseness, or difficulty in expressing an appropriate word or phrase, or may be unable to speak at all. In many cases, these students refrain from any class participation. Try these general strategies:

- **Don't prejudge.** Remember that students with speech impairments represent as wide a range of aptitudes and abilities as do students without such problems.
- **Speak normally.** Use normal communication patterns. Avoid completing statements or thoughts for the student.
- **Seek guidance.** Talk with specialists and counselors who see learners with speech impairments. These professionals may be able to provide you with guidelines, such as when to encourage or require that a particular student with a speech impairment enter group discussion, how to alter or defuse situations that seem to aggravate the speech problem, and so forth.
- **Communicate with students.** Once you and an individual student with a speech impairment have begun to get to know and be comfortable with each other, talk with him or her one-on-one about what classroom approaches do and do not work. Are there ways to make the class more effective and comfortable?

- **Encourage students' efforts to communicate.** Students who rely on electronic speaking devices or use body language to communicate should be encouraged in these efforts.
- **Make extra time.** Allow students to submit questions about particular lessons in writing. Set aside time to go over the questions with the student individually.

Students with speech impairments often do not feel comfortable participating in exercises devoted to interpersonal skills. From the very beginning of the course, try to encourage some degree of participation. You can start small, asking those who are not yet comfortable with speaking to watch and then to share written comments. Gradually, increase students' participation, moving toward full participation unless students begin to feel uncomfortable.

Even as you work toward improved speech function, allow plenty of opportunities for students with speech impairments to express themselves and know success in other ways. Written reports, bulletin boards and other visual displays, musical compositions—all offer authentic means of self-expression and communication.

HANDLING COMMON CLASSROOM PROBLEMS

Managing the Classroom

Even the most experienced teacher can experience problems in his or her classroom. The following discussion is designed to help you handle problems most commonly encountered by instructors.

Attendance Problems

First-term or first-year students sometimes do not understand how important it is to attend every class. They may be experiencing freedom for the first time or socializing too much. Here are some tips for handling attendance problems:

- **Expect regular attendance.** From the first day of class, announce that attendance, participation, and team cooperation will be graded. If a student misses class without telling you in advance, talk with the student in private and ask for a commitment. Point out that when students miss class, their teams suffer, too.
- **Grade attendance.** Remind students that attendance and participation are large parts of their grade. If attendance continues to be a problem, discuss this concern as a group. Attendance is important for teamwork, and the ability to come on time and prepared is important for both academic and career success.

Negative Attitude

A few students may sign up for the course feeling that it is either easy or a waste of time. They may be unsure of what is expected or skeptical about the value of the course. Occasionally, you may have a student who argues, is negative, or refuses to participate in team activities or contribute to class discussions. A negative attitude may indicate discomfort or fear. Here are some teaching tips for handling negative attitudes:

- **Expect responsibility.** Stress that students are responsible for their attitudes. Coaching and encouragement often inspire the negative student. Remind students of a major point in the book: Students are responsible for taking charge of their lives. They cannot blame others and be self-determined at the same time.
- **Isolate the problem student.** Meet with the disruptive student. Indicate that students who are disruptive during team exercises or class discussions will be asked to leave. Explain that students with negative attitudes affect the entire class. If the student complains or is uncooperative, ask him or her to answer this question: What can I do to correct this situation? Make students responsible for the solution.

Unmotivated Students

Increasing motivation is a major factor in helping students learn new material, complete assignments, work with others, and attend all classes. (Strategies for motivating students are discussed on pages 19–21.) Here are some teaching tips for handling unmotivated students:

- **Review motivational strategies.** Review the concepts of motivation (Chapter 7) and attitude (Chapter 5) and discuss how students can cope with low motivation. Discuss solutions as a group and assign a journal entry about motivation. Invite a guest speaker to address motivation and attitude.
- **Make learning active.** When energy is low (as is often the case around midterm time), you may want to go on a field trip. You could also vary assignments, role-play the Real-Life Success Stories, or discuss students' solutions for increasing their own motivation and developing a more positive attitude.
- **Focus on the benefits of the course.** Stress that forming positive habits will give students a sense of confidence and result in better grades in all their classes. Developing self-awareness will have lifelong benefits. Assure them that they will struggle less and enjoy life more.
- **Focus on real-world connections.** Again and again, focus on helping students relate the material to their lives.
- **Model enthusiasm.** When you, the instructor, are excited and enthusiastic about class, students are more likely to be motivated. Enjoy what you are doing and do not become discouraged by a lack of motivation on the part of some students.

Too Much Socializing

Sometimes students spend so much time socializing in class that they do not pay attention or complete projects. Here are some teaching tips for reducing student socializing:

- **Time exercises.** Set a certain amount of time for group and class discussions and exercises. Implementing a time limit helps students focus on the task at hand. You can always extend the time if necessary.
- **Stress doing "first things first."** Give students this rule of thumb for time management: Do first things first. Set priorities, follow through, and then have fun. Tell students that they will gain confidence when they learn this important habit. Their study teams will also benefit when they are more task-oriented.
- **Expect good manners.** Restate your expectations and rules for the class and be consistent. Encourage students to be courteous and respectful of all speakers.

- **Illustrate the disruption.** Often students think that if they are in the back of the classroom, the instructor does not see or hear them. Demonstrate the effects of side talking on a speaker and the class. Choose a student to speak in front of the classroom. Have a few other students talk among themselves. Ask the speaker what it was like to try and speak over conversations. Stress that public speaking and giving presentations are already difficult without distractions or rude behavior.
- **Clarify your feelings.** Use "I" messages to communicate how you feel: "I feel that what I am saying is being ignored or taken lightly when students side-talk."

Lack of Class Participation

You will have some students who are unwilling to participate in class. Here are some teaching tips for increasing class participation:

- **Explain why teamwork matters.** Tell students that, in the working world, organizations are run by teams and require employees to participate.
- **Review expectations.** Announce on the first day of the class and several times thereafter that teamwork and participation are essential. People who are successful learn to work with and handle various types of people, regardless of whether they personally like them or not. Stress that teamwork and participation are important factors in this course, in college, and in any career. Indicate that participation and sharing make the class much more effective and enjoyable.
- **Get involved.** Some students may feel more comfortable talking and participating in a small group. You may want to have teams of four or five students discuss Personal Journals or complete Exercises and then spend a few minutes discussing the topic with the class. Teamwork brings out participation even with shy students.
- **Model participation by sharing something about yourself.** Bring in periodicals occasionally and talk about the news and your opinions. Ask students about their opinions on current events, roommate problems, relating with instructors, and so on. Have a box where students can drop in topics they would like to discuss but do not want to introduce in front of the class.

Shy Students

You will always have some students who are shy and thus do not contribute as much as the more outgoing students. Here are some teaching tips for encouraging shy students:

- **Discuss personality traits.** Discuss how different personality traits can be sources of strength. Point out that some people are more extroverted than others and that people of all personality styles can attain success.
- **Encourage risk taking.** If students are shy, ask them to reach out and be more involved. Extroverted students should listen more to draw out the shyer students. Encourage your outgoing students to be supportive, to listen, and to help others express their views. You might want to ask students to shift their seating every few weeks so that shy students sit up front during some of the sessions. Discuss how you or other students overcame shyness.

Interrupting

Few things are more irritating than being interrupted. Here are some teaching tips for minimizing interruptions:

- **Expect good manners.** From the first day of class, stress the importance of listening courteously until others are finished talking. Emphasize that respect is essential to good communication.
- **Model respect.** Show respect to students by modeling good listening skills.

Personality Conflicts

Students may have personality conflicts with each other and at times with you. Most of the time, these conflicts can be resolved with a positive, diplomatic attitude. Here are some teaching tips for dealing with personality conflicts:

- **Don't take it personally.** Some students may have difficulty taking direction, dealing with authority figures, or letting anyone get close to them. Other students may be especially shy or unresponsive. These behaviors are not directed at you alone, and you are not to blame for them.
- **Communicate.** You may be misreading the behavior. Perhaps there is a misunderstanding, for example, or students are unclear about expectations. A student may have taken something you said the wrong way. Set judgments aside and begin a dialogue, practicing active listening and making constructive suggestions for improvement.
- **Discuss diversity.** You will have many opportunities to discuss diversity. Remind students that they will encounter people with a wide range of values, personality traits, beliefs, and attitudes, and that it is important to be able to relate to and communicate with all of them.
- **Be yourself.** Be confident, approachable, caring, and a good listener. Your goal is to support students in being successful. A student does not have to like you personally to learn from you.

Incomplete Work

You may have some students who are not turning in assignments. Here are some teaching tips to encourage students to complete their work:

- **Communicate expectations.** Explain the guidelines and expectations for receiving a good grade or credit for the course. Discuss what students want to learn from the course and what this means in terms of attendance, assignments, and participation. As suggested earlier, you may want to have students turn in note cards with their name, phone number, major, year in school, the grade they expect to earn, what they hope to learn from the course, and the areas they most want to work on. This is an excellent time to review goals and expectations.
- **Contact students.** Call or e-mail students when they miss class, repeatedly fail to participate, or do not turn in assignments. After this contact, it is up to students to produce results. Show your concern, but avoid rescuing them. They need to be responsible for their behavior.

Too Much to Do and Too Little Time

You do not have to cover every topic in detail. You might want students to take one topic and give a short presentation, then discuss it as a group. This assignment gives students a chance to improve their speaking skills, to research and present a topic, and to lead a discussion. As a group, students can also select the topics in which they are most interested. Instead of writing a paper about a large concept such as self-esteem, some students may want to explore a particular facet of that topic more thoroughly, then write a report or create a presentation and discuss the topic briefly in class.

ASSESSMENT AND EVALUATION

The Purpose of Assessment

Assessment is the gathering and analysis of information to improve student learning. Assessment can improve learning in many ways. It can boost students' motivation by showing them how much progress they have made and by helping them identify specific areas for improvement. It can help you gauge the effectiveness of activities, lectures, teaching materials, instructional methods, and the course as a whole.

What is good assessment? According to the American Association for Higher Learning, effective assessment is based on the following nine principles:

- Assessment is not an end in itself, but a vehicle for educational improvement.
- Because learning involves not only knowledge and abilities but also values, attitudes, and habits of mind, assessment must employ a variety of methods.
- Clear, specific educational goals are the cornerstone of focused, useful assessment.
- Assessment requires attention not only to outcomes but also and equally to the experiences that lead to those outcomes.
- Assessment works best when it is ongoing, not episodic.
- Assessment is collaborative and should involve stakeholders from across the educational community (on and off campus).
- Assessment makes a difference when it not only measures data but also illuminates questions that people really care about.
- Assessment is most likely to lead to improvement when it is part of a larger set of conditions that promote change.
- Assessment is a tool for educators to meet their responsibilities to their students and to the public.

Effective assessment can include much more than just testing. For example, talking with other student success instructors on your campus and other campuses can provide a way of gauging the success of your students and your teaching methods. Student self-assessment is another important form of assessment, especially since it can help students feel proud of their accomplishments and motivate them to work on improving their overall performance. The Personal Success Portfolio, along with any supplementary documents that you have students include, is also an excellent opportunity to assess students' overall progress.

The Grading Process

Exercises, Personal Journals, critical thinking and caption questions, and Application and Internet activities in *Psychology of Success* are designed to help students understand the concepts presented in the chapter and to prompt them to think more deeply and critically about their lives and their future. By definition, there are no "right" answers to critical thinking questions. Grading should be based on the sophistication and thoughtfulness of students' answers rather than on the specific opinions, ideas, or examples given in those answers. Below is a general scoring rubric.

SCORING RUBRIC	
Score	**Answer**
90–100%	Student fully understands the relevant chapter text and has done independent thinking about how these concepts can prove useful in his or her life. Student always backs assertions and opinions with critical thinking and specific examples. If an activity, answer shows evidence of originality and excellent planning and execution.
80–89%	Student understands almost all the relevant chapter text and has thought about how these concepts could apply in real-life situations. Student usually supports assertions or opinions with critical thinking and specific examples. If an activity, answer shows evidence of good planning and execution.
70–79%	Student has limited understanding of relevant chapter text. Student occasionally supports assertions or opinions with critical thinking and specific examples. If an activity, answer shows evidence of adequate planning and execution.
60–69%	Student understands only some chapter concepts and/or has not read all of the required text. Answer lacks adequate evidence of critical thinking. Student makes vague or opinionated statements without providing sufficient support or examples. If an activity, answer shows evidence of scanty planning and execution.
59% and below	Student misunderstands chapter concepts and/or has not read the required text. Answer shows no evidence of effort or thought or is lacking altogether.

Assessing the Course

The first place to start in assessing your course is to compare the goals of the course with its outcomes. What were the goals of the course? Did the course meet these goals? Did students make connections between what they learned in this class and what they are learning in other classes? Did students make connections between success in school, work, and life? Did students use critical thinking? Did they learn to be more self-confident, self-disciplined, and self-motivated?

Referring back to the specific course goals laid out on page 3, ask yourself:

- Did students gain an understanding of the basic principles of psychology?
- Did students develop a clear vision of what success means to them?
- Did students gain self-awareness and emotional awareness?
- Did students pinpoint their personality traits, values, skills, interests, and career preferences?
- Did students set specific, achievable short- and long-term goals?
- Did students learn strategies for coping with stress, anger, and other negative emotions?
- Did students break negative thought patterns and learn positive new ones?
- Did students learn to harness self-discipline to control impulses, break bad habits, and make positive life changes?
- Did students develop critical thinking and decision-making skills?
- Did students examine what motivates them and why?
- Did students overcome fear of failure and fear of success?
- Did students learn to manage their time and money effectively?
- Did students become effective speakers and active listeners?
- Did students appreciate diversity and reject stereotypes and prejudice?
- Did students build skills necessary for fulfilling, healthy relationships?

Gathering Data on Outcomes

You will also want to gather data and work with staff in research and development to measure outcomes. You can compare students who took the class to those who did not. You can also look at the retention rates of students over several years. This can help you justify the continuation of this course. To make the case for the importance of a student success course, it is also extremely helpful to have research data available about other student success programs and about student success programs as a whole. Schedule a meeting with your research and development staff and discuss questions such as:

- Do students who complete a student success course stay in school longer?
- Do students who complete a student success course get better grades?
- Are retention and graduation rates for these students higher?
- Are these students more successful in their jobs?

As you strive to improve this course to better meet students' needs, you may also want to look at other factors that affect the success of the course, such as:

- whether the course is offered for credit
- whether the course is graded
- whether the course meets at least twice a week

- whether the course meets for the entire semester
- whether the course is limited to twenty-five students or less
- whether experienced instructors teach the course
- whether the course includes peer teaching
- whether the book assigned to the course is new and mandatory
- whether the instructors receive training

You may want to suggest that a student success advisory committee be established to collect data, set goals, and assess the success of the program. This committee may be composed of student success instructors, administrators, and staff interested in student success and retention. The data can serve as a basis for ongoing conversations and continuous improvement.

Assessment of Instructors

Comments from students can be extremely helpful for assessing your effectiveness as an instructor, especially when you are teaching a course for the first time. Consider eliciting feedback on several different aspects of the course, including:

- general teaching approach
- instructor's accessibility/attitude
- clarity of explanations and examples
- sequencing and pacing of topics
- variety and suitability of assignments and activities
- difficulty level
- guidance of discussions and projects
- use of instructional media
- use of guest speakers and field trips

Students may feel more open to providing honest feedback if you ask each small group/team to give a review at midterm and then again at the end of the course.

Many standard evaluation forms are available for instructor and course assessment. Review several evaluation forms and modify them as necessary to meet your needs.

Assessment by Employers

Many colleges have advisory committees made up of local employers. Some colleges ask employers who hire their graduates to rate each employee's level of skill, competence, and professionalism. You may want to see what employer assessment instruments are available for you to use on your campus. Review past comments so that you know what employers expect from your graduates. This research can help you select relevant topics and activities for your classes.

Assessment by Accrediting Agencies

Many schools have accrediting agencies that review their programs. You may want to review their criteria and past suggestions to use as guidelines for your class. Ask if there are national exams or capstone courses that may also provide you with data.

PART 2
CHAPTER NOTES
AND ANSWERS

Psychology and Success

OVERVIEW

In this chapter, students are introduced to the building blocks of psychology and success. In Section 1.1 students learn how to define success for themselves and the relationship between success and happiness. They are also introduced to the discipline of psychology and how understanding this science will help them to better understand themselves. In Section 1.2 students take their first look at who they really are and the influences that have molded them. They read about how to build a healthy self-image and how their identities are shaped by society, culture, and gender role.

OBJECTIVES

After they complete this chapter, students should be able to:

- Define success.
- List several personal qualities that help people to be happy.
- Define psychology and cite its four major goals.
- Explain the relationship between thoughts, feelings, and actions.
- Define self, self-image, and identity.
- Describe the components of identity.

OUTLINE

Chapter Topics

UNDERSTANDING SUCCESS

What Is Success?

      Ingredients of Success

      Who Is a Success?

      Success and Happiness

      What Causes Happiness?

Understanding Psychology

      Why Study Psychology?

      Goals of Psychology

      Explaining Human Behavior

      Thoughts, Feelings, and Actions

      Cognition and Emotion

UNDERSTANDING YOURSELF

Your Inner Self

      Your Self-Image

      Building a Healthy Self-Image

You and Your Social World

      Identity

      Culture and Identity

      Gender and Identity

Chapter Activities

EXERCISE 1.1   **What Success Means to You** (pp. 5–6)

EXERCISE 1.2   **Your Role Model** (pp. 11–12)

EXERCISE 1.3   **How Happy Are You?** (pp. 14–15)

EXERCISE 1.4   **Wheel of Life** (pp. 28–30)

EXERCISE 1.5   **Sides of Yourself** (p. 32)

EXERCISE 1.6   **Identity Profile** (pp. 35–37)

Personal Journal 1.1   **Ingredients of Success** (p. 9)

Personal Journal 1.2   **Your Thoughts, Feelings, and Actions** (p. 21)

Personal Journal 1.3   **How Do You See Yourself?** (p. 26)

Personal Journal 1.4   **Gender Roles** (p. 39)

Chapter Features

PROFESSIONAL DEVELOPMENT   **You on Paper** (p. 7)

INTERNET ACTION   **Virtual Therapy** (p. 18)

Applying Psychology   **Are You a TV Addict?** (p. 25)

FOCUS

Introducing the Chapter

On the board, write the words *psychology* and *success*. Give students a total of five minutes to write a definition for each word. (Psychology—the scientific study of human behavior. Success—this may vary but should relate to a sense of achievement and/or fulfillment.) Then ask, "What is the relationship between psychology and success? How is a person's ability to be successful related to how a person behaves?" As a class, discuss the responses.

Real-Life Success Story "Am I Doing the Right Thing?" (p. 2)

Have a student read the Real-Life Success Story to the class. Then ask for volunteers to share a story about being in a similar situation. Ask, "Has anyone had to make a choice like Bill's? What did you do, and why?" Discuss what factors might make this a more or less difficult choice. For example, if you have a family to support financially, it could be more difficult to choose the job with lower pay. What could Bill do to make writing a more viable option?

Opening Quote (p. 3)

"What lies behind us and what lies before us are small matters compared to what lies within us."

Write the quote on the board or display a transparency of the reproducible master on page 241. Ask students what they think this statement means. What does "lies behind us" and "lies before us" mean? Does "lies within us" refer to character?

Ask students to think of a person they know who has great character. How did that person's past affect his or her character? How can his or her future be determined by that same character? Finally, ask if students agree with the quote. You may also wish to discuss some or all of the other quotes provided on the reproducible master.

INSTRUCT

Teaching Tips

The following topics are discussed in this chapter. You may want to expand on them in large or small class groups.

What Is Success? (pp. 4–16)

Discuss the relationship between success and happiness. Then ask a volunteer to give a definition for *happiness*. Compare the student's definition with the definition in the text (a state of well-being that comes from having a positive evaluation of your life). Then discuss the idea that factors such as wealth, youth, physical health, marital status, physical attractiveness, educational level, and social status have little effect on happiness. Ask students if they agree with that concept and have them explain why or why not, giving examples.

Understanding Psychology (pp. 17–23)

Ask students to review their definitions of psychology from the "Introducing the Chapter" activity. Allow students to share their definitions, then write the text's definition (the scientific study of human behavior) on the board. Explain that behavior is anything we think, feel, or do. Have students look at the behaviors listed on page 17 and give examples of how each behavior might affect a person's level of success. For example, how a person reacts to situations may help or hinder him or her in a certain career. Then introduce the idea that studying psychology can help students become more self-aware and that self-awareness can help them reach success.

Your Inner Self (pp. 24–30)

Write the terms *self* and *self-image* on the board and ask for volunteers to give definitions for each. Have students review page 25 of the text, which lists areas of our lives in which we have different self-images. Explain that having a healthy self-image means having a complex self-image, or having a variety of positive roles and ways of seeing yourself.

Bring an assortment of magazines and catalogs for the class to use. (Ask students to bring magazines and catalogs from home as well for variety.) Give students half an hour to go through the magazines and cut out images that they perceive as reflective of their own self-image and paste the images onto cardboard to make a collage. Ask students to talk in small groups about the areas of their lives they have depicted. (These might include school, home, spirituality, friendships, outdoor activities, sports, reading, playing or working on a computer, drawing, and writing.) Ask volunteers to share their collages with the rest of the class.

You and Your Social World (pp. 31–40)

Ask for a volunteer to explain the term *self-presentation*. Discuss as a class how people use self-presentation as a response to the desire for social acceptance. Ask students if they believe they engage in self-presentation; stress that self-presentation is entirely normal. What circumstances might encourage self-presentation? When might self-presentation have negative consequences? Positive consequences?

Have students work in groups of three or four to write and present a role-play that depicts the concept of self-presentation. Then ask if the role-plays affected how they think about how we present ourselves in society. Do we act our true selves, or are we a bit like actors on a stage?

In-Chapter Answers and Notes

EXERCISE 1.1

What Success Means to You (pp. 5–6)

A. Words or phrases associated with "success" will vary but should reflect a sense of fulfillment and/or achievement.

B. Answers will vary, but students should recognize whether their vision of success reflects public recognition or personal satisfaction.

C. Answers will vary but should address fulfillment and/or achievement.

D. Answers will vary. Many definitions will be similar to the text definition; however, some definitions will probably reflect the belief that success is something granted by others (e.g., through money, fame, or power).

E. Answers will vary. Those who agree with the text's definition of success should feel that it is within their power to become successful. Those who believe that success is something granted by others may feel less capable of achieving success.

F. The people chosen will vary. They may or may not be people personally known by the student, but students should be able to explain how the people they chose achieved success.

Exploring Further

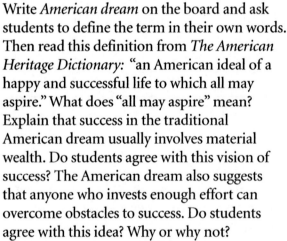

Write *American dream* on the board and ask students to define the term in their own words. Then read this definition from *The American Heritage Dictionary*: "an American ideal of a happy and successful life to which all may aspire." What does "all may aspire" mean? Explain that success in the traditional American dream usually involves material wealth. Do students agree with this vision of success? The American dream also suggests that anyone who invests enough effort can overcome obstacles to success. Do students agree with this idea? Why or why not?

The Center for a New American Dream is a nonprofit organization whose goal is a "shift of American culture away from its emphasis on consumption toward a more fulfilling, just, and sustainable way of life." Its motto is, "More Fun, Less Stuff!" The Center advocates working less, spending less, and finding a purpose in life outside of acquiring material goods. Explain these ideas to students and ask for their point of view. How important is wealth? Is it possible to be wealthy and unsuccessful?

You on Paper (p. 7)

Answers will vary. One example would be applying for an entry-level position in which many applicants have similar levels of education and job experience. Because the résumés would have similar information, an excellent cover letter could set one applicant apart from the others. A poorly written cover letter, by contrast, could keep an otherwise well-qualified candidate from receiving further consideration.

Personal Journal 1.1

Ingredients of Success (p. 9)

Student responses will vary but should recognize the following: self-awareness allows you to know what you want out of life; self-esteem helps you to keep believing in yourself; positive thinking helps you to focus on future possibilities instead of setbacks; self-discipline helps you to put your plans into action; self-motivation keeps you motivated and helps you overcome fears; and positive relationships are important because no one succeeds without the help, ideas, and emotional support of others.

EXERCISE 1.2

Your Role Model (pp. 11–12)

A. Students' role models will vary.

B-C. Answers will vary but should be realistic and demonstrate self-awareness.

Sample Answers

1. Name <u>Gwen Ifill</u>
2. Date and place of birth <u>New York, date unknown</u>
3. Special accomplishments <u>Moderator and Managing Editor of Washington Week in Review</u>

<u>Senior Correspondent on The NewsHour with Jim Lehrer</u>
<u>National correspondent for NBC</u>
<u>White House correspondent for The New York Times</u>

4. Obstacle(s) he or she overcame <u>growing up poor</u>
5. Ways he or she overcame these obstacles <u>Getting an education, believing she could do anything</u>
6. Special personal qualities <u>perseverance, intelligence</u>
7. Ways he or she shows or showed these special qualities <u>Becoming an African American role model in a field where few African Americans have achieved success</u>
8. Ways he or she acquired these special qualities <u>Hard work and family support</u>
9. Things you and your role model have in common (personal qualities, experiences, interests, challenges) <u>We both have an interest in journalism and we are both African American women</u>
10. Areas in which you would like to become more like your role model. <u>I would like to become a real journalist and eventually make my way into television news. I would also like to give back to my community and serve as a role model for other women in the media.</u>

EXERCISE 1.3

How Happy Are You? (pp. 14–15)

A-B. Responses and scores will vary.

C. Answers will vary. Students with average and above-average scores are likely to recognize that they have a positive evaluation of their lives. Students with below-average scores may recognize that they depend too much on the positive evaluation of others. Seeking the approval of others cannot lead to sustained happiness.

D. Answers will vary but could refer to some of the ways to foster happiness described on page 13.

E. Answers will vary, but students should recognize that it is healthier to base one's happiness on inner satisfaction than to base it on outside factors such as money or fame.

Virtual Therapy (p. 18)

Students' responses will vary. Some may feel that an advantage of online therapy is a certain amount of anonymity—being able to talk about a problem without having to actually meet the therapist. Others may agree that without personal contact, the therapy would have no lasting effect. Still others may feel that some online therapists may not be genuine.

FIGURE 1.1

Thoughts, Feelings, and Actions (p. 20)

Students' responses will vary, although students should recognize that thoughts and feelings both influence actions, so a person with conflicting thoughts and feelings might have trouble deciding how to act. Other students may answer the question by stating that logical thinking should prevail at all times, while others will probably say that happiness comes from "following your heart." Students should recognize that neither point of view is all right or all wrong and that everyone should evaluate each situation in his or her own way.

Personal Journal 1.2

Your Thoughts, Feelings, and Actions (p. 21)

Student responses will vary.

Sample Answers

I was hiking with a group last Saturday. I wasn't paying attention, and I walked straight into the web of a garden spider. Although I knew the spider was harmless, I panicked and ran back down the path for a half mile. I was embarrassed because I had to double back twice the distance in order to catch up with the rest of the group. Even though I knew the spider was harmless, I couldn't help feeling fear and anxiety, which made me panic and run away. This action led to an acute feeling of embarrassment.

Thoughts: knew the spider was harmless; realized my feelings were irrational
Feelings: fear and anxiety; embarrassment
Actions: panicking and running away

FIGURE 1.2

Positive and Negative Emotions (p. 22)

Student experiences of joy will vary, but may relate to relationships, spiritual experiences, or encounters with nature.

SECTION 1.1
SELF-CHECK (p. 23)

1. A role model is a person who has the qualities you would like to have.

2. Psychology helps to answer basic questions about what it means to be human, which helps us understand ourselves and others.

3. The nervous system is a system of nerve cells that regulates behavior by transmitting messages back and forth between the brain and the other parts of the body.

Applying Psychology

ARE YOU A TV ADDICT? (p. 25)
Answers will vary. Many students will probably recognize that watching TV does not require or encourage concentration; in fact, because of its fast pace, it makes concentration nearly impossible. People who watch a great deal of television can lose the patience necessary to pay attention to one thing for an extended period of time.

Personal Journal 1.3

How Do You See Yourself? (p. 26)

Students' ratings will vary depending on their self-image.

Exploring Further

Ask students to answer these follow-up questions: If a close friend or family member were to look at the 1–10 ratings you gave to each statement, do you think he or she would believe that you view yourself accurately? Why or why not? Whose views do you think would probably be more accurate—yours or those of the friend or family member? Why?

EXERCISE 1.4

Wheel of Life (pp. 28–30)

A-B. Responses and scores will vary.

C. Wheels will also vary but should reflect how much time is spent on each area and/or how important each area is to the student.

D. Answers will vary. By filling in the wheel, students may see a lack of balance of which they were previously unaware.

E. Answers will vary. Areas with scores of 10 or less may need more attention.

F. Answers will vary. Examples include giving up some time for hobbies and leisure to spend more time in the community, or spending less time on work and career to give more attention to spirituality.

G. Answers will vary. Some students may find hobbies and leisure or money less important at this stage of their lives.

EXERCISE 1.5

Sides of Yourself (p. 32)

A. Descriptions will vary.

B. Answers will vary; however, most students will recognize that they feel more comfortable with people with whom they are familiar, such as parents, siblings, and close friends. They may feel they are more "themselves" with these people.

C. Answers will vary, but should recognize that most people use self-presentation when they feel the need to make a good impression on others.

Sample Answers

A. Write how you think, feel, or act with the people named.

Parent(s)	Instructor
restrained	tongue-tied
polite	attentive
helpful	interested
respectful	exhausted
annoyed	stimulated

Sibling(s)	Close Friend
easygoing	honest
playful	curious
irritable	laughing
comfortable	relaxed
a little obnoxious	confident

Romantic Interest	New Acquaintance
excited	shy
happy	curious
nervous	standoffish
aroused	reserved
fascinated	fake

B. Are you more "yourself" with one of these individuals?

I am more open and comfortable with my siblings and my close friends, but I get more easily irritated by my relatives. I am more reserved in class and when meeting new people.

C. When do you use self-presentation?

I am very shy, so I use self-presentation a lot in the classroom, or when meeting new people. I try to present myself as an affable, even-tempered kind of person.

EXERCISE 1.6

Identity Profile (pp. 35–37)
Identity profiles will vary widely.

Exploring Further

Point out to students that people can also define their identities through what they are *not*. For example, a young adult who rejects her parents' conservative political beliefs might think of herself as "not conservative" and "not like her parents." Ask the class whether any of them think of themselves as "not" like something or someone, such as "not like my siblings," "not athletic," etc. Some students who are of minority ethnic heritage may not feel a tie with any particular ethnic group but may still describe themselves as "not white."

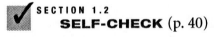

Gender Roles (p. 39)
Students' choices of adjectives will vary.

Exploring Further

Ask students whether they believe that the adjectives in the grey columns apply more to males than the adjectives in the white columns, and vice versa. Call on them to defend their opinions. Ask students how many of the "masculine" and "feminine" traits they think are positive. Are there any traits on this chart that they would *not* like to have? Why?

SECTION 1.2
SELF-CHECK (p. 40)

1. Self-image is all the beliefs a person has about himself or herself.

2. A social role is a set of norms (standards of behavior) that define how a person is supposed to behave in a given social position or setting.

3. The three components of identity are individual identity, relational identity, and collective identity.

Additional Activities

These additional activities are exclusive to this Instructor's Resource Manual. They are designed to meet the special needs of your students. The activities can be used as in-class activities or as take-home assignments. They can be assigned to individual students, pairs of students, or groups of students.

Application

THOUGHTS, FEELINGS, AND ACTIONS
Ask students to consider their most probable thought(s), feeling(s), and action(s) in the following situations. Working question by question, ask students to explain why they think they would act in the way they described. (A reproducible master of this list can be found on page 245.)

1. Gripping a hot pan
2. Seeing a great bargain at a store
3. Overhearing a funny comment
4. Smelling something burning
5. Seeing a friend crossing the street toward them
6. Seeing a nickel lying on the ground
7. Hitting head on cabinet door
8. Hearing an ambulance approaching while driving
9. Stepping on a tack while barefoot
10. Seeing a ball sailing through the air toward you

Ask students whether they believe they could alter their behavior (thoughts, feelings, or actions) in any of these situations. For example, would they be able to do anything other than dropping a hot pan? What about buying a bargain-priced item? Is there a difference between the two? Why or why not? If they *could* alter their behavior, would they want to? Why or why not?

POSITIVE QUALITIES   Ask students to select a magazine, television commercial, or television program. Which personal qualities does the magazine, commercial, or program equate or link with happiness and success? For example, does a certain magazine link happiness and success with wealth, style, fame, or self-esteem? Compare the qualities promoted in the magazine, commercial, or program to the qualities listed on page 16 of the textbook. (A reproducible master of this list can be found on page 246.) Do students believe that the images presented in the media are true indicators of happiness? Why or why not?

INDIVIDUALISM AND COLLECTIVISM

Have students imagine that they have accepted a job in a collectivist culture. (Point out that most societies in Asia and Africa embrace collectivism.) Ask students to choose a specific country and to research the business etiquette in this society. What are some of the cultural differences they will find when they get there? Ask them to cite three examples of how, as a Westerner from an individualist culture, they will need to change their usual behavior and why these changes are necessary.

CONSTRUCTING AN IDENTITY   Ask students to think of their favorite book series or television program and to create an identity for a new fictional character that is about to be introduced in the series or program. Students should create a profile of the individual, relational, and collective identity of the character, including descriptions of each of the elements listed on pages 33 and 34. If desired, divide the class into groups and ask each group to work together to create one such character profile. Groups could then be asked to present their characters to the rest of the class, and other students could be encouraged to ask questions about the character, such as "what did [the character] study in college? Why?" "Does [the character] have pets? Why?" The idea is to get students thinking about how the different parts of a person's identity come together to form a unified whole.

Internet Activities

STRENGTHS INVENTORY   Have students locate and complete the online strengths inventory offered by the Values In Action Institute (VAI). The 275-question survey, which takes about 20 minutes to complete, was created by adherents of the positive psychology movement to measure respondents' strengths of character in 24 areas. At the end of the questionnaire, an automatic scoring

system provides students with their top five strengths. Ask students to describe their top five strengths and to give specific examples of ways they have demonstrated these strengths in the past. Also ask students to describe the five strengths they would most like to develop further, and why. To facilitate class discussion, make a transparency of the reproducible master on page 247, "24 Strengths of Character."

MONEY AND HAPPINESS   Ask students to visit the Web site of the American Psychological Association and to locate an online article from the APA *Monitor*, "People Need Help Finding What Makes Them Happy." Then have them answer the following questions using the article: What evidence did two recent studies provide for the idea that money does not create happiness? What four reasons does psychologist Mihaly Csikszentmihalyi give to explain why people believe that more money will bring them more happiness? What three psychological theories provide an alternative to material pursuits to explain true happiness? Explain Csikszentmihalyi's "flow" theory. (Note: the concept of flow is briefly defined on page 77 in Chapter 2.)

ASSESS

Review and Activities Answers

Review Questions (p. 42)

1. According to the text, you are successful if you find a lifetime of personal fulfillment by creating meaning in your work and life. This kind of success comes from satisfaction with yourself and your achievements.

2. Thoughts, feelings, and actions are all connected. Each influences the other in a continuous cycle. For example, our thoughts about people, objects, events, and situations have a strong influence on our feelings about them.

3. Negative emotions encourage us to focus our attention on the specific thing that is troubling us. For example, if we experience anger, our mind will be filled with hostile thoughts for the object of our anger. Because negative emotions take up so much of our attention and energy, they make it hard to do productive things, like learning or working toward a goal.

4. Collectivism is a philosophy in many Eastern cultures that values group goals over individual goals and defines a person's identity more through group identifications than through personal attributes. Individualism, by contrast, is a philosophy in many Western cultures that values individual goals over group goals and defines identity more through personal attributes than through group identifications.

5. If you say, "I am Catholic," you are revealing a part of your collective identity because you are revealing the religious and sociocultural group to which you belong.

6. A social role is a set of norms, or standards of behavior, that define how we are supposed to act in a given social position or setting. We act according to social roles because we desire social acceptance. A gender role is a set of norms that define how males and females are supposed to behave. While social roles apply to everyone, regardless of sex, gender roles apply specifically to males or females. Gender roles and social roles can overlap: for example, the roles of "mother" and "father" have both a social and a gender component.

Critical Thinking (p. 42)

7. Answers may vary, but students should recognize that a person can raise the general level of his or her happiness by seeking out certain opportunities, such as creating a sense of purpose in your life and building deep connections with others. Most of the components of happiness must be sought—they do not arrive out of no-where, without effort and self-awareness. The very act of making effort to become happier can make a large difference in a person's self-esteem and level of well-being.

8. Answers will vary, although students should recognize that one's identity, or public self, is powerfully affected by factors such as culture and family. Growing up in another culture or family, a person would have different possessions, different beliefs and goals, different relationships, and possibly a different religion and social class, among many other things.

Application (p. 42)

9. Answers will vary, but should show critical thinking and an awareness of gender roles in our society. Although more and more gender-neutral toys and books are being produced, the majority still reflect entrenched gender roles. At Amazon.com, for example, games and books are grouped by age level and interest, but toys can be selected based on gender. The toys designated by gender do reinforce traditional gender roles. Boys' toys are divided into the categories of action figures, blocks and construction, home improvement, science and nature, and vehicles and die-cast. Girls' toys are divided into the categories of Barbie, real-food fun, arts and crafts, animal alley, and puzzles. If desired, ask students to bring photographs, printouts, or actual examples of merchandise that reinforces gender roles.

10. Answers will vary. Students should explain to participants that areas with scores of 10 or less may represent areas of their lives that need more attention.

Internet Activities (p. 43)

11. Summaries of biographies will vary but should include the names and accomplishments of the people selected, what inspired them, and their similarities to the other

individuals selected. Summaries should also include what the students learned from the life stories.

12. Reports will vary but should identify the five approaches: 1. psychodynamic, which is based on the ideas of Freud and holds that behavior stems from unconscious forces and conflicts; 2. behavioral, pioneered by Watson and Skinner and based on the belief that psychology should only examine observable human behavior, not subjective thoughts and feelings; 3. humanistic, developed by Rogers and Maslow, which takes the view that people are complex, unique individuals who naturally strive to reach their full mental and spiritual potential; 4. cognitive, which focuses on cognition, the functions of processing, storing, and remembering information and experiences; and 5. biological, which investigates the biological basis of human behavior.

Real-Life Success Story "Am I Doing the Right Thing?" (p. 43)

Stories will vary but should reflect an understanding of how this chapter defines success.

Sample Answers

Although some of his friends didn't understand his decision, Bill decided not to take the job. He realized that advancing his movie production career would only be the right move if it would help him to achieve success on his own terms. His real dream was to become a published writer and to achieve a balance between his personal and work lives. By listening to his feelings and considering his vision of success, Bill made a choice that he could be happy with. He also faced the future with greater focus and self-confidence.

CLOSE

Culminating Activity

Have students work in pairs to interview one another about their definition of success. Students should ask each other:

- What does success mean to you? Why?
- Has reading this chapter changed your ideas about success?
- Do you feel like a success now? If so, why? If not, what would make you feel like a success?

After students have finished their dicussions, reunite the class and discuss what students learned from their classmates.

Personal Success Portfolio

Have students complete the Personal Success Portfolio worksheet for Chapter 1 on page 231. Refer to pages 9 and 10 for suggestions on presenting this activity.

For Chapter 1, additional materials you may wish students to add to their Personal Success Portfolios include:

- a personal essay reflecting on one or two people who have achieved success according to the student's definition
- a cover letter written according to the guidelines presented in the "Professional Development" feature on page 7
- a first-person letter addressed to a living role model asking for advice in one or two areas (students can mail the letter and keep a photocopy or printout in their portfolios, along with any answer received)
- a technology project, such as a PowerPoint presentation, a digital photo project, or a simple Web page or HTML file documenting some aspect of the student's identity in which he or she takes particular pride
- a brief research project, bibliography, or book report on a chapter topic that interests the student

ADDITIONAL RESOURCES

The following books and periodicals offer information on personal success strategies, general and positive psychology, emotion and cognition, and identity and the self.

Books

Baltus, Rita. *Personal Psychology for Life and Work.* 5th ed. Columbus: Glencoe/McGraw-Hill, 2000.

Bandura, Albert. *Social Foundations of Thoughts and Action.* Englewood Cliffs, New Jersey: Prentice-Hall, 1986.

Bellah, R. et al., *Habits of the Heart: Individualism and Commitment in American Life.* Berkeley: University of California Press, 1985.

Brown, Jonathon D. *The Self.* New York: McGraw-Hill, 1998.

Choquette, Sonia, Patrick Tully, and Julia Cameron. *Your Heart's Desire: Instructions for Creating the Life You Really Want.* New York: Random House, 1997.

Czikszentmihalyi, Mihaly. *The Evolving Self: A Psychology for the Third Millennium.* New York: Harper Perennial, 1993.

Damasio, Antonio. *Descartes' Error: Emotion, Reason, and the Human Brain.* New York: Grosset/Putnam, 1994.

Damasio, Antonio. *The Feeling of What Happens: Body and Emotion in the Making of Consciousness.* San Diego: Harcourt, Inc., 1999.

Diener, E. and C. Diener. "Most People Are Happy." *Psychological Science* 7 (1996): 181–185.

Dyer, Wayne. *10 Secrets for Success and Inner Peace.* Carlsbad, CA: Hay House, 2002.

Feldman, Robert S. *Understanding Psychology.* 4th ed. New York: McGraw-Hill Higher Education, 2002.

Frankl, Victor. *Man's Search for Meaning.* 3rd ed. New York: Simon & Schuster, 1984.

Gilbert, D., S. Fiske and G. Lindzey, eds. *Handbook of Social Psychology.* 2 vols. 4th ed. New York: McGraw-Hill, 1998.

Jeter, Derek and Jack Curry. *The Life You Imagine: Life Lessons for Achieving Your Dreams.* New York: Crown Publishing Group, 2000.

LeDoux, Joseph. *The Emotional Brain: The Mysterious Underpinnings of Emotional Life.* New York: Simon & Schuster, 1996.

Lewis, M. and J. M. Haviland, eds. *Handbook of Emotions.* 2nd ed. New York: Guilford Press, 2000.

Passer, Michael and Ronald Smith. *Psychology: Frontiers and Applications.* New York: McGraw-Hill, 2001.

Qubein, Nido R. *Stairway to Success: The Complete Blueprint for Personal and Professional Achievement.* Hoboken, NJ: John Wiley and Sons, 1997.

Rafaeli-Mor, Eshkol, I. H. Gotlib, and W. Revelle. "The Meaning and Measurement of Self-Complexity," *Personality and Individual Differences* 27 (1999): 341–356.

Seligman, Martin and Mihaly Csikszentmihalyi, "Positive Psychology: An Introduction," *American Psychologist* 55 (2000): 5–14.

Snyder, C. R. and Shane J. Lopez, eds. *Handbook of Positive Psychology.* New York: Oxford University Press, 2001.

Strack, F., M. Argyle and N. Schwarz. *Subjective Well-Being: An Interdisciplinary Perspective.* Oxford: Pergamon Press, 1991.

Tesser, Abraham and Nobert Schwartz, eds. *Blackwell Handbook of Social Psychology: Intraindividual Processes.* Malden, MA: Blackwell Publishers, 2001.

Triandis, H.C. *Individualism and Collectivism.* Boulder, CO: Westview Press, 1995.

Waitley, Denis. *Empires of the Mind: Lessons to Lead and Succeed in a Knowledge-Based World.* New York: Quill, 1996.

Waitley, Denis. *The Joy of Working: The 30-Day System to Success, Wealth, and Happiness on the Job.* New York: Ballantine Books, 1993.

Waitley, Denis. *The New Dynamics of Goal Setting.* London: Nicholas Brealey, 1997.

Waitley, Denis. *The New Dynamics of Winning: Gain the Mind-Set of a Champion.* New York: Quill, 1995.

Waitley, Denis. *The Psychology of Winning.* New York: Berkley Books, 1992.

Waitley, Denis. *Seeds of Greatness: The Ten Best-Kept Secrets of Total Success.* New York: Pocket Books, 1986.

Waitley, Denis. *The Winner's Edge.* New York: Berkley Books, 1994.

Ziglar, Zig. *Over the Top.* Revised and updated edition. Nashville, TN: Thomas Nelson, 1997.

Ziglar, Zig. *See You at the Top: 25th Anniversary Edition.* 2nd ed. New York: Pelican Books, 2000.

Ziglar, Zig. *Success for Dummies.* Hoboken, NJ: John Wiley and Sons, 1998.

Ziglar, Zig. *Top Performance: How to Develop Excellence in Yourself and Others.* New York: Berkley Books, 1991.

Periodicals

American Psychologist

Contemporary Psychology: APA Review of Books

New York Times, Science Times section (appears Tuesdays)

Psychology Today

Self and Identity

Self-Awareness

OVERVIEW

This chapter helps students to know themselves better and understand how self-knowledge can help them achieve their life goals. In Section 2.1 students will read about self-awareness and how their dreams and values can give their lives direction. In Section 2.2 they will explore their personalities, skills, and interests and learn how these can help them make satisfying career choices.

OBJECTIVES

After they complete this chapter, students should be able to:

- Define self-awareness and cite its benefits.
- Explain the factors that influence people's values.
- Define personality and list the "big five" personality traits.
- Compare and contrast skills, knowledge, and interests.
- Explain how personality, skills, and interests relate to career choice.

OUTLINE

Chapter Topics

FINDING YOUR DIRECTION
Developing Self-Awareness
      The Importance of Self-Honesty
      Self-Consciousness
      Emotional Awareness
Defining Your Dreams
      The Importance of Purpose
      What Should a Dream Be?
Getting In Touch With Your Values
      Examining Your Values
      Your Values at Work

DISCOVERING YOUR STRENGTHS
Personality and Individuality
      Personality Traits
Exploring Your Skills and Interests
      Types of Skills
      Multiple Skills, Multiple Intelligences
      Discovering Your Interests
Putting It All Together: Self-Awareness and Work
      Why Work Matters
      Personality Types and Work

Chapter Activities

Exercise 2.1   **How Self-Conscious Are You?** (pp. 49–50)
Exercise 2.2   **Values Inventory** (pp. 59–60)
Exercise 2.3   **Personality Self-Portrait** (pp. 64–65)
Exercise 2.4   **Skills Assessment** (pp. 69–71)
Exercise 2.5   **Discover Your Multiple Intelligences** (pp. 73–75)
Exercise 2.6   **Interest Survey** (pp. 82–84)

Personal Journal 2.1   **How Well Do You Know Yourself?** (p. 47)
Personal Journal 2.2   **What Are Your Dreams?** (p. 55)
Personal Journal 2.3   **Your "Big Five" Personality Traits** (p. 67)
Personal Journal 2.4   **Exploring Your Interests** (p. 78)

Chapter Features

Applying Psychology **Projective Tests** (p. 56)
INTERNET ACTION **Online Personality Profiles** (p. 63)
PROFESSIONAL DEVELOPMENT **Career Fulfillment** (p. 80)

FOCUS

Introducing the Chapter

Write *self-awareness* on the board and ask students to write a brief definition of the term. (The process of paying attention to oneself.) Ask for specific examples of behavior that show self-awareness. Then ask, "What does self-awareness have to do with being successful?" and discuss their ideas as a class. If necessary, remind students of the meaning of success. Guide students to the idea that self-awareness helps you know yourself better, which helps you choose the life paths best suited to your values, personality, skills, and interests. This, in turn, leads to greater personal fulfillment.

Real-Life Success Story "What Do I Really Want?" (p. 44)

Ask a volunteer to read the Real-Life Success Story to the class. Then ask students what they would do if they were in Mariah's situation. Ask, "Would you take the temp-to-hire job? Why or why not? What are Mariah's other options?" Ask students to think of ways that Mariah could take inventory of her skills and interests. Lead students to understand that taking the job is not necessarily limiting if she investigates what kind of work she would prefer in the long run.

Opening Quote (p. 45)

"Few people even scratch the surface, much less exhaust the contemplation of their own experience."

Write the quote on the board or make a transparency of it from the reproducible master on page 248 and ask students what they think this quote means. What does "exhaust the contemplation of their own experience" mean? Why would people choose not to contemplate their lives? Finally, ask students whether they agree with the statement. Why or why not?

Exploring Further

Begin each class meeting by discussing a new quotation that relates to the chapter topic you will be covering that day. A collection of relevant quotations is provided on the reproducible master. Alternatively, ask one or two students to bring in a quotation relevant to that day's topic.

INSTRUCT

Teaching Tips

The following topics are discussed in this chapter. You may want to expand on them in large or small class groups.

Developing Self-Awareness (pp. 46–52)

Write *self-honesty* on the board and have a student define the term. Discuss the difficulties and benefits of being honest with oneself. Ask why it can be difficult to see your strengths and weaknesses clearly. Point out that some people can underestimate their strengths and overestimate their weaknesses as readily as others can overestimate their strengths and underestimate their weaknesses. Make sure students understand that "clearly" means "realistically."

Ask a student to explain the benefits of self-honesty. Point out that by recognizing your strengths you can see what you have to offer, and by recognizing your weaknesses you can see what you need to do to become the person you want to be.

Defining Your Dreams (pp. 53–55)

Discuss Dr. Viktor Frankl's findings about human behavior in his book *Man's Search for Meaning* and ask students how they felt when they read about his experience. Ask if any students know of similar situations, such as a gravely ill grandparent who waited for the birth of a grandchild or other special event before dying. You may wish to point out that both John Adams and Thomas Jefferson died on the 50th anniversary of Independence Day

(July 4, 1826). Then ask, "Does reading this motivate you to define a dream for your life? Why or why not?"

Getting in Touch With Your Values
(pp. 56–61)
Have a student retell the story of the missionary and the two tourists as told by author Rita Baltus. Then ask, "How does this story show that different people have different values? Do your values align more with the missionary's or the tourists'?" Help students see how this story can help them define their own values.

Personality and Individuality (pp. 62–66)
Have students think of a classmate in this class and, without naming him or her, make a list of that classmate's personality traits. Then make a comprehensive list on the board of all the personality traits listed by the class as a whole and compare it to the list in Exercise 2.3. Are there traits in the class list that are not in the exercise list and vice versa?

Ask students whether they agree that no personality trait is better than any other. Point out that it may be the way a personality trait is expressed that makes it less pleasing to others. A person who is honest but tactless, for example, would be very different from a person who is honest and tactful.

Exploring Your Skills and Interests
(pp. 66–78)
Write *skills, interests,* and *career fields* on the board and ask students to define these terms and explain the relationship between them. Remind students that skills are the result of knowledge combined with experience. Skills and interests are related because people are usually skilled at the things they are interested in and interested in the things at which they are skilled. Have students draw a simple illustration of the relationship as they see it. The reproducible master on page 250 contains a Venn diagram in which *skills* and *interests* overlap to form *career fields*.

You may also wish to introduce students to workplace (SCANS) skills. SCANS skills are skills that were determined by the Department of Labor's Secretary's Commission on Achieving Necessary Skills (SCANS) to be crucial for career success. SCANS skills are listed on the reproducible master on page 257. This list can help students target the core skills they need to improve. Ask students why they think the government decided that these skills are so important for success in the world of work.

Putting It All Together: Self-Awareness and Work (pp. 79–84)
Write the myths about work on the board without labeling them as such. Ask students which statements they agree or disagree with, and discuss why they feel that way. Then point out that these statements are myths that spring from a negative attitude toward work. As a class, look at each statement and discuss why it is a myth. Then ask, "Now that you know these statements are myths, will your attitude about work be different?"

In-Chapter Answers and Notes

Personal Journal 2.1

How Well Do You Know Yourself?
(p. 47)
Students' statements will vary. Point out to students the sentences at the bottom of the activity: *Did you have trouble completing any of these statements, especially the last one? If so, you will benefit from taking a closer look at yourself and what you want out of life.* Remind students that the point of this chapter is to learn more about themselves.

EXERCISE 2.1

How Self-Conscious Are You?
(pp. 49–50)
A-B. Students' responses and scores will vary.
   The highest total score possible is 68.
   The highest possible score for private self-consciousness is 40, and the highest possible for public self-consciousness is 28.

C. Answers will vary but should demonstrate whether the student feels more or less self-consciousness than average.

D. Answers will vary but should demonstrate an understanding of the benefits and drawbacks of public and private self-consciousness.

E. Answers will vary, but students may suggest that working toward a higher level of private self-consciousness while working toward a lower level of public self-consciousness could provide greater self-awareness with less anxiety.

FIGURE 2.1

Feeling Words (p. 52)

Students should understand that developing a large vocabulary of feeling words can help them get in touch with the wide range of their emotions and therefore become more emotionally aware.

Personal Journal 2.2

What Are Your Dreams? (p. 55)

Completed sentences will vary. Remind students to write down what first comes into their minds without judging the thought. These tend to be the ideas that in some way represent what we really want from life.

Sample Answers

I've always wanted to <u>be able to travel for my job.</u>

If I were to receive an award, I would want it to be for <u>environmental work of some kind.</u>

The things that make life worth living are <u>art, the beauty of nature, music, friends, family, and good food.</u>

The best thing that could possibly happen to me is <u>that I would be able to support myself as an environmental activist.</u>

If I were nearing the end of my life, I would regret not having <u>visited more than one other country.</u>

Applying Psychology

PROJECTIVE TESTS (p. 56)
Answers will vary. Some students may say that the Rorschach test could reveal how a person sees the world; an aggressive person, for example, might be more likely to interpret an abstract shape as a scene of violence than a passive person would. Other students may say that the Rorschach test could reveal whether a person has recurring thoughts or fears about a certain person, thing, or situation. Still others may say that the results of a Rorschach test would vary from culture to culture and from person to person, since each test taker interprets inkblots based on his or her individual experiences.

Exploring Further

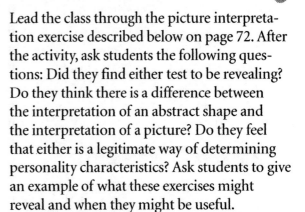

Lead the class through the picture interpretation exercise described below on page 72. After the activity, ask students the following questions: Did they find either test to be revealing? Do they think there is a difference between the interpretation of an abstract shape and the interpretation of a picture? Do they feel that either is a legitimate way of determining personality characteristics? Ask students to give an example of what these exercises might reveal and when they might be useful.

EXERCISE 2.2

Values Inventory (pp. 59–60)

A-B. Values and rankings will vary.

C. Students' top three values will vary, but answers should reflect an understanding of the values chosen and give a specific example of putting these values into practice.

D. Answers will vary but could include people, such as parents, teachers, clergy, and friends; events, such as the death of a loved one or a national conflict; or experiences, such as familial alcoholism or an encounter with unexpected generosity or love.

E. Values in friends and romantic partners will vary. Some students may seek out people who have most of the same values as they do, while others may feel an affinity to people who share just one of their core values. Situations and explanations will vary.

Exploring Further

Ask small groups of students to share their values rankings with one another and explain why they find certain values more important than others. Ask them to pay particular attention to their top-ranked and bottom-ranked values. Within each team, how are the students' lists similar? How are they different?

SECTION 2.1
SELF-CHECK (p. 61)

1. Self-awareness is the process of paying attention to oneself.
2. Having dreams gives our lives meaning, helps us make choices, and helps us persevere in the face of obstacles or hardship.
3. Values are the beliefs and principles one chooses to live by.

INTERNET ACTION

Online Personality Profiles (p. 63)
Answers will vary but should include some of the following information. Some personality tests assign each test-taker to a single personality type. The Myers-Briggs Type Indicator, for example, assigns each test-taker to one of 16 types. Tests based on the Enneagram model assign each test-taker to one of nine types, and the Keirsey Temperament Sorter has four major types. Tests based on the personality trait theory assess how strongly test-takers show each of the traits being tested.

Exploring Further

Many personality tests are available online. Popular online personality tests include the Keirsey Temperament Sorter and the Type A Personality Test, which assesses whether you are a Type A personality (competitive and driven) or a Type B personality (relaxed and noncompetitive). Ask each student to take an online personality test and then discuss the results. Do students believe that the results were accurate? Why or why not? Did they learn anything from the test? Why or why not?

EXERCISE 2.3

Personality Self-Portrait (pp. 64–65)
A-B. Personality traits and the top five traits will vary.
C. Specific personality traits will vary, but students should provide a well thought-out explanation of why they value these particular traits.
D. Answers will vary. Some students may say that their personality traits are similar to their family members' for genetic or environmental reasons. Other students may say that their traits developed as a reaction to those around them. For example, if a student has an older sibling who is very outgoing, the student may have become more introverted in order to fill a different niche.

Personal Journal 2.3

Your "Big Five" Personality Traits (p. 67)
Scores will vary but should fall between zero and five for each trait. Answers to the follow-up question will also vary, although students may recognize that each of the "big five" personality traits is a general category used to distinguish people from one another, not to describe individuals in precise detail.

EXERCISE 2.4

Skills Assessment (pp. 69–71)
A. Skill descriptions will vary but should be meaningful and realistic.
B-C. Skills that students are proud of and skills that need improvement will vary. Students

should recognize that this activity is leading them toward self-honesty—seeing their strengths and weaknesses clearly.

Sample Answers

A. What are your skills? Think of anything and everything that you know how to do and write it down below.

managing money
creating HTML documents
mentoring children/teenagers
remembering numbers
speaking to small groups of people
understanding complex ideas
describing events
explaining concepts
identifying plants
growing plants from seed
caring for animals
learning foreign languages
listening to music
repairing cars
expressing myself in words
taking apart and repairing machines
inventing new words
motivating people
performing in theater
setting up experiments
making observations
drawing objects and faces
negotiating prices

B. Look over all the skills you wrote down and select three. For each one describe a situation in which you used that skill to accomplish something.

Skill #1
describing events
worked as news announcer at college radio station

Skill #2
speaking to groups of people
gave a presentation on book-banning and free speech at city council meeting

Skill #3
mentoring children/teenagers
involved in volunteer program for at-risk youth at community center

C. Now list three skills you would like to improve. For each one, think of some specific things you could do to improve it.

Skill #1
organizing my schedule
buy a day planner to keep track of important dates
make to-do lists each week for errands and bills
set aside specific times for chores

Skill #2
repairing cars
take a class in basic automobile repair
research car problems on Web
listen to "Car Talk" on the radio every weekend

Skill #3
managing money
start balancing checkbook
buy and use money management software
keep track of and reduce wasteful expenses

Exploring Further

If desired, follow up Exercise 2.4 with the "Skills Inventory" provided as a reproducible master on page 254.

EXERCISE 2.5

Discover Your Multiple Intelligences
(pp. 73–75)

A-B. Totals and scoring will vary.

C. Answers will vary. An example would be using logical/mathematical intelligence to do well in math classes, manage finances, or analyze legal arguments.

D. Answers will vary. An example would be using interpersonal intelligence to mediate a problem between two friends or coworkers.

E. Answers will vary but should probably refer to two intelligences that the student has not yet developed.

Exploring Further

Intelligence is one of the most controversial topics in psychology. Psychologists disagree about the existence of a general intelligence (known as *g*) that represents global mental ability. Most psychologists believe that a person's *g* is less important to success than how he or she uses it. For example, students who apply what they learn in school to the solution of real-world problems are making better use of their intelligence than students who use their thinking skills simply to get good grades. This has long been recognized in many nonwestern cultures. In China, for example, personal effort is considered both a sign of intelligence and a source of intelligence. Ask students to suggest various ways of defining intelligence. What does it mean to them to be "intelligent"? How can a person demonstrate intelligence in ways other than getting a high score on an IQ test?

FIGURE 2.2

Expanding Your Intelligences (p. 76)
Answers will vary but could include any of the action tips given in the figure. Model answers will also include original ideas.

Personal Journal 2.4

Exploring Your Interests (p. 78)
Students' responses will vary but should show honest self-reflection.

Sample Answers

What activities make you feel energized and alive?
<u>playing music, taking care of my nieces and nephews, writing, playing basketball</u>

If you were at a library, bookstore, or newsstand, which subject area(s) would you enjoy browsing?
<u>music, history, and sports</u>

What courses or subjects have you enjoyed the most in school?
<u>criminal psychology, 20th century history, music</u>

What subject(s) could you talk about endlessly?
<u>music and basketball</u>

What were you enthusiastic about as a child?
<u>sports</u>

Now examine your answers. Does any subject, theme, or key word appear more than once? These are probably your strongest interests.

PROFESSIONAL DEVELOPMENT

Career Fullfillment (p. 80)
Answers will vary but should include some of the following: consulting print and Inter-net references, such as the *Dictionary of Occupational Titles*, the *Guide for Occupational Exploration*, and the *Occupational Outlook Handbook* (also available online); conducting informational interviews; browsing career Web sites such as Monster.com and O*NET; and gathering advice from career professionals and career counselors.

EXERCISE 2.6

Interest Survey (pp. 82–84)
A-B. Students' responses and scores (three-letter codes) will vary.

C. Answers will vary but could mention some or all of the resources listed in the answer directly above.

Exploring Further

There are many books, such as *Do What You Are: Discover the Perfect Career for You Through the Secrets of Personality Type*, and online tests, such as the Career Key, that help job seekers find careers to match their personality types. Ask students to search the World Wide Web for information on John Holland's career theory. If desired, ask them to locate and complete the online Career Key and to bring their results to class.

1. The "big five" personality traits are openness, conscientiousness, extroversion, agreeableness, and emotional stability.

2. The eight types of intelligence are verbal/linguistic, logical/mathematical, visual/spatial, bodily/kinesthetic, musical, interpersonal, intrapersonal, and naturalistic.

3. No, no one should stick with a career no matter what. You have the freedom to change jobs or careers as you gather experience and learn more about yourself.

Additional Activities

These additional activities are exclusive to this Instructor's Resource Manual. They are designed to meet the special needs of your students. The activities can be used as in-class activities or as take-home assignments. They can be assigned to individual students, pairs of students, or groups of students.

Critical Thinking

CONFLICTING DREAMS   Ask each student to imagine that his or her dreams for the future are completely different from the dreams that his or her family, peers, or partner have for his or her future. Ask students to write a paragraph explaining why they would be in a better position than their family, peers, or partner to know what dreams would be best and most fulfilling for them.

PERSONALITY AND PERSONAL STYLE
Personal spaces such as bedrooms and offices can reveal a great deal about the personalities of their inhabitants. As an example, a creative, distinctive decorating style tends to indicate someone with a high degree of openness, while a very tidy and orderly space suggests a person high in conscientiousness. Ask students to briefly describe their bedrooms or office spaces as they usually look on any given day. How might a stranger rate them on the "big five" personality traits? Why? Do they think a neutral observer could gain an accurate picture of them from observing their personal space? Why or why not?

To extend the activity, ask students to search the journals page of the American Psychological Association Web site (**www.apa.org**) for the article "A Room With a Cue: Personality Judgments Based on Offices and Bedrooms" by Samuel D. Gosling, Sei Jin Ko, Thomas Mannarelli, and Margaret E. Morris (Journal of Personality and Social Psychology 82 [2002]: 379–398). Ask students to summarize the studies described in the article and the researchers' conclusions.

Application

SELF-AWARENESS EXPERIMENT   Ask students to unplug their television, CD player, DVD player, and radio for a day or an entire weekend. Have them use the silence to pay attention to their thoughts and feelings. How do they feel? Agitated? Relaxed? Sad? What types of cognitions are they experiencing? Remembering? Visualizing? Solving problems? Ask students to describe at least one thing they learned about themselves during this experiment and to explain whether they would want to do such an experiment again.

SELF-AWARENESS AND CAREER CHOICE
Ask students to work in pairs or small groups to review the Exercises they completed in Chapter 2 and to make a list of several careers and jobs suggested by their answers to these exercises. Emphasize that this exercise is about self-exploration and is equally useful for all students, regardless of their previous work experience. For example, a student who highly values independence and adventure might think of careers such as a travel writer or an overseas reporter. A student who possesses a strong naturalistic intelligence might want to explore careers in ecology. To extend the exercise, ask students to choose one particular job or career and to set up an interview with someone who is currently working in that

field. In class, ask students to work in small teams to create a list of 10 specific questions they would like to ask their interviewees. As a class, combine the teams' suggestions into a top-ten or top-five list of insightful questions. Give students a week to complete their interviews and write up a one-page summary in question-and-answer format. Discuss students' findings in class, asking for volunteers to describe what they learned. If desired, compile the students' work into a binder for your school's career office or library.

PICTURE INTERPRETATION　What you see in a picture says something important about who you are. People generally identify with the main character in a picture and believe that he or she shares their hopes, fears, desires, and concerns. Using this idea, the picture interpretation technique (also known as the Thematic Apperception Test) investigates the way people interpret a series of photographs or sketches. Let's say that you are shown a photograph of a man sitting alone at a café table. What might the man be thinking? What do you imagine he might do next? Display a photograph or painting featuring a man or woman. (Many images can be found in online image banks such as Getty Images at **www.gettyimages.com**.) Select a photograph or illustration that is interesting enough to encourage discussion but vague enough to allow for multiple interpretations.

Let students look at the illustration for a few minutes. Then ask them to write down brief answers to the following questions:

- What is this person thinking about?
- Where is he/she?
- What does he/she do for a living?
- How old is he/she?
- What is his/her name?

Discuss the students' responses as a class, emphasizing that there are no right or wrong answers. What does the range of responses reveal about the students in the class? Why do people perceive the same image in such different ways?

SENSATION SEEKING　Reproduce and distribute the "Sensation Seeking Questionnaire" on page 255. Explain to students that everyone has a need for a certain level of sensation, or excitement. Everyone suffers boredom when their environment doesn't provide enough sensation, such as challenges and new experiences. Each individual, however, shows a different level of sensation seeking. *Sensation seeking* is an attraction to varied, novel, complex, and intense sensations and experiences and a willingness to take physical, social, and financial risks for the sake of such experiences. Ask students to complete the questionnaires individually and tally their results. Then ask students to work in small groups to discuss their results. Students should discuss whether their jobs or educational programs provide too little sensation, too much sensation, or about the right amount. They should also consider how being aware of their level of sensation seeking can help them choose a career. A high sensation seeker might enjoy working in a busy hospital emergency room, for example, while a low sensation seeker might prefer to work in quiet solitude. What careers would be good for high and low sensations seekers? Reunite the class and discuss their answers.

EXPLORING CAREERS　Ask students to select a career field that interests them and to complete the following sentences through research:

- A magazine I could read to expand my knowledge of this field is

　_____.

- An educational television program I could watch to learn more about this field is

　_____.

- A book I could read this month to learn more about this field is

　_____.

- This month I could attend the following lecture, meeting, or group discussion about this field: _____.

- I could talk to the following people who work or have worked in this field:

_____.

Ask students to follow through on one of these ideas. If desired, this can be assigned as a month-long project.

Internet Activities

PERSONALITY TYPES Ask students to find and complete the online Keirsey Temperament Sorter II. The Temperament Sorter assigns each test taker to one of four personality types—artisan, guardian, idealist, or rational. Ask students to take the questionnaire online and bring their results to class. Make a transparency of the "Keirsey Personality Types" reproducible master on page 256 and lead the class in a discussion of the personality types. What is the distribution of types in the class? How well do students feel their test results fit them? Are they interested in the careers that are suggested for their personality type? Finish the discussion by asking whether they think that personality types are an accurate way to describe individuals.

EMOTIONAL INTELLIGENCE Ask small groups of students to use an Internet search engine to investigate the concept of *emotional intelligence*. Ask each group to prepare brief answers to the following questions:

- What is emotional intelligence?
- Why is emotional intelligence important?
- What individual qualities or skills make up emotional intelligence?
- What is the relationship between emotional intelligence and emotional awareness?
- How can people increase their emotional intelligence?

Review the answers as a class. Point out that emotionally intelligent people consider the effect their words and actions may have on others. Ask students to recall a situation in which another person misunderstood their intention in saying or doing something. How could they use emotional intelligence to prevent similar misunderstandings in the future?

ASSESS

Review and Activities Answers

Review Questions (p. 86)

1. Private self-consciousness is the tendency to be aware of the private, inward aspects of yourself. Public self-consciousness is the tendency to be aware of the aspects of yourself on display in social situations.

2. The three questions are: How is my body feeling? What happened right before I started to experience this emotion? Can I put a specific name to this emotion?

3. Our value choices are influenced by our family, religious beliefs, teachers, friends, and personal experiences.

4. People develop skills as a result of learning and practice.

5. Interpersonal intelligence involves skill at person-to-person communication and relationships, while intrapersonal intelligence involves skill at self-awareness and self-reflection. While both are concerned with awareness of thoughts and feelings, interpersonal intelligence involves sensitivity to others, while intrapersonal intelligence involves sensitivity to oneself.

6. The six personality types in John Holland's model are realistic, investigative, artistic, social, enterprising, and conventional.

Critical Thinking (p. 86)

7. Answers will vary, but most students will recognize that seeing oneself clearly and realistically is difficult for many people.

8. Answers will vary, but most students will recognize that you can resolve values conflicts by remaining flexible and employing creativity and imagination. For example,

people who value generosity and financial security could look for work with a philanthropic organization. They could also spend less on themselves in order to save more and give more.

Application (p. 86)

9. Answers will vary, but most students will recognize that by thinking about your emotions, keeping track of them, and answering questions about them, they can become more emotionally aware.

10. Students' collages will vary. If necessary, suggest that students refer to the personality traits listed in Exercise 2.3 for inspiration.

Internet Activities (p. 87)

11. Students' writing will vary but should choose one from each of the following characteristics: extroverted or introverted, sensing or intuitive, thinking or feeling, judging or perceiving. This will give the student a personality type expressed as a four-letter sequence of letters. For example, someone who is an INFJ is introverted and intuitive, makes decisions based on feeling, and looks at life from a judging perspective.

12. Students' career selections will vary. Allow students to exchange their findings to increase their exposure to different career possibilities.

Real-Life Success Story "What Do I Really Want?" (p. 87)

Answers will vary but should mention strategies presented in the chapter for taking stock of one's values, personality traits, skills, and interests.

CLOSE

Culminating Activity

Ask students to create a project that sums up what they have learned about self-awareness in Chapter 2. Suggest that each student use his or her strongest intelligence to design the project. For example, students strong in musical intelligence might choose to create a poem or song, students strong in bodily/kinesthetic intelligence might create a skit, and students strong in verbal/linguistic intelligence might write an essay. Projects should describe at least three ways in which students have become more self-aware and how their increased self-awareness can help them plan their futures.

Personal Success Portfolio

Make handouts or a transparency of the Personal Success Portfolio worksheet for Chapter 2 on page 232. Refer to pages 9 and 10 for suggestions on presenting this activity.

For Chapter 2, additional materials you may wish students to add to their Personal Success Portfolios include:

- students' descriptions of themselves as children and what they dreamed of becoming when they grew up
- a list of ten statements beginning, "When I grow up, I want to be…" or "When I grow up, I will be…"
- ideas for how the student could express his or her top three values in a positive way
- a project in which the student uses one of his or her strongest skills to do something positive for the school or community
- a short bibliography of books and magazines for a subject of interest to the student, such as car repair, ballet, animal care, physics, etc.

ADDITIONAL RESOURCES

The following books and periodicals offer information on self-assessment, values, personality, multiple intelligences, and career choice.

Books

Bernstein, Alan B. and Nicholas Reid Schaffzin. 4th ed. *The Princeton Review Guide to Your Career.* New York: Random House, 2000.

Bolles, Richard. *What Color Is Your Parachute? 2003: A Practical Manual for Job-Hunters and Career-Changers.* Berkeley: Ten Speed Press, 2002.

Brownmiller, Susan. *Femininity.* New York: Fawcett Books, 1994.

Cervone, D. and Y. Shoda, eds. *The Coherence of Personality: Social-Cognitive Bases of Consistency, Variability, and Organization.* New York: Guilford Press, 1999.

Choquette, Sonia, Patrick Tully, and Julia Cameron. *Your Heart's Desire: Instructions for Creating the Life You Really Want.* New York: Random House, 1997.

Clawson, James G. et al. *Self-Assessment and Career Development.* 3rd ed. Englewood Cliffs, NJ: Prentice-Hall, 1992.

Farmer, Richard F., LaRita L. Jarvis, Matthew K. Berent, and Alicia Corbett. "Contributions to Global Self-Esteem: The Role of Importance Attached to Self-Concepts Associated with the Five-Factor Model." *Journal of Research in Personality* 35 (2001), 483–499.

Fellman, Wilma R. *Finding a Career That Works for You: A Step-By-Step Guide to Choosing a Career and Finding a Job.* Chicago: Independent Publishers Group, 2000.

Funder, D.C. *The Personality Puzzle.* 2nd ed. New York: W.W. Norton, 2000.

Furnham, Adrian and Patrick Heaven. *Personality and Social Behaviour.* London: Hodder Arnold, 1999.

Gardner, Howard. *Frames of Mind: The Theory of Multiple Intelligences.* New York: Basic Books, 1983.

Goleman, Daniel. *Emotional Intelligence.* New York: Bantam, 1997.

Goleman, Daniel. *Working with Emotional Intelligence.* New York: Bantam, 2000.

Langston, Christopher A. and W. Eric Sykes. "Beliefs and the Big Five: Cognitive Bases of Broad Individual Differences in Personality." *Journal of Research in Personality* 31 (1997): 141–165.

Lynn, Adele B. *The Emotional Intelligence Activity Book: 50 Activities for Promoting EQ at Work.* New York: AMACOM, 2001.

Nardi, Dario. *Multiple Intelligences and Personality Types.* Huntington Beach, CA: Telos Publications, 2001.

Pervin, L.A. and O. P. John, eds. *Handbook of Personality: Theory and Research.* 2nd ed. New York: Guilford Press, 1999.

Pinker, Stephen. *How the Mind Works.* New York: W.W. Norton, 1997.

Pinker, Stephen. *The Blank Slate.* New York: Viking Penguin, 2002.

Sher, Barbara, and Barbara Smith. *I Could Do Anything If I Only Knew What It Was: How to Discover What You Really Want and How to Get It.* New York: Delacorte Press, 1994.

Stock, Gregory. *The Book of Questions.* New York: Workman Publishing, 1987.

Strein, William. "Assessment of Self-Concept. ERIC Digest" Greensboro, NC: ERIC Clearinghouse on Counseling and Student Services, 1995.

Tieger, Paul D. and Barbara-Tieger. *Do What You Are.* 3rd ed. Boston: Little Brown and Company, 2001.

Periodicals

Journal of Personality and Social Psychology

Journal of Psychological Type

Journal of Research in Personality

Occupational Outlook Quarterly

Goals and Obstacles

OVERVIEW

In this chapter students use the foundation of self-knowledge built in Chapters 1 and 2 to formulate specific life goals. They learn the characteristics of well-set goals and how short- and long-term goals work together. Students also learn how to handle the inevitable obstacles that arise when they set goals, as well as how stress and anger affect goal achievement. They examine strategies for managing stress and anger that will help them overcome internal obstacles to success.

OBJECTIVES

After they complete this chapter, students should be able to:

■ Explain the importance of setting goals.

■ List the characteristics of well-set goals.

■ Distinguish between short-term and long-term goals.

■ Cite common obstacles to reaching their goals.

■ Recognize the causes and symptoms of stress.

■ Describe several strategies for relieving stress.

■ Explain ways to deal with anger constructively.

OUTLINE

Chapter Topics

SETTING AND ACHIEVING GOALS
What Are Your Goals?
    Setting Goals
    Short-Term and Long-Term Goals
    Tying Your Goals Together
    Staying on Track
    Adjusting Goals as You Go
Overcoming Obstacles
    Trying to Please Someone Else
    Not Really Wanting It
    Being a Perfectionist
    Going It Alone
    Resisting Change

HANDLING STRESS AND ANGER
Stress and Stressors
    Symptoms of Stress
    Escape Responses
    Stress Management
Coping With Anger
    Responses to Anger
    Handling Anger Constructively

Chapter Activities

Chapter Features

FOCUS

Introducing the Chapter

Most of your students probably do not have specific goals for the future. Ask for a show of hands of students who have a clear vision of where they want to be in five years. (You might point out that "Where do you see yourself in five years?" is a common question in job interviews.) Ask for another show of hands of students who have a clear vision of where they want to be in twenty years. Ask these students to explain how they plan to get from where they are now to where they want to be in the future. Do they have a clear, step-by-step plan for reaching their life goals? If not, how to they plan to get where they want to be? Engage students in a discussion about the value of setting goals for their future.

Real-Life Success Story "Where Do I Go From Here?" (p. 88)

Have students read the first part of the Real-Life Success Story, "A New Direction," while covering up the second part, "New Goals, New Challenges." Then ask, "What would you do if you were Trinh? What goals might you set if you were in her situation?" Discuss what obstacles might arise for each of the different goals. For example, going back to school could overextend her financial resources. Then read the second part of the story and discuss the goal Trinh chose and what she could do to address the obstacles she may face.

Opening Quote

"Whoever wants to reach a distant goal must take small steps."

Write the quote on the board or display a transparency of the reproducible master on page 257 and ask students what they think this statement means. What do "small steps" mean? Why would small steps be necessary? Do they agree that this is true?

Ask students to think of a major achievement in human history, such as the building of the pyramids or the development of the loom. What small steps do they think went into such an achievement?

INSTRUCT

Teaching Tips

The following topics are discussed in this chapter. You may want to expand on them in large or small class groups.

What Are Your Goals? (pp. 90–99)

Ask students to share their New Year's resolutions. How many students made a resolution? How many can remember what it was? How many followed through on it? Ask students who did follow through how they did it. Ask students who did not follow through to explain what held them back from keeping their promises to themselves. This would be a good time to discuss SMART goals.

Overcoming Obstacles (pp. 99–103)

Ask for a volunteer to define *obstacle* (any barrier that prevents us from achieving our goals) and explain the difference between an *internal obstacle* and an *external obstacle*. Have students give examples of different types of obstacles and compare them to those given in the text: trying to please someone else, not really wanting it, being a perfectionist, going it alone, and resisting change. Which do they think creates more problems, internal obstacles or external obstacles? Why? Finally, ask a volunteer to give a personal example of an opportunity that originally appeared to be an obstacle.

Stress and Stressors (pp. 104–115)

Explain to students that *stress* is a physical or psychological tension and that *stressors* are causes of stress. As a class, brainstorm a list of common stressors and write them on the board. Compare them to the list of stressors on page 105 in the textbook. Then ask students how they cope with stress and whether or not their current stress management strategies work.

Coping With Anger (pp. 116–122)

Begin by asking, "What makes you angry?" As students respond, make a list on the board. (If students have trouble responding, ask them to recall the last time they got angry and to explain why.) Then, alongside this list, write what students say they do when they get angry. Are some responses to anger more productive than others? Point out that controlling your anger allows you to channel your energy into positive action. Refer to the example in the text that suggests studying in the library if you know your home will be noisy. Finally, have students suggest positive strategies for coping with the anger-causing situations they thought up at the beginning of class.

In-Chapter Answers and Notes

FIGURE 3.1

SMART Goals (p. 91)

Research has shown that the act of writing down ideas helps to better encode them in our long-term memory. The experience of forming the letters and words taps into memory more fully than speaking the words or simply thinking them through. Writing goals down on paper also creates a visible reminder of them.

EXERCISE 3.1

Setting Smart Goals (pp. 92–93)

A-B. Students' responses will vary depending on their schedules, finances, lifestyles, and academic goals. Their SMART goals will vary, but should contain all SMART elements.

C. Students' goals will vary depending on the dreams they selected in Chapter 2. However, the final written version of each goal should contain all SMART elements and should clearly relate to the dream(s) selected.

D. Answers will vary but should show that students have a realistic idea of how much effort their goals will require.

Sample Answers

1. Complete my certificate or degree.
   Missing Factor: T
   SMART Goal: Complete my associate degree by end of spring semester.
2. Give more time or money to charity.
   Missing Factors: S, M, T
   SMART Goal: Volunteer three hours every Saturday at city animal shelter.
3. Find out in next two weeks how to get financial aid.
   Missing Factors: S, M
   SMART Goal: Find out in next two weeks how to apply for Pell Grant for next academic year.
4. Pay off my credit cards by the end of the month.
   Missing Factors: A, R
   SMART Goal: Pay off my credit cards by the end of the year.
5. Eat healthfully three times a day.
   Missing Factors: S, T
   SMART Goal: Eat according to Food Guide Pyramid three times a day for next ten days.
6. Work out in gym for an hour three times a week.
   Missing Factor: R
   SMART Goal: Work out in gym for twenty minutes three times a week.
7. Spend more time with my family and friends.
   Missing Factors: S, M, T
   SMART Goal: Spend Saturday afternoons with family and friends.
8. Find something to do for fun.
   Missing Factors: S, M, T
   SMART Goal: See a good movie this weekend.
9. Read more.
   Missing Factors: S, M, T
   SMART Goal: Read one new novel every month.
10. Join a volunteer program.
    Missing Factors: S, M, T
    SMART Goal: Join Habitat for Humanity by next week.

11. Raise GPA to 3.8 by end of semester.
    Missing Factors: A, R
    SMART Goal: Raise GPA to 3.4 by end of school year.
12. Set aside $10 each week in a savings account.
    Missing Factors: none (OK)
13. Get annual physical exam.
    Missing Factor: T
    SMART Goal: Make appointment for physical exam by Friday.
14. Update my résumé.
    Missing Factor: T
    Update my résumé by the end of this month.
15. Watch less TV.
    Missing Factors: S, M, T
    SMART Goal: Watch only my three favorite shows each week.

EXERCISE 3.2

Generating Short-Term Goals (pp. 95–96)

A. Content of students' long-term goals will vary, but all goals should contain the five SMART elements.

B. Short-term goals will vary, but should be realistic and relate specifically to the long-term goals listed in question A. Students should be able to list at least eight short-term goals for each long-term goal.

C. Short-term goals should be listed in chronological order and should represent a logical progression toward the long-term goal.

D. Answers will vary, although students' plans of action should be realistic. Students should also understand that they have the opportunity to get started on their long-term goals immediately.

E. Answers will vary. Students should take this promise seriously and make a concerted effort to follow through on it.

Exploring Further

Assign this exercise as homework, but instruct students not to sign the promise to themselves at the end of question E until they come to class. Ten or fifteen minutes before the end of

the class period, ask students to take out their homework and sign the promise to themselves. Then ask students whether they think they will follow through on this promise, and why. When you return the checked exercise to students, ask for a show of hands of students who followed through on their promise. Ask a few students who did not follow through to describe why they didn't. Can they identify why? Then ask a few students who did take action to describe what they did and why. How did the action relate to their short- and long-term goals? How did taking this action make them feel about themselves? Were they inspired to take any further action on their goals? Why or why not?

Goal Cards (p. 98)

Check that students have filled out all four cards and provided a do-by date on each one. If desired, supply pairs of scissors and ask students to cut out the cards and place them in their wallets.

Exploring Further

For an in-class activity, have students work in pairs to help each other set reasonable deadlines for each goal. As a follow-up activity a week later, ask students to take out their goal cards and evaluate how much progress they have made toward accomplishing the goals. Some students will not have taken any action toward their goals. Ask why they think this is so. Use this opportunity to discuss obstacles, such as perfectionism and lack of commitment, that may be standing in their way. This can be structured as a class discussion or a group activity.

INTERNET ACTION

Surfing the Day Away (p. 101)

Students' responses will vary, but should explain that the Internet is an extremely useful tool for research and communication, but that it also contains many sites that distribute out-dated or misleading information.

Exploring Further

Many younger students may take the convenience of the Internet for granted and not realize how much this technology has simplified everyday tasks. Ask more experienced students to describe one or two specific ways that the Internet has saved them time with everyday tasks. Areas they may mention include banking, shopping, paying bills, searching a library catalog, or filling out government forms.

EXERCISE 3.3

Anticipating Obstacles (pp. 102–103)

A. As in Exercise 3.2, content of students' long-term goals will vary, but all goals should contain the five SMART elements.

B. Answers will vary, but should reflect an understanding of internal and external obstacles. Answers should also demonstrate that students have thought about the effort and resources necessary to reach their goals.

C. Answers will vary depending on the nature and severity of the obstacles.

Sample Answers

Goal:
Own my own business selling scented candles.

Possible Obstacles:
Don't know how to start a business.
Not sure I'm creative enough.
Need money for start-up costs.
Might not qualify for a business loan.
Business might take too long to become profitable.
Market might be saturated.
Rental space might be too expensive.
Qualified employees might be hard to find.
Competition might have better or cheaper product.
Unforeseen expenses might arise.

Cost of insurance might be too high.
Supplies might be too expensive.
I might not want to put in the work required.

 SECTION 3.1
SELF-CHECK (p. 103)

1. A goal is an outcome you want and toward which you direct your effort.

2. SMART stands for specific, measurable, achievable, realistic, and time-related.

3. One good way to make sure that your long-term and short-term goals are in synch is to start with your long-term goal(s) and then work backwards in time, thinking of all the steps necessary to achieve each long-term goal. These steps represent short-term goals.

FIGURE 3.2

The ABC Model (p. 104)

Students should understand that being aware of their personal stressors allows them to anticipate the situations that will cause them stress. This can help them avoid these situations when possible, recognize the irrational thoughts that contribute to their stress in these situations, and select appropriate stress management strategies.

Applying Psychology

ARE YOU TECHNOSTRESSED? (p. 105)
Students' experiences with technology will vary. Younger students, or those who like cutting-edge technology, may be less affected by technostress than older students and technophobic students because they may be more comfortable with the pace of technological change.

EXERCISE 3.4

How Stressed Are You? (pp. 107–108)
A-B. Responses and scores will vary.

C. Answers will vary. Some students may say they feel more stressed than their score indicates. These students may not even be aware that they are experiencing certain symptoms of stress, such as nervous habits or muscle tension. They may also misattribute some symptoms, such as nausea or tiredness, to causes other than stress. A few students may have symptoms not described on the questionnaire. These include headache, loss of sense of humor, poor concentration, forgetfulness, increased drinking or smoking, grinding teeth, and lowered resistance to illness.

D. Answers will vary, although postsecondary students often undergo major life changes such as leaving home, making new friends, beginning new romantic relationships, encountering new people and ideas, and making important self-discoveries.

PROFESSIONAL DEVELOPMENT

Job Stress (p. 111)

Answers will vary, but should demonstrate an understanding that a balanced life includes time for the areas depicted on the Wheel of Life in Exercise 1.4: relationships (friends and family); work and career; community activities; school, continuing education, or self-improvement; health and fitness; hobbies/leisure; spirituality; and money/ financial security.

Personal Journal 3.2

Stress Management Techniques (p. 113)
Students' choices of stress relief strategies will vary according to their personalities, interests, and lifestyles.

Exploring Further

To use this Personal Journal as an in-class activity, ask students to work together in pairs to review the various stress relief strategies

presented in the chapter, then the five strategies that they believe would work best for them. Ask pairs to describe the strategies they selected. Why did they pick these strategies? Ask students who chose other strategies to explain why they chose differently.

EXERCISE 3.5

Personal Stressors and Relievers
(pp. 114–115)

A. Students' stressors and stress relief ideas will vary. Common stressors for students include financial responsibilities, academic demands, balancing work and school, choosing a major and career, and relationship conflict and uncertainty.

B-C. Students' ideas will vary, but should reflect an understanding of the strategies described in the chapter.

Personal Journal 3.3

Stress Relief Reminders (p. 116)
Students' stress relief strategies will vary.

Sample Answers

To reduce the stress caused by <u>working full-time and going to school,</u> I will <u>schedule time for meditation each morning.</u>
To reduce the stress caused by <u>my job,</u> I will <u>play racquetball at lunch.</u>
To reduce the stress caused by <u>living with my parents,</u> I will <u>schedule plenty of time away from home and keep up with my housework.</u>
To reduce the stress caused by <u>going through final exams,</u> I will <u>get plenty of exercise and sunshine.</u>
To reduce the stress caused by <u>living in a big city,</u> I will <u>plan weekend hikes and drives to the country.</u>
To reduce the stress caused by <u>my 1½-hour commute,</u> I will <u>use a small tape recorder for an audio journal while sitting in traffic.</u>

Anger Triggers (p. 120)
Students' answers will vary, but should identify specific events that cause anger for them, rather than annoyances or time-wasters that cause inconvenience for almost everyone.

 SECTION 3.2
SELF-CHECK (p. 122)

1. The body reacts to stress by emitting adrenaline and cortisol, hormones that regulate our mood. Adrenaline prepares our bodies for "fight or flight," while cortisol counteracts those effects. Over the long term, the body reacts to stress by going through three stages: alarm, resistance, and exhaustion.

2. An escape response is a behavior or thought that helps get your mind off your present troubles.

3. Constructive ways of dealing with anger include understanding the causes of the anger, staying calm, and taking positive action to correct the problem causing the anger. Being assertive, rather than passive, passive-aggressive, or aggressive, is a good way to resolve interpersonal problems. Another useful way to deal with anger is to deal with problems and potential problems *before* they become anger-provoking situations.

Additional Activities

These additional activities are exclusive to this Instructor's Resource Manual. They are designed to meet the special needs of your students. The activities can be used as in-class activities or as take-home assignments. They can be assigned to individual students, pairs of students, or groups of students.

Internet Activities

PERFECTIONISM Some psychologists believe that perfectionism is a double-edged sword. While it can make people feel bad about themselves for not meeting their own impossibly high standards, it can also spur them to maximize their potential and achieve seemingly impossible goals. Activate students' background knowledge by asking whether there is a difference between having high personal standards and being a perfectionist. Do any students see a positive value in perfectionism, either in their life or in others' lives? If desired, ask students to complete an online perfectionism self-quiz. Then ask students to visit the Web site of the University of Texas at Austin Counseling & Mental Health Center. Ask them to find and read the article on perfectionism on the site and to summarize the myths and realities about perfectionism. In class, discuss the parable of the South Indian Monkey Trap, which is described at the end of the online article. How is a perfectionist like a monkey that will not let go of the rice to free itself from the trap?

STRESS AND INFORMATION OVERLOAD
One relatively new cause of stress is *information overload*, an inability to find the information one needs or wants amidst the immense quantity of information available. Ask students to use the Internet to research information overload. Why is there more information available today than in the past? What are the effects of information overload? How can people cope with it?

If desired, ask students to locate the "How Much Information?" project on the Web site of the University of California, Berkeley, School of Information Management and Systems. How much information does the study say is produced every year? How much of it is in print? How many hours of television does the average household consume in one year? How much and what kinds of data do individuals generate? Ask students to prepare their responses for a class discussion.

Application

FORMULATING SHORT-TERM GOALS
Give students a challenging long-term goal, such as organizing a new political party,

completing a triathlon, or developing a new vaccine. What would it take to accomplish this goal? What short-term goals would be involved? How long would each one take? For an in-class activity, divide the class into small teams and allow them a specified length of time to come up with a step-by-step plan for reaching the long-term goal. Ask teams to prepare oral or written presentations outlining their plan. If desired, take a vote to select the best (most realistic and detailed) plan.

UNDERSTANDING PASSIVE-AGGRESSION

Reproduce and distribute the "Passive-Aggression Questionnaire" on page 261. Review the definition of passive-aggression (indirect, disguised aggression toward others) and ask students how common they think passive-aggressive behavior is. Have they ever encountered a highly passive-aggressive person? Ask each student to take the quiz and answer the two follow-up questions. Alternatively, ask each student to administer the quiz and questions to two different interviewees of their choosing. (Students should first explain the purpose of the quiz to the interviewees and define passive-aggression.) Discuss the results as a class. Which passive-aggressive behaviors are most common? What situations provoke them? How can people replace passive-aggressive behavior with more positive behavior?

To extend the activity, ask pairs or groups of students to work together to rewrite each of the fifteen statements in a positive way. For example, instead of "People don't understand me or my feelings," students might suggest, "The important people in my life understand me and my feelings" or "I have friends who understand me and my feelings."

Follow-Up Questions

Select one or two statements that the interviewee answered "sometimes" or "often." Reread these statements to the interviewee and then ask these questions:

1. What situations provoke you, or have provoked you, to think or act this way? Why?

2. Is there another, more constructive way of thinking or acting that you could use in these situations in the future? Explain.

STRESSFUL LIFE EVENTS   Create an overhead slide of the reproducible master "Stressful Life Events" on page 262. This scale is the work of stress researchers T. H. Holmes and R. H. Rahe, who saw stress as the amount of life change that an individual is facing at any given time. Explain to students that these researchers drew up a list of major life changes, both positive and negative, that contribute to stress. Ask students what they think the most stressful events in a person's life would be. What have been the most stressful events in their lives so far? Show the scale and ask students whether they agree with the ranking of events on the scale. Which of the events on the scale could be both positive and negative? Why?

Ask students to check off all the stressors on the scale that they have faced in the last year, then add up the total point value. Anyone who scores over 300 has reached a critical stress level, with an 80 percent chance of developing stress symptoms such as ulcers and high blood pressure within one year. What is the range of scores in the class? Group students by stress score and ask each group to come up with the top ten stressors that they face on a regular basis. Compare the groups' lists in a class discussion.

If desired, guide the class in agreeing on a top-ten list of their stressors and brainstorming several ways of coping with the most stressful events on the list.

STRESSFUL JOBS   This activity is designed to help students think about job stress and how it could affect their choice of career. Ask students what jobs they think are the most stressful, and why. What factors can students think of that would cause stress on the job? Two factors repeatedly cited to cause job stress are poor or dangerous working conditions and low pay. Other factors include overwork, long hours, exhausting pace, risk of personal injury, interaction with abusive people, lack of job security, lack of advancement opportunities, lack of autonomy, and lack of recognition. After students generate several job titles, display a transparency of the reproducible master on page 263, which contains a list of the most stressful jobs and a table citing jobs with different work environments and salaries. Did students think of any of these jobs? For the ones they did not think of, ask students for ideas on why these jobs would be particularly stressful. Do students think that more stressful jobs should have higher salaries than less stressful jobs? Why or why not? Would they be interested in any of the high-stress jobs on the list? Why or why not?

ASSESS

Review and Activities Answers

Review Questions (p. 124)

1. "Goals are dreams with deadlines" means that goals are tools for translating dreams into concrete, time-related plans of action.

2. Goals should be specific because this makes it easier to plan a course of action. Goals should be measurable because this allows us to gauge our progress and know when we have reached our target.

3. Answers will vary but should recognize that a short-term goal has a short time frame for achievement (less than a year) and a long-term goal has a longer time frame for achievement (over one year). An example of a long-term goal could be to work as a teacher in South America. Related short-term goals could include finding out the requirements for such a job, completing an educational program, gaining teaching experience, and so on.

4. Stress can be positive when it is eustress, a desirable stress felt in exciting and challenging situations, such as playing a sport or going on a date.

5. Aggression is behavior that is intended to harm or injure a person or object, while passive-aggression is a way of dealing with emotional conflict by indirectly expressing aggression toward others. Passive-aggression is a disguised form of aggression.

6. Assertiveness allows you to express and control your anger by standing up for your rights without hurting others.

Critical Thinking (p. 124)

7. The essence of this statement is that anger hurts its owner more than its recipient. Students may or may not agree with this statement, although they should understand that anger, regardless of its source or target, has negative physical and psychological consequences for the angry person.

8. Answers will vary. Many people have difficulty being assertive when they fear rejection or feel that their thoughts and feelings are not respected. Some people, particularly some women, have difficulty being assertive because they are afraid of causing trouble or being "difficult." Low self-esteem often contributes to this fear.

Application (p. 124)

9. Answers will vary. Students will likely find that most people do not take the time to set goals or give much thought to their life's direction. Those who do have probably accomplished more and feel that they are leading more fulfilling lives.

10. Stress logs will vary but should include stress management strategies in addition to the list of stressors. Students should understand that they can develop coping skills to deal with stress and that no matter what their problems are, they can work on them in a way that is healthy and constructive.

Internet Activities (p. 125)

11. Answers will vary. Areas for goal setting at myGoals.com include health & fitness, family & relationships, time management & organization, personal finance, career, education & training, personal growth & interests, recreation & leisure, and home improvement & real estate. Each category contains subcategories with lists of pre-made Goalplans, such as "to watch less television" and "to reduce my caffeine intake." Each Goalplan has a list of obstacles and strategies to overcome these obstacles. Some students may find the service informative and may be encouraged by the thought that others are facing the same obstacles. Other students may prefer to use their own goal system.

12. Students' reports will vary. Chronic anger has been associated with high blood pressure, heart disease and other cardiovascular disorders, risk of diabetes, kidney malfunction, urinary problems, weakened immune system, digestive disorders, prolonged headaches, and even cancer. Women go through the same processes of dealing with anger as men, but research suggests that women are more likely to feel shame or regret about experiencing anger.

Real-Life Success Story "Where Do I Go From Here?" (p. 125)

Stories will vary, but should reflect an understanding of the stress management strategies introduced in the chapter.

Sample Answer

When the instructor had the students introduce themselves at the beginning of the class, Trinh realized that most of the other students felt as nervous as she did. She also realized that she had a head start over many of the others: She already had a job with an accounting firm and was familiar with much of the work she would be learning to do. Trinh took control of her stress by scheduling time for meditation and relaxation, taking brisk walks at lunchtime, and making an extra effort to eat well to sustain her energy. When she felt herself becoming overwhelmed, she took several deep breaths and a quick step back from the situation. Trinh focused on the big picture: She was making progress toward her degree. She could succeed.

CLOSE

Culminating Activity

Ask students to complete this sentence: "My favorite stress management strategy is _____, because _____." Then discuss how the chosen strategies will help students achieve their goals. For example, a student might answer, "By walking every morning, I have more energy to complete my schoolwork, and, therefore, my grades are likely to improve and I'm more likely to complete my degree on schedule."

Personal Success Portfolio

To bring the chapter full circle, have students fill out the Chapter 3 worksheet of the Personal Success Portfolio.

Additional chapter-related materials for students' Personal Success Portfolios could include:

- a one-page report or bulleted list describing stressors that are common in a job or career that interests the student and positive ways of handling those stressors

- a photocopy of the student's goal cards from Personal Journal 3.1

- a list of hassles and uplifts experienced over the course of one week

- a paragraph describing one of the student's anger triggers and how he or she will use self-awareness and anger-management strategies to reduce his or her reaction to this trigger

ADDITIONAL RESOURCES

The following books and periodicals offer information on goal setting, stress relief, and anger management.

Books

Allen, David. *Getting Things Done: The Art of Stress-Free Productivity.* New York: Viking Press, 2001.

Bremner, Douglas J. *Does Stress Damage the Brain? Understanding Trauma-Related Disorders from a Neurological Perspective.* New York: W. W. Norton & Company, 2002.

Cairo, Jim. *Motivation and Goal Setting: How to Set and Achieve Goals and Inspire Others.* Franklin Lakes, NJ: Career Press, 1998.

Davis, Martha, Elizabeth Robbins Eshelman, and Matthew McKay. *Relaxation and Stress Reduction Workbook.* 5th ed. Oakland: New Harbinger Publications, 2000.

Ellis, Keith. *The Magic Lamp: Goal Setting for People Who Hate Setting Goals.* New York: Three Rivers Press, 1998.

Gable, Cate. *Strategic Action Planning Now: Setting and Meeting Your Goals.* Boca Raton: CRC Press, 1998.

Karvelas, Katherine, ed. *The Power of Goals: Quotations to Strengthen Your Climb to New Heights.* Franklin Lakes, NJ: Career Press, 1998.

McKay, Matthew and Peter Rogers. *The Anger Control Workbook.* Oakland: New Harbinger Publications, 2000.

McKay, Matthew, Peter Rogers, and Judith McKay. *When Anger Hurts: Quieting the Storm Within.* Oakland: New Harbinger Publications, 1989.

Sapolsky, Robert M. *Why Zebras Don't Get Ulcers: An Updated Guide to Stress, Stress-Related Diseases, and Coping.* New York: W.H. Freeman, 1998.

Periodicals

International Journal of Stress Management

Stress and Health

Stressfree Living

Yoga Journal

Self-Esteem

OVERVIEW

In Chapter 4 students read about self-esteem and how it fits into the success equation. In Section 4.1 they learn what self-esteem is, where it comes from, and how it helps them achieve their goals. They also experiment with strategies to develop their self-expectancy (self-efficacy). In Section 4.2 students read about self-acceptance and why it is important to self-esteem. They also develop strategies to accept themselves as they are now. Finally, they learn how to handle criticism effectively without letting it erode their self-esteem.

OBJECTIVES

After they complete this chapter, students should be able to:

- Define self-esteem and explain its importance.
- Describe how childhood experiences affect self-esteem.
- Define self-expectancy and explain two ways to boost it.
- Explain why self-acceptance is important for high self-esteem.
- Explain how to change negative self-talk into positive self-talk.
- Explain how to handle criticism well.

OUTLINE

Chapter Topics

UNDERSTANDING SELF-ESTEEM
The Power of Self-Esteem
      Effects of High and Low Self-Esteem
      Origins of Self-Esteem
      Shyness and Self-Esteem
      Raising Your Self-Esteem
Self-Expectancy and Self-Esteem
      Building Your Self-Expectancy

LEARNING TO LIKE YOURSELF
Self-Acceptance and Self-Esteem
      You, Flaws and All
      Mending a Negative Self-Image
      Kick the Comparing Habit
      Real or Ideal?
Using Positive Self-Talk
      Negative Self-Talk: Your Inner Critic
      Using Affirmations
Criticism and Self-Esteem
      Destructive and Constructive Criticism
      Handling Constructive Criticism
      Handling Destructive Criticism
      Assertiveness and Self-Esteem

Chapter Activities

EXERCISE 4.1   **Test Your Self-Esteem** (pp. 131–134)
EXERCISE 4.2   **Social Support and Self-Esteem** (pp. 138–139)
EXERCISE 4.3   **Accomplishment Inventory** (pp. 144–145)
EXERCISE 4.4   **Personal Inventory** (pp. 151–153)
EXERCISE 4.5   **Negative Self-Talk Log** (pp. 162–163)
EXERCISE 4.6   **Handling Criticism** (pp. 171–173)

Personal Journal 4.1   **Examine Your Self-Expectancy** (p. 142)
Personal Journal 4.2   **Learning to Cope** (p. 146)
Personal Journal 4.3   **Social Comparison Log** (p. 156)
Personal Journal 4.4   **Your Ideal Self** (p. 159)

Chapter Features

INTERNET ACTION   **The Digital Divide and Self-Esteem** (p. 141)
PROFESSIONAL DEVELOPMENT   **Image Consulting** (p. 149)
Applying Psychology   **CULTURE AND BODY IMAGE** (p. 154)

FOCUS

Introducing the Chapter

Write *self-esteem* on the board and ask volunteers for definitions (confidence in and respect for oneself). Then ask, "What do you think is the relationship between self-esteem and success?" and discuss their answers as a class. Explain that if you have self-esteem, you have confidence in yourself and your ability to reach your goals. People with high self-esteem are not roadblocked by people or circumstances. Finally, tell students that in this chapter they will find out more about their own self-esteem and learn how to develop it in order to reach their goals and achieve success.

Real-Life Success Story "Do I Have What It Takes?" (p. 126)

Have a student read the Real-Life Success Story aloud and ask what effect Paul's parents and sister are having on Paul. Ask, "Do you think they are being fair to Paul? Do they seem concerned with Paul's best interests?" Point out that constant criticism and underestimating what a person can do can seriously undermine that person's self-esteem. Finally ask, "What would you do if you were Paul?"

Opening Quote (p. 127)

"Allow yourself to fail and you will be more likely to succeed."

Write the quote on the board or make a transparency of it using the reproducible master on page 264. Ask students what they think this statement means. Ask, "How can allowing yourself to fail lead to success?" Ask, too, if they agree with this statement.

Have students think of inventors or innovators, such as George Washington Carver, Marie Curie, or Bill Gates. Ask, "Do you think they were successful the first time they tried to invent something, or do you think they had to make many attempts before their ideas really worked?"

INSTRUCT

Teaching Tips

The following topics are discussed in this chapter. You may want to expand on them in large or small class groups.

The Power of Self-Esteem (pp. 128–140)

Have students compare the benefits of high self-esteem listed on page 129 of the textbook with the effects of low self-esteem listed on page 130. Ask students how having confidence in and respect for yourself could lead to the benefits listed and how having little or no confidence in yourself could lead to the negative effects listed. For example, if you have confidence in yourself, it is easier to try out new ideas and experiences. Conversely, if you have little confidence, you are more likely to fear mistakes and to avoid trying new things.

Self-Expectancy and Self-Esteem (pp. 141–147)

Write *self-expectancy* on the board and ask a volunteer for its definition (the belief that you are able to achieve what you want in life). Then ask students how they think self-esteem affects self-expectancy. Lead them to understand that people with low self-esteem expect to fail, and this is usually what comes true for them. On the other hand, people with high self-esteem expect to succeed, and this is what usually comes true for them.

Self-Acceptance and Self-Esteem (pp. 148–158)

Write *self-acceptance* on the board and ask a volunteer for its definition (recognizing and accepting what is true about yourself). Then read the following: "The difference between people who accept themselves and people who reject themselves isn't the number of weaknesses they have. It's the way they look at them." Ask students, "Given this statement, how does self-esteem affect self-acceptance?" Students should see that people with high self-esteem focus on their strengths, while people with low self-esteem concentrate on their weaknesses.

Ask students what they see as the relationship between self-expectancy and self-acceptance. Explain that both are necessary ingredients of self-esteem. If desired, draw a Venn Diagram on the board in which the circles labeled "self-expectancy" and "self-acceptance" overlap to form the concept "self-esteem."

Using Positive Self-Talk (pp. 158–165)

Ask students if they ever talk to themselves. "Do you say nice things or critical things to yourself? Have you ever thought how you'd feel if a good friend said critical things to him- or herself? Would you ever criticize a friend as harshly as you would criticize yourself?" Lead students to recognize that we are often our own harshest critics. Then ask, "How do critical thoughts make you feel about yourself?" Explain that we can actually change how we feel about ourselves by changing the way we talk to ourselves.

Criticism and Self-Esteem (pp. 165–174)

Have students work in pairs to create two role-plays to illustrate constructive and destructive criticism. Both role-plays should address the same problem, but one role-play should use destructive criticism and the second should use constructive criticism. Allow students to present their role-plays to the class and discuss what makes criticism destructive or constructive.

In-Chapter Answers and Notes

EXERCISE 4.1

Test Your Self-Esteem (pp. 131–134)

A-B. Students' responses and scores will vary.

C. Answers will vary but should reflect the number of C's scored. 0–10 C's suggests that the student has low self-esteem, and 11 or more C's suggests that the student likes him- or herself.

D. Answers will vary. Students who score 8 or more A's have an aggressive behavior pattern, those with 7 or more B's have a passive behavior pattern, and those with a near equal number of A's and B's show a mix.

E. Behaviors and examples will vary.

FIGURE 4.1

Childhood Origins of Self-Esteem
(p. 136)

Answers will vary but could include grandparents, aunts, uncles, siblings, teachers, coaches, and friends.

EXERCISE 4.2

Social Support and Self-Esteem
(pp. 138–139)

A-B. Checks and scores will vary. Suggestions for building more social support will also vary but could include showing more interest in others, being social support for others, join a school group, neighborhood club, or volunteer project, and work on communication skills, such as empathy and active listening.

C. Responses and situations will vary. People can experience loneliness regardless of whether they are physically alone.

D. Diagrams will vary. People referred to could include parents, spouse or partner, roommate, siblings, friends, and neighbors.

E. Opinions will vary. Students should mention some of the strategies described on page 140.

INTERNET ACTION

The Digital Divide and Self-Esteem
(p. 141)

Answers will vary. Students should recognize that in order to verify Internet information they should find other sources (at least two is best) that give the same information. Students should also consider the stability and reputation of the Internet source. For example, information taken from a *BusinessWeek* Web site is likely to be more reliable than information gathered from a chat room.

Personal Journal 4.1

Examine Your Self-Expectancy (p. 142)

Students' responses will vary. Remind students to review the long-term goals they set for themselves in Chapter 3 and to think about how confident they are about achieving them. Point out that this will also help them better understand their self-expectancy.

Sample Answers

Put a check mark in the box next to the statements with which you agree.

☑ I know I can accomplish my goals.

☑ When something unexpected comes my way, I find resourceful ways to handle it.

☑ I can solve almost any problem if I try hard enough.

☑ Stress and anger aren't a problem for me because I have good coping skills.

☑ I can handle whatever comes my way.

☑ If someone else can do something, then I can probably do it, too.

☑ I am capable of success.

My long-term goals are to complete my degree and to own my own business in the next 10 years. I am very confident that I will complete my degree because I am working hard at school and doing well. So far, I've been able to meet all the challenges that school has thrown at me. As far as owning my own business—I'm not sure how long this will take. I'm intimidated by the state of the economy and the fact that I haven't done it before. Right now I know I have a lot to learn, but I have some good ideas, and after I finish school, I know I will be better prepared to be a successful entrepreneur.

EXERCISE 4.3

Accomplishment Inventory
(pp. 144–145)

A. Accomplishments will vary.

B. Skills will vary. Point out that some people find it difficult to recognize their own skills but readily recognize the skills of others. That is why thinking of someone else can help a person to acknowledge his or her own skills.

C. Skills will vary but should focus on mid- to long-term goals.

D. SMART goals will vary. If necessary, have students review SMART goals in Chapter 3.

E. Students' responses will vary. Confidence in achieving the first goal may be higher than confidence in reaching the last, but students should recognize that each goal achieved helps to prepare you for the next goal.

Personal Journal 4.2

Learning to Cope (p. 146)

Students' responses will vary but should recognize that while avoiding a problem reduces short-term discomfort, coping will help you feel better about yourself overall and improve self-esteem.

Exploring Further

Begin a class discussion by asking students to name other coping strategies that could provide a temporary solution to a problem or crisis. Examples might include denying that the problem exists and blaming others for the problem. Ask students to think about why these strategies are so widely employed, not only by individuals but also by politicians and other public figures. What benefits do people derive from these negative escape responses? Have students think about whether there is ever a case where it would be appropriate to use nonproductive coping strategies such as denying the problem or blaming others.

SELF-CHECK (p. 147)

1. People with self-esteem appreciate their value or worth as a person. They are confident in their ability to cope with life's challenges, and they believe that they are worthy of success and happiness. This motivates them to work hard and succeed.

2. Unconditional positive regard is the love and acceptance of a person, particularly a child, regardless of his or her particular behavior.

3. Avoidance reduces short-term discomfort, but leaves you with the feeling that you are incapable of dealing with the situation, which lowers self-esteem.

PROFESSIONAL DEVELOPMENT

Image Consulting (p. 149)

Personal stories will vary, but students should recognize that people with high self-esteem try to make a good first impression—not because they are insecure, but because they want to make the other person feel comfortable and because they want others to see them at their best.

Exploring Further

Ask students to imagine that they are applying for a new job. They have worked hard in school and gotten good grades, and have assembled some relevant work experience. Their task now is to let their interviewer know they are the perfect person for the job. The interviewer does not know much about them, and they have only four minutes to make that important first impression. (Studies have shown that four minutes is about how long it takes to make a first impression.) What kind of things might make a positive first impression on an interviewer? What kinds of things might make a negative first impression? Why? Ask students to discuss how much first impressions depend on appearance and how much they depend on other factors.

EXERCISE 4.4

Personal Inventory (pp. 151–153)

A. Good points and bad points will vary. Make sure students have included items in all six areas.

B. Students' responses will vary but should follow the rules listed.

C. Letters will vary.

Sample Answers

A. Write down what you see as your good points and bad points in each of the following areas of your life.

APPEARANCE
Beautiful skin
(Frizzy hair)

ROMANTIC RELATIONSHIPS/SEXUALITY
(Can't communicate with my partner)
Physically open and responsive

SOCIAL SKILLS/POPULARITY
(Never make friends easily)
Good listener, loyal
Compassionate

THINKING SKILLS/INTELLIGENCE
(Completely spaced out about everyday stuff)
Analytical and probing

SCHOOL
(Terrible at math)
Do well on essays and artistic work
Quick and accurate

WORK
(Not ambitious or creative enough)

B. Look over what you wrote about yourself, circling all the negative items. Rewrite each negative item.

APPEARANCE
My hair becomes dry at the ends between trims

ROMANTIC RELATIONSHIPS/SEXUALITY
Although we have a good relationship, my partner and I sometimes have communication problems

SOCIAL SKILLS/POPULARITY
It takes me a while to get to know people

THINKING SKILLS/INTELLIGENCE
I can be absentminded about details, but I never lose track of the big picture

SCHOOL
I receive an average of a B in math courses

WORK
Satisfied with my current position at work, and have other outlets for my interests

C. Write a letter describing yourself to someone you have never met.

May 12, 2003

Dear Tom,

Mimi's brother Carlo gave me your name and told me that we'll both be attending the motivational workshop. I look forward to meeting you next weekend. Let me tell you a little about myself. I hope you'll be able to recognize me at the booth: I'm about 5'6, sturdy, brown hair, brown eyes, and olive skin, and I tend to wear a lot of black and red.

Like you, I just graduated a few months ago with a degree in architecture. I thought about doing industrial engineering for a while, but I struggled to maintain decent grades in math so I decided to stick with the more creative side of things. I am twenty-two years old and work as a production assistant at a design firm.

I just moved in with Mimi in Los Angeles—that's going pretty well, though some things take getting used to. She gets after me for forgetting to do small stuff like taking the recycling out or turning off the stove, but once we figure out how to talk it through, we get along just fine. The design firm keeps me pretty busy, but there's not a lot of room for growth there at the moment, so to keep my skills sharp I also volunteer at an agency which helps nonprofits establish their own Web sites and online newsletters. It's definitely cool to put my design skills to use for a good cause. It's also helped me get to know people in the area. I'm pretty shy, so it usually takes me a while to make friends, but once I do, I'm a friend for life. I'm a great listener, and I hope we get to connect soon! I look forward to meeting you at the workshop.

Sincerely,
Joo-ri Kim

Applying Psychology

CULTURE AND BODY IMAGE (p. 154)
Students' responses will vary. Some students may feel that these images represent a standard that they should try to achieve, especially if the models in the images are from a similar ethnic background. Many students, however, will feel that they cannot relate to the images of models, regardless of ethnic background, because the body types portrayed tend to be extremes.

Exploring Further

Have each student collect and bring to class examples of media images that they feel present unrealistic standards for physical appearance, as well as some they feel represent realistic standards. Break the class into small groups and ask the students to share their images with one another and to discuss the similarities and differences among their examples and among their own ideals of physical appearance. You may also wish to draw students' attention to the blank facial expressions of the models shown in the illustration that accompanies this feature. Why do students think that so many fashion ads feature unsmiling models? Why might advertisers use these kinds of images, and how might these images make consumers feel?

Personal Journal 4.3

Social Comparison Log (p. 156)
Students' responses will vary, but this activity should help them recognize whether or not they have the comparing habit, and if so in what areas.

FIGURE 4.2

You and Your Ideal (p. 157)
Answers may vary, but one response is that instead of focusing on a fantasy ideal, you can think about your possible selves—the

person(s) you think you might realistically become in the future.

Personal Journal 4.4
Your Ideal Self (p. 159)
Students' responses will vary. Only unrealistic fantasies and things that are truly not needed or wanted should be crossed off.

Sample Answers

Write down how you would like to look, act, and feel and what you would like to be, achieve, and own in an ideal world. Then cross out every item that represents either an unrealistic fantasy or something that you don't truly want or need.

confident
~~the richest person who ever lived~~
~~own apartments in New York, San Francisco, Paris, London, and Prague~~
~~travel to a distant planet~~
be happy
married
write a book
decorate my apartment
~~win a Nobel prize, an Oscar, and a Grammy~~
own my own plane
~~be a secret agent like James Bond~~
~~become taller~~
~~look like a supermodel~~
~~own a dinosaur~~
volunteer 20 hours a week
finish my bachelor's degree
be debt-free
keep the house clean
start my own business
~~find a giant bag of money~~
adopt a child
travel to Africa

Exploring Further

Ask each student to note things he or she ended up crossing off and why. Ask students to share the characteristics of their ideal self with

one other person in order to help them evaluate their choices. Does the other person think that some of the "unrealistic" ideals or expectations are actually realistic or possible? Does the other person think that some of the "realistic" ideals or expectations are actually unrealistic and impossible? Why or why not?

EXERCISE 4.5

Negative Self-Talk Log (pp. 162–163)
A-B. Students' responses will vary.

C. Statements and their origins will vary. Many students will recognize that their parents, guardians, or other influential adults may be the origin of their inner critic. It might help students to recognize that in many cases those adults weren't trying to inflict pain but may not have known how to offer constructive criticism.

D. Affirmations will vary. An example would be changing "I'm always late" to "I have the power to be on time."

FIGURE 4.3

Responding to Constructive Criticism (p. 167)
Students' responses will vary but should recognize that constructive criticism (addressing specific behavior, mentioning positive points, and offering helpful suggestions) can be helpful to employees if offered in an empathetic and positive way.

FIGURE 4.4

Responding to Destructive Criticism (p. 169)
Answers will vary, but some may suggest that when the criticism is not valid or if the critic is baiting you into an argument, it may be best not to respond.

Exploring Further

In this chapter the author states, "no matter what you do or say, or don't do or don't say, you will receive criticism at some point."

Challenge groups of students to think of an action or statement that no one, or almost no one, could possibly criticize. Then have groups present the ideas to the class, asking the rest of the students to think of situations in which someone could indeed criticize the behavior. For example, if one group says that no one could criticize tending the sick and homeless, the class could point out that some people might say that charity work is a waste of time and money, or that homeless people "want" to be that way.

EXERCISE 4.6

Handling Criticism (pp. 171–173)

A. Responses to constructive criticism will vary.

B. Responses to destructive criticism will vary.

C. Responses will vary, but some may recognize that even constructive criticism is hard to accept.

D. Responses will vary but will probably acknowledge that destructive criticism is very difficult to accept gracefully and that it often angers those being criticized.

E. Students should cite several positive self-statements that they can use to protect their self-esteem. Students should also understand that being criticized is not a reason to feel badly about themselves. Criticism often stems from a difference of opinion or from the critic's personal difficulties. Everyone therefore receives criticism at some point. Criticism can also provide the self-knowledge necessary for developing self-acceptance.

Sample Answers

A. Write a response to each constructive criticism that 1) restates the criticism and 2) asks for specific suggestions.

Instructor: "You always have interesting things to say in your homework. It's disappointing that you don't speak up more in class."

Restate: Yes, I'd like to talk more in class than I have been.

Ask for suggestions: How involved in class discussion would you like me to be?

Roommate: "I love the color you chose for the living room walls. It might be even better if the paint was a little more even."

Restate: It's true that sometimes the thickness of the coats is not consistent.

Ask for suggestions: Would you mind pointing out where it looks uneven to you so I can try to fix it?

Boss: "I see how much effort you've put into this spreadsheet, but the small type makes it hard for me to read."

Restate: Yes, it's not so easy to read at that point size.

Ask for suggestions: Is there a specific type size that you prefer I use in the future?

Parent: "You forgot Michael's birthday last week, and his feelings were hurt. You need to make a point to remember family occasions."

Restate: I would like to be more organized about remembering family occasions so I don't offend anyone.

Ask for suggestions: Would you mind sharing any ways of keeping track of family events that might work for me?

B. Write a response to each destructive criticism that 1) acknowledges the facts and 2) asserts yourself by correcting the part of the criticism that is mistaken, unfair, or insulting.

Instructor: "You never have anything to contribute in class."

Acknowledge: I don't speak up in class very often.

Assert yourself: However, I do put forth most of my ideas in my papers.

Roommate: "You did a terrible job painting the living room walls."

Acknowledge: It's true that it looks uneven in some places.

Assert yourself: However, I did manage to paint the entire thing without leaving any blank spots or dripping on the furniture.

Boss: "I practically need a microscope to read this spreadsheet. Please make it look like a professional did it."

Acknowledge: I can see that this font is difficult to read at that size.

Assert yourself: <u>However, all of the information is there, and this was the standard template that was provided to me by the department.</u>

Parent: "You forgot Michael's birthday again. It's important to remember family occasions."

Acknowledge: <u>I know he was upset because I got the date wrong like last year.</u>

Assert yourself: <u>I haven't missed anyone else's birthday, and Michael accepted my apology.</u>

Exploring Further

The ability to formulate solid constructive criticism is a valuable skill. Divide the class into small groups and ask each group to create a role-play that involves the giving and receiving of constructive feedback, such as a supervisor giving an employee feedback on a presentation or a coach giving a player comments on his or her game. Ask students to come up with four or five statements of feedback and to phrase them in both a constructive fashion and a destructive fashion. Remind students that constructive statements focus on behavior, make mention of positive points, and provide specific suggestions for improvement.

SECTION 4.2
SELF-CHECK (p. 174)

1. Self-acceptance means recognizing and accepting what is true about yourself.

2. By using positive self-talk, you can give yourself praise and encouragement, which can change the way you feel about yourself and build your self-esteem.

3. An example of destructive criticism is "You're totally out of shape." An example of constructive criticism is "I'm concerned about your health. What if we went speed-walking together a few times a week?"

Additional Activities

These additional activities are exclusive to this Instructor's Resource Manual. They are designed to meet the special needs of your students. The activities can be used as in-class activities or as take-home assignments. They can be assigned to individual students, pairs of students, or groups of students.

Critical Thinking

PHYSICAL EXERCISE AND SELF-EXPECTANCY   Being fit and active can raise a person's self-esteem. People with high self-esteem are usually motivated to be fit and active because they value themselves and their physical health. People with low self-esteem, however, may avoid exercise because they doubt their ability to perform athletically or stick to an exercise plan. This means they miss out on the positive psychological and physical effects of exercise. Ask students to think of a list of objections that a person with very low self-esteem could raise against the idea of beginning an exercise program. For example, a person with low self-esteem and a poor body image might be afraid of going to a gym or even of walking in public. Have students discuss the list and try to come up with positive rebuttals to each objection.

SELF-ESTEEM AND VIOLENCE   Several studies have linked high self-esteem with aggression. Bullies and gang members, for example, often appear to have high levels of self-esteem and self-expectancy. According to one recent study, people with high self-esteem are more likely to be criminal, racist, and violent than people with low self-esteem. Ask students whether they are surprised by these findings. Is there a difference between self-esteem based on realistic confidence in one's own abilities and self-esteem based power and violence? To motivate the discussion, read students the following quotation by Rollo May: "Deeds of violence in our society are performed largely by those trying to establish their self-esteem, to defend their self-image, and to demonstrate that they, too, are significant." Ask students to interpret this statement. (The statement implies that people with low self-esteem use violence to acquire a false, inflated sense of self-esteem.) Ask students to cite examples from their own experience to support or contradict this statement.

Application

CHILD AND ADULT SELF-ESTEEM   This activity takes students back in time to their childhood and adolescence. Make handouts or a transparency of the reproducible master on page 270, "History of Your Self-Esteem." Ask students to provide answers to each of the questions as honestly as they can and to the best of their memory. Then ask students to discuss whether their self-esteem has grown higher or lower over time, and why. You may wish to ask them to plot a simple line graph of their level of self-esteem over time. Discuss students' answers in class. What ups and downs in self-esteem have students experienced over their lives? As an example, some painfully shy children grow into self-confident adults, while some confident children grow into adults with low self-esteem. Engage the class in a discussion of the reasons why a person's self-esteem might rise or fall as he or she grows up and finds a place in the world.

THE ART OF COMPLIMENTING   Divide students into pairs. Ask them to write down on a sheet of paper a short statement about how they are feeling about themselves that day. Set a timer for 10 minutes or note the time on the clock. Tell the students that they will be practicing making compliments. One student should begin the exercise by making only positive statements about the other student for the first five minutes. The students will then reverse roles for the next five minutes. Afterwards, ask the students to describe the differences between how they felt before, during, and after the exercise. Did they feel happy? Embarrassed? Upset? Exposed? Surprised? Discuss whether the exercise was more or less challenging for the student who went first or for the one who went second.

Internet Activities

ROSENBERG SELF-ESTEEM SCALE   The Rosenberg Self-Esteem Scale, developed in 1965 by sociologist Manny Rosenberg, is one of the most frequently used and reliable self-esteem inventories. Ask students to find and print out the inventory on the Internet, then administer the test to three friends or family members whom they know at least fairly well. (A copy of the scale is also provided in reproducible master form on page 271.) Ask students to predict each interviewee's score before he or she takes the test, then compare this prediction to the real score. Ask students to describe their reactions to the scores. Were they surprised by the results? Why or why not?

SHYNESS   Ask students to locate an online version of the shyness questionnaire known as the "Revised Cheek and Buss Shyness Scale (RCBS)." Have them take the questionnaire and add up their totals. Are they more or less shy than average? Are they surprised by the results? Ask students to write a paragraph discussing how their shyness, or lack of shyness, affects their self-esteem and their behavior in social settings.

MOTIVATIONAL SPEAKERS   Organizations such as companies and schools sometimes hire motivational speakers to give presentations on motivation, self-esteem, communication, body image, addiction, and other topics. Many of these speakers have developed specific programs that people should follow in order to achieve their goals (a 12-step program, for example). First ask students to define what they think a motivational speaker is. Then have students use the Internet to find information about at least two professional motivational speakers and their methods. Ask students to write a one-page critique of each speaker: do they find that person's methods informative and inspirational? How do this person and their methods compare to the student's original ideas of what a motivational speaker should be or do?

COSMETIC SURGERY AND BODY IMAGE

Plastic surgery is usually performed for a medical reason, such as to correct a physical abnormality. However, more and more cosmetic (medically unnecessary) surgery is being performed on healthy people who want to feel better about their appearance. Between 1992 and 2001, for example, the number of women receiving breast enlargement surgery rose more than 500 percent. Ask students to research the benefits and drawbacks of plastic surgery on the Internet and answer these questions:

- How many people sought cosmetic surgery in the previous year?
- Which cosmetic procedures are currently the most popular?
- What are some medical risks of these procedures?

Ask students to bring their answers to class for discussion. In class, ask students, "Do you believe that cosmetic surgery is a good way to improve body image and self-esteem? Why or why not? Would you ever consider cosmetic surgery? Why or why not?"

ASSESS

Review and Activities Answers

Review Questions (p. 176)

1. Effects of high self-esteem include accepting your strengths and weaknesses, expressing your true thoughts and feelings, establishing emotional connections to other people, giving and receiving compliments, giving and receiving affection, trying out new ideas and experiences, expressing your creativity, standing up for yourself, handling stress and anger calmly, and seeing the future with optimism. Effects of low self-esteem include mistrusting other people, experiencing difficulty developing intimate relationships, fearing mistakes and having trouble making decisions, criticizing yourself relentlessly, being extremely sensitive to criticism from others, anticipating problems, crises, and failure, ignoring your own needs, giving in to unreasonable requests, disliking being the center of attention, withholding your true thoughts and feelings from others, living in fear of rejection and disapproval, worrying about being a burden on others, feeling out of control of your life, and missing out on the joy of life.

2. If your childhood experiences include encouragement from nurturing parents, teachers, coaches, and friends, you will probably have high self-esteem. If your childhood experiences include abusive or neglectful relationships, repeated rejection, family dysfunction, or intense criticism from others, you will probably have low self-esteem.

3. When you expect something and dwell on it, you direct the bulk of your time and energy to it. You experience it in your mind and prepare for it. This makes it almost inevitable that it will come to pass.

4. To change a distorted self-image, you must first accept that it is distorted and then look at yourself objectively to reassess your strengths and weaknesses. Having an accurate view of your strengths helps you set challenging goals, overcome obstacles, and take advantage of opportunities, which in turn helps improve your self-image.

5. Answers will vary but should recognize that a downward comparison is one in which we compare ourselves to people "below" us, such as fellow students earning lower grades or coworkers who have received fewer promotions. An upward comparison is one in which we compare ourselves to people "above" us, such as students with higher grades or coworkers who have been promoted above us.

6. The three steps in handling constructive criticism are: 1. Listen carefully and check

for understanding; 2. Restate the criticism; and 3. Ask for suggestions.

Critical Thinking (p. 176)

7. Answers will vary but should recognize that working around your weaknesses and coping with your problems, rather than avoiding them, is not a contradiction. Working around your weaknesses is ultimately the same thing as focusing on your strengths. Working around your weaknesses does not mean avoiding them, but rather acknowledging, accepting, and adapting to them.

8. Answers will vary but should recognize that people who often criticize or make fun of others may very well have low self-esteem. Some people with low self-esteem can be aggressive, pushy, critical, or hostile. Being critical or making fun of others can be a type of downward comparison that enables the critic to feel better about him- or herself. If you have self-acceptance, you don't need downward comparison to feel good about yourself.

Application (p. 176)

9. Journal entries will vary. Students will probably recognize that their self-esteem is high when their social support system functions well, when they accomplish something, when they cope with a problem, and when they use positive self-talk. They may also recognize that their self-esteem is low when they feel anxious, when their social support system lets them down, when they avoid a problem, when they compare themselves to others too often, and when they succumb to negative self-talk.

10. Interviews will vary but should illustrate the value of accomplishment in building self-expectancy. Students should recognize the cyclical nature of accomplishment and self-expectancy. Through the accomplishment of a goal, you gain self-expectancy,

which enables you to strive for additional accomplishments.

Internet Activities (p. 177)

11. The ten effects or outcomes of having negative "self-scripts" include over-dependence on the approval of others, lack of self-esteem and low self-concept, immobilization, negativity, pessimism, self-pity, cynicism, the "guard-all shield," fulfillment of the prophecy, and depression. Affirmations will vary.

12. Answers will vary but should recognize that shyness can vary from mild social awkwardness to totally inhibiting social phobia. One way to describe the relationship between shyness and self-esteem is that shyness leads to avoidance behavior, which in turn reduces self-esteem. One positive aspect of shyness is greater self-awareness.

Real-Life Success Story "Do I Have What It Takes?" (p. 177)

Answers will vary but should demonstrate knowledge of the techniques discussed in the chapter.

Sample Answer

Paul talked to his adviser about quitting school. The advisor asked Paul why he had decided to enter veterinary technician school in the first place. As Paul talked about his experiences with animals, his enthusiasm began to return. He realized that he had developed a self-defeating attitude—and that he had the power to change his attitude. He learned to use positive self-talk and to visualize himself in his future role as a veterinary technician, helping people and animals. His self-confidence grew, and he developed a resistance to negative comments by his family.

CLOSE

Culminating Activity

Read the following quotation by Eleanor Roosevelt: "No one can make you feel inferior without your consent." Ask students to discuss the relationship between this statement and the concept of self-esteem discussed in this chapter. Ask students to touch on what these words might mean, whether it is significant to them personally, and in what contexts this statement might be true or untrue. Have students come up with a real-life situation in which Roosevelt's quotation would be helpful or applicable.

Personal Success Portfolio

Make handouts or a transparency of the Personal Success Portfolio Worksheet for Chapter 4 on page 234. Refer to pages 9 and 10 for suggestions on presenting this activity.

For Chapter 4, additional materials you may wish students to enclose in their portfolios are:

- an action plan for expanding the student's social support network
- a collection of five or six goal cards, one for each of the goals the student generated in Exercise 4.3, question D
- an action plan for coping with a problem the student has been avoiding
- a list of affirmations the student can use to replace the negative self-talk generated by social comparison
- using the student's answers to Personal Journal 4.4, a list of ten statements that begin, "I am good enough the way I am, without..."
- a depiction of a large red stop sign that the student can visualize whenever he or she needs to stop negative self-talk

ADDITIONAL RESOURCES

The following books offer a variety of theoretical and practical perspectives on self-esteem, self-talk, self-acceptance, and self-efficacy (self-expectancy).

Books

Ball, Carolyn. *Claiming Your Self Esteem: A Guide Out of Codependency Addiction and Other Useless Habits.* Berkeley: Celestial Arts, 1995.

Bandura, Alfred. *Self-Efficacy: The Exercise of Control.* New York: W. H. Freeman and Company, 1997.

Baumeister, R. F., ed. *Self-Esteem: The Puzzle of Low Self-Regard.* New York: Plenum Press, 1993.

Branden, Nathaniel. *The Power of Self-Esteem.* Deerfield Beach, FL: Heath Communications, 1992.

Branden, Nathaniel. *The Six Pillars of Self-Esteem.* New York: Bantam Books, 1994.

Brown, Byron. *Soul Without Shame: A Guide to Liberating Yourself from the Judge Within.* Boston: Shambhala Publications, 1999.

Felder, Leonard and Harold H. Bloomfield. *Making Peace With Yourself: Transforming Your Weaknesses into Strengths.* New York: Ballantine Books, 1996.

Hay, Louise L. *Self-Esteem Affirmations: Motivational Affirmations for Building Confidence and Recognizing Self-Worth.* Audio CD. Carlsbad, CA: Hay House, 1998.

Hay, Louise L. *Change Your Thoughts, Change Your Life.* Audio CD. Carlsbad, CA: Hay House, 1999.

Heldman, Mary Lynne. *When Words Hurt: How to Keep Criticism from Undermining Your Self-Esteem.* New York: Ballantine Books, 1990.

Helmstetter, Shad. *What to Say When You Talk to Your Self.* New York: Pocket Books, 1990.

Leary, Mark R. "Making Sense of Self-Esteem." *Current Directions in Psychological Science* 8 (1999): 32–35.

Mecca, A. M., N.J. Smelser, and J. Vasconcellos, eds. *The Social Importance of Self-Esteem.* Berkeley: University of California Press, 1989.

Sorensen, Marilyn J. *Breaking the Chain of Low Self-Esteem.* Sherwood, OR: Wolf Publishing, 1998.

Positive Thinking

OVERVIEW

Chapter 5 explores the relationship between positive thinking and success. In Section 5.1 students read about the habits associated with positive thinking and learn how their attitude can influence their mental and physical health. In Section 5.2 they learn why having positive expectations for themselves makes a huge difference in getting what they want out of life. They also investigate several types of negative thinking and learn techniques for transforming unpleasant thoughts and feelings into positive ones.

OBJECTIVES

After they complete this chapter, students should be able to:

- Define positive thinking and cite its benefits.
- List six habits that can help them become more positive thinkers.
- Explain the link between positive thinking and good health.
- Describe how self-defeating attitudes create a vicious cycle.
- Define cognitive distortions and irrational beliefs and give an example of each.
- Summarize the ABCDE method for overcoming irrational beliefs.

OUTLINE

Chapter Topics

BECOMING A POSITIVE THINKER
Positive Thinking and Optimism
>Why Positive Thinking Matters
>Thinking and Attitude

Adopting Positive Habits
>Look for the Good
>Choose Your Words
>Surround Yourself With Positive People
>Accept, Don't Judge
>Limit Complaints
>Don't Worry

Thinking Style and Health
>Good Attitude, Good Health
>Negative Thinking and Mental Health
>Getting Healthy

CONQUERING NEGATIVE THOUGHTS
Overcoming Self-Defeating Attitudes
>The Power of Attitude
>A Vicious Cycle
>Changing Your Attitude

Recognizing Distorted Thoughts
>Irrational Beliefs

Changing Your Negative Thoughts
>Learning Your ABCDEs

Chapter Activities

Chapter Features

FOCUS

Introducing the Chapter

To introduce the chapter, ask the class, "How do you think positive thinking affects success?" and briefly discuss their responses. Then display a transparency of the chapter's Keys to Success and ask a student to read aloud the Keys to Success from Section 5.1. Finally, have each student choose a Key to Success statement to write on a file card to keep in his or her notebook or Personal Success Portfolio.

Real-Life Success Story "Will Things Go My Way?" (p. 178)

Have a volunteer read the first part of the story and then ask, "Well, how can Jessica make today's interview different? What can she do to feel less nervous and more confident?" Lead students to recognize that concentrating on her positive qualities (being bilingual, having great people skills, and earning top grades) can help calm her nerves. Students may also be familiar with interview strategies that can help, such as rehearsing with a friend, choosing clothes carefully the day before, arriving early, and so on.

Then read the second part of Jessica's story and discuss Jessica's attitude about herself, the interview, and the job. Students should recognize that Jessica is setting herself up for failure. Contrast this with the strategies suggested above to show how Jessica's own actions and attitude may sabotage her career dreams.

Opening Quote (p. 179)

"Hope is not a dream, but a way of making dreams become reality."

Write the quote on the board or make a transparency of it using the reproducible master on page 272. Ask students what they think this statement means. Ask, "How can hope make a dream come true? Is there a relationship between hope and positive thinking?"

Have students each envision a personal dream and think about how their hopes for that dream can help make that dream come true. What happens to a dream when a person loses all hope of attaining it? If desired, discuss one or more of the other quotations on the reproducible master. Then allow students several minutes to write down their thoughts on their dreams and hopes to keep in their private journals or add to their Personal Success Portfolios.

INSTRUCT

Teaching Tips

The following topics are discussed in this chapter. You may want to expand on them in large or small class groups.

Positive Thinking and Optimism (pp. 180–185)

Write the following terms on the board: *positive thinking, negative thinking, optimism, pessimism,* and *attitude.* Ask volunteers for definitions for each term, referring to the text if necessary. Then ask students to draw a simple chart to reflect the relationship among the five terms. Charts will vary but should show that positive thinking and optimism are opposites of negative thinking and pessimism and that both positive and negative thinking are attitudes about life.

Adopting Positive Habits (pp. 186–191)

Point out that there are six important positive habits of thought and action and write them on the board or display them on a transparency made from the reproducible master on page 274. The habits are: look for the good, choose positive words, surround yourself with positive people, accept, don't judge, limit complaints, and don't worry. In small groups or pairs, have students choose one of the positive habits and write a brief scenario or role-play that illustrates it. Allow them to share their scenarios or role-plays with the class.

Thinking Style and Health (pp. 191–200)
Ask students if they have ever heard of the book *Anatomy of an Illness* by Norman Cousins. In the book, Cousins writes about how he battled a crippling and supposedly incurable disease with, among other things, humor. He watched Marx brothers films and the TV show *Candid Camera* while sick in bed in order to laugh. He determined that by laughing he could increase certain antibodies that helped him defeat his illness.

Ask students if they believe that their attitude has any effect on their health and have them explain why or why not. Then have a volunteer read out loud the text at the bottom of page 191 and the top of 194 on how the body's immune system is affected by negative and positive thoughts.

Overcoming Self-Defeating Attitudes (pp. 201–204)
Project a transparency of Figure 5.3, "Self-Defeating Attitudes: A Vicious Cycle." Explain that a self-defeating attitude leads to self-defeating behavior, which leads to a negative outcome, which strengthens the self-defeating attitude. Then ask, "How can a person overcome this cycle?" Discuss students' responses and point out that we can overcome self-defeating attitudes in two steps and write them on the board.

1. Awareness—realize what our self-defeating attitudes are doing to us.
2. Positive self-talk—replace our negative attitudes with positive self-statements.

Recognizing Distorted Thoughts (pp. 204–212)
Have students scan this section to find the types of cognitive distortions identified by Aaron Beck. (They are: all-or-nothing thinking, overgeneralizing, filtering, helpless thinking, self-blame, personalizing, mind reading, emotional reasoning, and catastrophizing.) Write them on the board as students identify them and discuss each. Point out that they all have one important thing in common: a

pessimistic outlook that transforms the frustrations and disappointments of everyday life into earth-shattering disasters. If desired, ask students to give an original example of each cognitive distortion from their own lives.

Changing Your Negative Thoughts (pp. 212–218)
As a class or in small groups, have students create a scenario to explain how the ABCDE method works. Make sure they specify which parts of their scenarios reflect the five parts of the method: A–activating event; B–belief; C–consequences; D–dispute; and E–exchange.

In-Chapter Answers and Notes

Applying Psychology

AGING WITH AN ATTITUDE (p. 181)
Fears will vary but could include becoming immobile, losing independence, losing one's health, being alone, being found unattractive, losing mental faculties, becoming physically disabled, losing hearing or sight, or not having enough money to live comfortably.

Exploring Further

Ask students to cite their fears of growing older. Make a list on the board or on a transparency of the fears that are mentioned the most often. Then ask students to work in pairs or small groups to think of one positive thing about growing older for every negative thing on the class's list.

FIGURE 5.1

The Power of Positive Thoughts (p. 182)
Answers will vary. Students should recall from Chapter 4, however, that through positive self-talk you can change negative thoughts and feelings about yourself. The subconscious

mind can affect the conscious mind, but the conscious mind can also affect the subconscious mind.

Are You a Positive Thinker?
(pp. 184–185)

A.-B. Students' responses and scores will vary. Students with scores of 31 and higher are mostly positive thinkers. Scores of 17–30 reflect a mix of positive and negative attitudes. These students need to pay more attention to their negative thoughts and work to replace them with positive ones. Students with scores of less than 17 are negative thinkers and need to adopt new habits of thinking.

C. Responses will vary but should be consistent with scores and should include examples. Students should understand that negative thinking is a habit, not a character flaw.

D. Responses will vary, although people generally think negatively about areas in which they have a negative self-image or in which they have had negative experiences in the past.

Personal Journal 5.1

Focusing on the Good (p. 187)
Students' responses will vary. Make sure students focus on what went right rather than what didn't go wrong.

Sample Answers

What do you feel good about today?

Today I'm grateful for:
  1. The love of my nephew and nieces
  2. Having a comfortable home
  3. Having a steady job and a promising career

Three good things that happened to me today:
  1. I finished cleaning my kitchen in record time.
  2. I found at $10 bill in my back pocket.

  3. A letter I had been waiting for came in the mail.

Three good things that I have to look forward to in the future:
  1. Starting a family
  2. Summer trip to Bali
  3. Getting a raise at the end of the month

PROFESSIONAL DEVELOPMENT

Thinking Positive at Work (p. 189)

Actions will vary but could include anything from bringing in treats to share, to organizing an activity, to hanging art work, to personalizing one's personal space or desk.

Exploring Further

As a class, make a list of several things that students think would help make the school campus a more positive place to be. Break the class into groups and assign each group to follow up on one of the ideas. For example, a group following up on an idea to redecorate or replant a certain drab area of the campus might go to the grounds department or administration and ask about the possibility of such an idea, find out how much the project would cost, design a fundraiser or solicit business donors for the project, and so on. As a class, discuss the feasibility of each idea. Choose one and work together as a class to make it happen.

Banishing Worry (pp. 192–193)

A. Responses will vary but could include money, health, school, career and job issues, relationships, children, crime, terrorism, and war.

B-D. Responses will vary. Students should realize that worst-case scenarios are not likely to happen and learn to distinguish between worst-case scenarios and realistic, probable outcomes.

E. Worries will vary. Point out that the process of writing down your worries and stashing them in a worry jar or box will help to separate you from your worries.

Sample Answers

A. Describe the biggest worry you have right now.
<u>I am worried that my relationship with Laura will not work out. I want to grow closer and one day get married and have a family, but I worry that she thinks I am not good enough for her, that she doesn't care about me the way I care about her, and so on.</u>

B. Describe the worst-case scenario. What would happen if all your worst fears came true in this situation?
<u>In the worst-case scenario, I dare to bring up my worries with Laura and she finds this clingy and pushy. She confirms my worst fears about myself and breaks up with me. I never see her again.</u>

C. How likely is it that the worst-case scenario will come true?
<u>It is highly unlikely, because Laura is a sensitive person who has a kind way of voicing her feelings. It is also unlikely because Laura probably wouldn't be close to me in the first place if she thought I wasn't good enough for her or if she didn't care about me.</u>

D. What is the most likely *realistic* outcome?
<u>The most likely realistic outcome is that Laura wants to continue the relationship but doesn't really know what she wants in her future. This would be painful, but it wouldn't necessarily mean that I have done something wrong.</u>

E. Write down six things you are worried about right now.

WORRY #1
My relationship with Laura will crumble.

WORRY #2
I won't be able to pay off my credit card bills, and they will continue to mount.

WORRY #3
I will be laid off and won't be able to find another job.

WORRY #4
My car will need a huge repair and I won't have the money to pay for it.

WORRY #5
I won't achieve any of my long-term goals.

WORRY #6
I will regain the weight I lost over the last three months.

Personal Journal 5.2

Depression Self-Check (p. 195)
Students' responses will vary. Make sure students take all warning signs of depression seriously.

Exploring Further

Depression is poorly understood by the general public, and people who suffer from depression are often stigmatized. Ask students whether any of them have had first-hand experiences with depression, either personally or with a close friend or family member. Without calling on any student in particular, ask students to talk about their experience and to talk about the serious effects of depression. Ask students why they think the illness is stigmatized. If desired, ask two or three students who have experience with the disease to give a short presentation about the causes and symptoms of depression and how it can be successfully treated.

EXERCISE 5.3

What's Your Health Attitude?
(pp. 196–198)

A-B. Students' responses and scores will vary.

C. Students' responses will vary. Students with higher scores for Section I and lower scores for Sections II and III have a generally positive attitude toward their health. Students with lower scores for Section I and higher scores for Sections II and III have a generally negative attitude toward their health.

D. Responses will vary but should recognize that the more responsibility you take for your well-being, the more motivated you will be to treat yourself right.

E. Responses will vary. Students should recognize that when you "make an effort to get well" you are acknowledging your responsibility for your health.

F. Answers will vary but could include eating a healthier diet, getting more exercise, getting more sleep or more rest and recreation, and having a more positive attitude.

FIGURE 5.2

The Food Guide Pyramid (p. 200)
Answers will vary but could include perceived lack of time, lack of experience cooking healthy foods, and lack of attention to the importance of a healthy diet.

Exploring Further

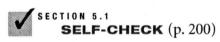

Display Figure 5.2 on a transparency made from the reproducible master on page 276. Ask students to think about what they ate the previous day or about what they have eaten today so far. Do their daily diets follow the recommendations of the Food Guide Pyramid? If not, how far off are they? What specific obstacles are preventing them from eating a more healthy diet?

SECTION 5.1
SELF-CHECK (p. 200)

1. Positive thinking means focusing on what is good about ourselves, other people, and the world around us. Negative thinking means focusing on the flaws and problems in ourselves, other people, and the world around us.

2. Being judgmental is a negative thought habit that is hurtful. People who find fault with others usually find fault with themselves, too.

3. The two main types of exercise are aerobic and anaerobic. Aerobic exercise is sustained, rhythmic physical activity that causes a temporary increase in heart and breathing rates, which strengthens the cardiovascular system. It includes activities such as jogging, basketball, and swimming. Anaerobic exercise is higher intensity wexercise that strengthens muscles and involves short bursts of intense exertion. It includes push-ups, stomach crunches, and weight training.

FIGURE 5.3

Self-Defeating Attitudes: A Vicious Cycle (p. 203)
Answers will vary but should recognize that you can overcome self-defeating attitudes through self-awareness and positive self-talk.

EXERCISE 5.4

Challenging Self-Defeating Attitudes (pp. 205–208)

A. Students' responses will vary but should recognize the vicious cycle that can be established.

B. Students' responses will vary but should recognize how positive self-talk can help to break the vicious cycle.

C. Statements will vary. Students should recognize that repeating the positive self-statements can reinforce a positive attitude.

Sample Answers

1. **Self-Defeating Attitude:** "I'm no good at making friends."
   Positive Self-Talk: Just because I'm shy around strangers doesn't mean that I'm bad at making friends. It just means that I need to practice more. I can look at meeting people as a fun opportunity to learn new things rather than as a scary situation in which people are judging me and I'm likely to put my foot in my mouth.
   Positive Behavior: Going out more, seeking out

new social events, introducing myself to new people
Positive Outcome: More friends and acquaintances

2. **Self-Defeating Attitude:** "I'm going to make a fool of myself at this dance class."
Positive Self-Talk: So what if I look awkward? If I already knew how to dance, I wouldn't need a class. Anyway, the other students will probably be more concerned with following along than with judging my performance. Dancing is fun, and I'm going to enjoy myself.
Positive Behavior: Attend class and dance with fewer inhibitions
Positive Outcome: Faster progress and greater self-confidence

3. **Self-Defeating Attitude:** "This date is going to be a disaster."
Positive Self-Talk: It's normal to be nervous before a date. However, just because I feel nervous doesn't mean the date will go poorly. I'm a fun person and I have interesting things to say. Even if we don't hit it off, it won't be a "disaster."
Positive Behavior: More outgoing and fun on date
Positive Outcome: Feel better about myself; enjoy date

4. **Self-Defeating Attitude:** "I'll never find another job."
Positive Self-Talk: "I haven't found a job yet, but that doesn't mean I never will. It took me almost a year to find my last job, but I persevered and finally found the right position. Soon my résumé will land on the desk of someone who will appreciate my education and accomplishments."
Positive Behavior: Keep searching and applying for promising job openings
Positive Outcome: Find new job

5. **Self-Defeating Attitude:** "Someone like that would never be interested in me."
Positive Self-Talk: "I have a lot to offer— humor, intelligence, sensitivity, interesting knowledge and hobbies. Why wouldn't someone be interested in me? Besides, if someone isn't attracted to me, that doesn't mean I'm unattractive, it just means that that particular individual isn't attracted to me.
Positive Behavior: Act more true to self; don't

become overly concerned with what that one person thinks of me
Positive Outcome: Find person who does appreciate me

6. **Self-Defeating Attitude:** "I'm too lazy to stick with an exercise program."
Positive Self-Talk: It's true that I don't usually stick with exercise programs, but that doesn't mean I'm lazy. I just need to pick an activity that works with my personality and schedule. I can pick something I enjoy doing, like dog walking, that will be exercise as well as fun.
Positive Behavior: Try something that fits my personality and schedule
Positive Outcome: Stick to the new program and get fit

 INTERNET ACTION

Inspiration by E-Mail (p. 210)
Books, poems, and quotations will vary. Allow time for students to share what they find to be inspirational.

Exploring Further

Circulate a sign-up sheet and ask students to each select a class day to bring in and discuss their book, poem, or quotation. Begin or end each class with an inspirational reading by a student.

`Personal Journal 5.3`

From Irrational to Rational (p. 213)
Students' responses will vary but should reflect the guidelines presented in the second paragraph on page 212.

Sample Answers

Irrational Belief: I must succeed at everything.
Rational Belief: It's impossible to succeed at everything. I will focus on succeeding at the things that really matter to me.

Irrational Belief: If _____ doesn't love me, then I'm worthless.

Rational Belief: I am not worthless just because a particular individual doesn't love me. I want _____ to love me, but if he or she doesn't, that doesn't affect my worth as a person.

Irrational Belief: I can't do anything about my feelings.

Rational Belief: I don't have to be a prisoner of my feelings. I can become aware of them and find ways to change them.

Irrational belief: I can't do anything about my bad habits—they're stronger than I am.

Rational Belief: I have the power to control my bad habits. It may take determination, patience, and perseverance, but I can replace bad habits with good habits.

FIGURE 5.4

The ABCDE Method (p. 214)
Answers will vary but should reflect the list of questions on page 215.

EXERCISE 5.5

Disputing Negative Thoughts
(pp. 216–218)
A. Students' responses will vary.
B. Students' experiences will vary.

Exploring Further

Allow students to share what they have written for question A and to discuss and compare their responses. For question B, ask students to share their activating events, irrational beliefs, and negative consequences. Then ask the rest of the class to suggest effective disputes to the particular irrational belief. Encourage students to generate as many effective disputes as possible.

 SECTION 5.2
SELF-CHECK (p. 218)

1. Self-defeating attitudes are negative attitudes about ourselves that doom us to failure.

2. According to Ellis, the three faulty assumptions behind irrational beliefs are: 1. I must do well. (If I don't, I'm worthless.) 2. You must treat me well. (If you don't, you must be punished.) 3. The world must be easy. (If it isn't, it's intolerable.)

3. ABCDE stands for activating event (A), belief (B), consequences (C), dispute (D), and exchange (E).

Additional Activities

These additional activities are exclusive to this Instructor's Resource Manual. They are designed to meet the special needs of your students. The activities can be used as in-class activities or as take-home assignments. They can be assigned to individual students, pairs of students, or groups of students.

Critical Thinking

DO NEGATIVES OUTWEIGH POSITIVES?
According to the National Institutes of Health, research consistently shows that negative qualities often command more attention and seem more important than positive qualities. Examples of this phenomenon are listed on the reproducible master on page 279, "Do Negatives Outweigh Positives?" Display a transparency of the reproducible master (temporarily covering up the last paragraph) and ask a student to read each bulleted point out loud. Why do students think these statements are true? Lead students to the answer by asking them why negative thinking might benefit a person in the struggle for survival. Then uncover the last paragraph and ask a student to read it out loud. What can students do to counteract the distressing effects of "built-in" negative thinking?

MURPHY'S LAW We've all heard of Murphy's Law: "anything that can go wrong will go wrong." There are many other variations on Murphy's Law, which are presented on the reproducible master on page 280, "Murphy's Laws."

Although Murphy's Law is intended to be humorous, it also reflects the negative attitude that everything always ends in some kind of disaster. Ask students whether they think that making jokes about everything going wrong is a positive coping strategy, or whether it focuses too much on the negative. Ask students to add a statement to the end of each of Murphy's Laws that points out the silver lining in negative events. For example, to the law "Everything goes wrong at once," students could add, "and this really teaches you how to handle a crisis." To the law "Toast always falls with the buttered side down," students might add, "which forces you to finally mop the kitchen floor." Encourage students to be humorous and creative and to have fun with the activity.

Application

CULTIVATING GRATITUDE Ask students to telephone or visit three people who have done something kind for them over the last year. Have them express their gratitude toward the person (even if they have already done so at an earlier time). Ask students to write a brief description of each interaction and how they felt at the end of the exercise. Does feeling and expressing gratitude give a boost to their positive attitude?

LOOKING FOR THE GOOD This activity lends itself well to being used as a brief warm-up exercise. Have students write down the names of everyone in the class. Next to each name, ask them to write the nicest thing they can about that person. Instruct them to say something positive about everyone, even about students whom they may not know well or whom they may even dislike for some reason. After this activity, ask students how it made them feel to be forced to "look for the good" in others. Does thinking positively about others make them feel good about themselves, too? Type up students' responses (or ask volunteers to type them up) so that each student can receive a sheet with all his or her classmates' positive comments.

FALSE MEMORY TEST AND PERCEPTION
The false memory test is a well-known psychological exercise designed to demonstrate that people can "remember" things that never happened. Without telling students the purpose of the exercise, simply explain that you are going to read them a list of words. (Students should not write while you read.) Read one of the lists provided on the reproducible master on page 281, "False Memory Test." Then ask them whether they recall hearing the word printed below the list in italics. Continue with the remaining lists, if desired. Now reveal to students that none of the lists contained the italicized word. Most students will be surprised. Explain that people can easily be tricked into having false perceptions, such as "hearing" a word they did not hear. Suggest to students that negative thinking is a kind of false perception. Discuss this idea.

Internet Activities

RATIONAL-EMOTIVE BEHAVIOR THERAPY Albert Ellis, the theorist of the ABCDE model and the ABCDE method, is known as the founder of rational-emotive behavior therapy (REBT). Ask students to research REBT on the Internet. What is REBT? What ideas is it based on? How does it work? How is it similar to and different from other types of therapy? Who practices REBT? Would students be interested in trying it? If desired, ask students to continue their investigations by conducting an interview on REBT via e-mail with a local psychologist or professor of psychology. Have students print out their correspondence and place it in their Personal Success Portfolios.

DEFENSIVE PESSIMISM According to psychologist Julie K. Norem, author of the book *The Positive Power of Negative Thinking*, people are either strategic optimists or defensive pessimists. Defensive pessimists are people who suffer from such anxiety that, Norem says, it is impractical for them to adopt a more optimistic attitude. Instead, they can harness the power of negative thinking (worrying, imagining worst-case scenarios, etc.) to be successful. Ask students to locate Norem's Web site to read about her theory, and to take the "Are You a Defensive Pessimist?" quiz. Have students print out their quizzes and write a brief summary of Norem's ideas. In class, ask students whether they think that the "defensive pessimism" theory makes sense. Is defensive pessimism a good strategy for success? Can defensive pessimists enjoy life and attain happiness? Why or why not?

ASSESS

Review and Activities Answers

Review Questions (p. 220)

1. Having positive expectations of success helps you attain it because positive thinking gives you the drive to work hard to make good things happen. Positive thoughts lead to positive feelings and positive actions.

2. Psychologists believe that negative thinking makes you more vulnerable to depression. Negative thinking is also a symptom of depression.

3. Healthy eating habits will vary but could include some of the following: listen to your body's internal cues; take time out for meals; shop with a list; try a variety of foods; read and understand nutrition labels; and aim to feel and look healthy, not to be a certain weight. Healthy exercise habits will also vary but could include some of the following: try to be physically active for at least 20 minutes each day; vary your activities; listen to your body; set SMART exercise goals; learn about health and fitness; and exercise for strength and energy, not to look a certain way.

4. Students' examples of self-defeating attitudes will vary, but their answers should demonstrate an understanding of the vicious cycle: the self-defeating attitude leads to self-defeating behavior, which leads to a negative outcome, which strengthens the self-defeating attitude.

5. The cognitive distortion that involves the false belief that you are not in control of your life is known as helpless thinking.

6. To dispute irrational beliefs means to confront them with the facts of the situation. It involves separating your emotional reaction from the reality of the situation. A good way to dispute irrational beliefs is to use some of the questions listed on page 215 (such as, "Am I exaggerating?" and "Is it really as bad as it seems?").

Critical Thinking (p. 220)

7. Answers will vary but should recognize that just feeling bad or worrying will not change a past or future event; however, if worry or bad feelings cause you take a positive action, you may be able to affect a future event.

8. Answers will vary but should recognize that optimism is the tendency to expect the best possible outcome. Optimists focus their energy on making their goals happen, rather than bracing for the worst. Therefore, optimistic college students are likely to be more focused on being successful in college. This would likely lead to better academic performance.

Application (p. 220)

9. Answers will vary but may suggest that negative stories can create a sense of fear or anxiety in viewers and that this emotional tension may capture viewers' attention more than positive stories.

10. Answers will vary, but most students will recognize that helping others helps them to feel better about themselves.

Internet Activities (p. 221)

11. Answers will vary but should show that students understand each statement and how it might apply to their lives. For example, for the item "Be so strong that nothing can disturb your peace of mind," a student might write, "I'm going to be totally confident when I take the exam tomorrow because I know I studied hard and deserve to do well."

12. Responses will vary, but students should show evidence that for one full day they recorded everything they ate or drank. Also have them print out the reports generated at the Web site.

Real-Life Success Story "Will Things Go My Way?" (p. 221)

Answers will vary but should show an understanding of the material covered in the chapter, particularly the concept of self-defeating attitudes and the vicious cycle and how positive self-talk can help to change ingrained negative attitudes.

CLOSE

Culminating Activity

Write the words *self-esteem* and *positive thinking* on the board and ask students to define both terms. (Self-esteem is confidence in and respect for oneself; positive thinking is focusing on what is good about oneself, other people, and the world). What do these two concepts have in common? Students should see that positive thinking is necessary for self-esteem and that self-esteem is necessary for positive thinking. Positive thinking is inherently related to self-esteem because it involves focusing on what is good about oneself. Many of the distorted thought patterns that characterize negative thinking—cognitive distortions such as personalizing and self-blame as well as irrational beliefs such as "I must succeed at everything"—are self-attacking and erode self-expectancy and self-acceptance. There are many other specific links between positive thinking and self-esteem. For example, positive thinkers tend to choose positive friends, who are more likely to provide the emotional and instrumental support that is crucial for self-esteem. Ask students to work in small groups to look through Chapter 5 and find examples of negative or distorted thinking that could be both a cause of and an effect of low self-esteem.

Personal Success Portfolio

Make handouts or a transparency of the Personal Success Portfolio worksheet for Chapter 5 on page 235. Refer to pages 9 and 10 for suggestions on presenting this activity.

Additional documents that you may wish students to create for their Portfolios worksheet include:

- an action plan for becoming a more positive thinker
- an essay describing people the student knows (or knows of) who think positively and what the student can learn from these people about living life to the fullest
- an essay describing people in the student's life who think negatively and how the student can help protect him- or herself from these people's negativity
- a photocopy of the worry slips on page 193, cut up into slips and placed in a sealed envelope
- a hand-sketched reproduction of the Food Guide Pyramid on page 200, along with a list of foods in each food group that the student either has never tried or would like to eat more of (such as a variety of unusual fruits and vegetables)

ADDITIONAL RESOURCES

The following books and periodicals offer information on positive thinking, healthy diet and exercise, and overcoming cognitive distortions and irrational beliefs.

Books

Beck, Aaron. *Cognitive Therapy: Basics and Beyond.* New York: Guilford Press, 1995.

Benson, Herbert and Eileen M. Stuart. *The Wellness Book: The Comprehensive Guide to Maintaining Health and Treating Stress-Related Illness.* New York: Fireside, 1993.

Burns, David D. *Feeling Good: The New Mood Therapy.* Revised edition. New York: Wholecare, 1999.

Copeland, Mary Ellen. *The Worry Control Workbook.* Oakland: New Harbinger Publications, 1998.

Dyer, Wayne. *Your Erroneous Zones.* New York: Harper Books, 1997.

Ellis, Albert. *How to Stubbornly Refuse to Make Yourself Miserable About Anything—Yes, Anything.* New York: Lyle Stuart, 1988.

Ellis, Albert. *Overcoming Destructive Beliefs, Feelings, and Behaviors: New Directions for Rational Emotive Behavior Therapy.* Amherst, NY: Prometheus Books, 2001.

Ellis, Albert and Irving Becker. *Guide to Personal Happiness.* North Hollywood, CA: Wilshire Book Company, 1986.

Goldberg, Burton, John W. Anderson, and Larry Trivieri. *Alternative Medicine: The Definitive Guide.* 2nd ed. Berkeley: Ten Speed Press, 2002.

Greenberger, Dennis and Christine Padesky. *Mind Over Mood: Change How You Feel by Changing the Way You Think.* New York: Guilford Press, 1995.

McKay, Matthew and Patrick Fanning. *Prisoners of Belief: Exposing and Changing Beliefs That Control Your Life.* Oakland: New Harbinger Publications, 1991.

McKay, Matthew, Martha Davis, and Patrick Fanning. *Thoughts and Feelings: Taking Control of Your Moods and Your Life.* 2nd ed. Oakland: New Harbinger Publications, 1998.

Peiffer, Vera. *Positive Thinking: Everything You Have Always Known About Positive Thinking but Were Afraid to Put Into Practice.* Boston: Element Books, 1991.

Reivich, Karen and Andrew Shatté. *The Resilience Factor: 7 Essential Skills for Overcoming Life's Inevitable Obstacles.* New York: Broadway Books, 2002.

Seligman, Martin. *Authentic Happiness: Using the New Positive Psychology to Realize Your Potential for Lasting Fulfillment.* New York: The Free Press, 2002.

Seligman, Martin. *Learned Optimism: How to Change Your Mind and Your Life.* New York: Pocket Books, 1998.

Snyder, C. R., Hal S. Shorey, Jennifer Cheavens, Kimberley Mann Pulvers, Virgil H. Adams III, and Cynthia Wiklund. "Hope and Academic Success in College." *Journal of Educational Psychology* 94 (2002): 820–826.

Willett, Walter C., P. J. Skerrett, and Edward L. Giovannucci. *Eat, Drink, and Be Healthy: The Harvard Medical School Guide to Healthy Eating.* New York: Simon and Schuster, 2001.

Periodicals

Cognitive Psychology

Cook's Illustrated

Cooking Light

Fitness Magazine

Health Magazine

Journal of Rational-Emotive and Cognitive-Behavior Therapy

Men's Health Magazine

Prevention

Self-Discipline

OVERVIEW

In Chapter 6 students read about the importance of developing self-discipline in achieving their goals. In Section 6.1 they explore the benefits of self-discipline and learn about the key concepts of self-determination and persistence. They also learn how to control impulses by considering the long-term consequences of their actions. They then look at how self-discipline can help them make difficult changes, including changing bad habits into better ones. In Section 6.2 students learn about self-disciplined thinking by exploring the elements of critical thinking and learning how to make logical, step-by-step decisions.

OBJECTIVES

After they complete this chapter, students should be able to:

■ Define self-discipline and cite its benefits.

■ Explain how to control impulses.

■ Describe the process of replacing bad habits with good ones.

■ Define critical thinking and list its seven standards.

■ List the steps in the decision-making process.

OUTLINE

Chapter Topics

TAKING CONTROL OF YOUR LIFE
What Is Self-Discipline?
    Elements of Self-Discipline
    The Power of Persistence
    Self-Determination
Controlling Impulses
    Thinking Long-Term
Embracing Change
    Do You Resist Change?
    What's Holding You Back?
Conquering Bad Habits

DISCIPLINING YOUR THINKING
Learning to Think Critically
    Benefits of Critical Thinking
    Are You a Critical Thinker?
    Standards of Critical Thinking
Becoming a Better Decision Maker
    Why Good Decisions Matter
    Handling Mistakes
    Steps in the Decision-Making Process

Chapter Activities

EXERCISE 6.1   **Do You Control Your Life?** (p. 229)
EXERCISE 6.2   **Making Positive Changes** (pp. 234–235)
EXERCISE 6.3   **Overcoming Resistance to Change** (pp. 237–238)
EXERCISE 6.4   **Getting to Know Your Bad Habits** (pp. 241–242)
EXERCISE 6.5   **How Critical Is Your Thinking?** (pp. 248–250)
EXERCISE 6.6   **Developing Your Critical Thinking** (pp. 256–257)
EXERCISE 6.7   **Using the Decision-Making Process** (pp. 264–266)

Personal Journal 6.1   **Going Against the Odds** (p. 227)
Personal Journal 6.2   **Thinking Long-Term** (p. 232)
Personal Journal 6.3   **Habit Change Chart** (p. 244)
Personal Journal 6.4   **Pros and Cons** (p. 262)

Chapter Features

Applying Psychology   **Improving Memory** (p. 231)
INTERNET ACTION   **Artificial Intelligence** (p. 247)
PROFESSIONAL DEVELOPMENT   **Sought: Multitaskers** (p. 253)

FOCUS

Introducing the Chapter

Ask a volunteer to define *self-discipline*. Write his or her definition on the board and compare it to the definition in the text (the process of teaching oneself to do what is necessary to reach important goals). Then ask students to brainstorm ways self-discipline can and does help them in their lives. Write these ideas on the board as well. Point out that students probably have developed self-discipline in many areas without even realizing it, because self-discipline is a habit. For example, they may have a regular study routine, exercise regularly, or stick to a budget. Finally, discuss how a person benefits from these examples of self-discipline.

Real-Life Success Story "Should I Make a Change?"

(p. 222)

Have a volunteer read the Real-Life Success Story aloud. Remind the class that they have now read about self-awareness, goals and obstacles, self-esteem, and positive thinking. Ask them what they have learned already that could help Jeanette. For example, ask, "What do you know about overcoming obstacles that could help Jeanette? What about positive thinking or positive self-talk?" Help them recognize that self-discipline is the key to helping Jeanette put these ideas into action.

Opening Quote (p. 223)

"Not everything that is faced can be changed, but nothing can be changed until it is faced."

Write the quote on the board or make a transparency of it from the reproducible master on page 282 and ask students what they think this statement means. What does facing something have to do with changing it? Do students agree that this is true? Ask students to think of a situation that they felt needed to be changed. How

did they handle it? Did they face, or recognize, the problem? If not, did the situation ever get better? Was the problem really solved?

You may wish to open subsequent classes by discussing one of the other quotes provided on the reproducible master.

INSTRUCT

Teaching Tips

The following topics are discussed in this chapter. You may want to expand on them in large or small class groups.

What Is Self-Discipline? (pp. 224–228)

Have students recall the definition of self-discipline discussed above in "Introducing the Chapter." Then explain that self-discipline helps you to achieve your goals by strengthening your ability to do the following:

- control your destiny
- persist in the face of setbacks
- weigh long-term consequences of actions
- make positive changes
- break bad habits
- think critically
- make effective decisions

Ask students to suggest ways self-discipline helps a person do each of the above. (Preview the definition of critical thinking if students are not familiar with the term.) Discuss their ideas.

Controlling Impulses (pp. 228–232)

Ask volunteers to give examples of "acting on impulse" and list them on the board. Have students think of one thing they did on impulse and then write down the answers to these questions: How did you feel when you acted on the impulse? Were you pleased with the outcome? Why or why not? Would you do the same again? If not, what would you do differently next time? Guide students to the idea that impulses can lead us away from, rather than toward, our goals.

Embracing Change (pp. 233–236)

(Present this material in conjunction with Exercise 6.3.) Have students review the section "Overcoming Obstacles" in Chapter 3, and remind them that there are two main kinds of obstacles—internal and external—and that resistance to change is one type of internal obstacle. Then ask them to think of a change they may need to make in their lives and to answer the two key questions posed in the text: "Do You Resist Change?" and "What's Holding You Back?" Give them a few minutes to write a brief response. Ask a volunteer to explain *hidden resistance* (an unwillingness to change because we do not want to give up the rewards that we get from staying the way we are), and ask students to contemplate whether or not hidden resistance does or has kept them from making a needed change.

Discuss how and why people resist new ideas and ways of doing things. Share with the students some of your own beliefs that may have changed. For example, an instructor might offer examples such as, "I used to believe that I shouldn't make reference to my personal experiences in the classroom" or "I used to believe that I had to have all the answers and could never admit to a student that I didn't know something."

Ask students what ideas or beliefs might be limiting their success. You might share common limiting beliefs that many students have expressed in the past, for example:

- I work best under pressure, so I like to wait until the night before a paper is due.
- I can study with the television on.
- Smoking helps me deal with stress/ concentrate/relax/lose weight.
- Working in groups is a waste of time.
- I can't apply anything I'm learning in class to the real world.
- Classroom discussions are much less important than lectures.
- Getting good grades is a matter of smarts, not effort.

Conquering Bad Habits (pp. 236–245)

Ask the class to brainstorm a list of bad habits. (Examples of some common bad habits are found on page 239 of the student text.) As ideas are generated, write them on the board. Then have students, individually or in pairs, choose a common bad habit and write a short story describing how a person goes through the three steps to change the habit. Step 1 should include a description of the three stages (precontemplation, contemplation, and preparation). Step 2 should describe how the person answers the five questions on page 240 that will help in understanding the habit. Step 3 should describe how the person replaces the habit and give examples of the positive self-talk he or she used along the way. Allow students to share their stories.

Learning to Think Critically (pp. 246–257)

Review the seven standards for critical thinking using the reproducible master on page 284. Discuss each standard by having students use a piece of paper to cover up the before-and-after examples of each standard (pp. 251–255). First have a student read aloud the description of the standard. Then have students uncover only the first example and ask them to explain what is wrong with it. (With clarity, for example, students would uncover the first "Unclear:" and you would ask, "Why is this unclear?") Then allow students to reveal the explanation ("Why It's Unclear") and to compare their responses with the information in the text. Continue in this way for all seven standards. If desired, follow this activity with a review of the characteristics of critical thinkers, which are listed on the reproducible master on page 285.

Becoming a Better Decision Maker (pp. 258–266)

Have students work in pairs to write a scenario describing a person making an important life decision. Students should create the decision to be made and include and identify the seven steps necessary to make the decision.

Alternatively, give students a scenario in which a person finds him- or herself in a difficult or unwelcome situation but does not know how to fix the situation—in other words, does not know what he or she needs to decide. For example, have students imagine that they have held the same position at the same company for five years and have realized that it is a dead-end job. They are unhappy, but what exact decision do they need to make? Students should formulate a clear statement of the decision to be made and then describe the seven steps necessary to make the decision. During the activity, display a transparency of the reproducible master on page 286, "The Decision-Making Process."

In-Chapter Answers and Notes

FIGURE 6.1

Ingredients of Self-Discipline (p. 225)
Answers will vary but should recognize that the ability to accomplish your goals and cope with difficult situations is an important part of self-esteem. By practicing self-discipline, you can accomplish more and be more in control of your life, which will raise your self-esteem.

Personal Journal 6.1

Going Against the Odds (p. 227)
Responses will vary but should demonstrate persistence. Allow students to share their responses in a class discussion so that they can hear other creative ideas for overcoming the various obstacles.

Sample Answers

Title of Your Novel: *Cecil: A Love Story*

Not enough free time for writing
Set aside 30 minutes at the same time each day to write.

Don't know how to start novel
Begin in the middle of the novel. Work on beginning later when a good idea comes to me.

Life isn't interesting enough
Focus on rich inner experiences rather than on mundane outward events.

Writer's block
Do creativity exercises such as brainstorming, sketching, or simply writing down sentence fragments.

Accidentally delete first five chapters from computer
Dig out printouts from recycling bin and scan them back into computer.

Rejected by publisher
Refine novel using publisher's suggestions and resubmit it.

Rejected by publisher again
Self-publish.

EXERCISE 6.1

Do You Control Your Life? (p. 229)
A-B. Students' responses and scores will vary.

C. Answers will vary. Some students may suggest making attitude changes in certain areas, such as deciding to take personal responsibility for the course of their lives. Other students may list specific actions they could take in certain areas of their lives, such as handling their finances more responsibly or eating more healthful meals in order to take charge of their health and feel better physically.

Applying Psychology

IMPROVING MEMORY (p. 231)
Answers will vary but should recognize that the feelings, sights, sounds, and even smells associated with the place where you learned something new can help trigger the memory of learning it.

Thinking Long-Term (p. 232)

Students' responses will vary but should reflect the *think* and *decide* aspects of the stop-think-decide approach to dealing with impulses.

Sample Answers

Impulse

To eat box of chocolate-chip cookies

1. What are the satisfying or pleasurable short-term consequences of giving in to this impulse?

Satisfy chocolate craving; get mood boost from caffeine in chocolate; experience sugar high

2. What are the possible negative long-term consequences for you, your goals, or the people you care about?

Eating empty calories instead of nutritious food; gaining a half-pound in one sitting; feeling ashamed of my lack of self-discipline; having negative influence on children

3. Do the positive short-term consequences outweigh the negative long-term consequences? Explain.

No, because the temporary good feelings will be replaced by longer-lasting negative feelings. Also, giving in to temptation will make it harder to resist next time.

EXERCISE 6.2

Making Positive Changes (pp. 234–235)

Responses will vary. Students should be aware that the questions grow progressively more specific.

Exploring Further

Ask students to complete questions A through C at home. In class, assign students to small teams. Each student should pick a specific day and time to take action on his or her selected change and write it down with the other students in the team as "witnesses." The following week (without announcing this beforehand),

reunite the students in the same small teams. Team members should review one another's pledges and discuss whether or not they followed through on making the change. (Encourage students to be supportive and inquisitive, not punitive.) Ask for volunteers to discuss why they did or did not take action. Ask those who did take action to explain how they found the self-discipline to do so.

EXERCISE 6.3

Overcoming Resistance to Change (pp. 237–238)

A-D. Responses will vary but should reflect how students answered the questions presented in the teaching tips presented for "Embracing Change" on page 128.

Sample Answers

A. Think of one life change that you would like to make but that you have been avoiding.

I would like to become more outgoing and meet more people. My social support network is too small, and I have recently dissolved some friendships that were not rewarding.

B. Why do you think you have been avoiding making this change?

I've been avoiding meeting new people because I am a relatively shy, private person and am afraid of rejection. I often feel different from other people, and the types of places people often congregate (parties, clubs, etc.) make me uncomfortable. I think I'm also afraid of investing effort without getting results—I've tried taking self-enrichment courses and volunteering at various organizations, but these strategies have not been very successful.

C. Do you ever pretend to yourself that you don't need to change? Explain.

I sometimes tell myself that it's okay to have just a few close friends, which is true, but I think I do this in order to make myself believe that everything is fine and I don't need to take action. In fact, I am often lonely and I know that I do need to reach out to others; no one is going to come knocking on my door.

D. Drawbacks of Staying the Same

Loneliness

Feeling of having missed opportunities

Lack of exposure to new ideas and points of view

Will be hard to meet people of opposite sex for possible romantic relationship

Boredom with same activities

Too much dependence/reliance on family members, who are often not supportive

Benefits of Changing

More social interaction

Greater self-expectancy from having made real effort

Will meet people with new ideas and points of view

Might meet partner with whom I could build a future

Might find new activity partners for outings

Can develop broader social support network of people who appreciate me for who I am.

The benefit that is the most important to me is the chance to meet potential partners. I would like to have a family, and in order to develop a committed romantic relationship I need to make a greater effort to reach out to others.

E. Describe the specific actions you would need to take to make this change. Which of them would be most difficult for you?

There are several things I could do to meet more people. I could follow up on the invitations I receive from the people I already know. I could participate in activities that are offered by the clubs I belong to. I could go to social places by myself and introduce myself to people. I could also make an effort to get to know people I see often but don't really know, such as my coworkers and the other volunteers at the animal shelter. For me, the hardest of these would be going out by myself and introducing myself to new people. I am not used to making the first move, and I would worry about saying the wrong thing or giving people a false impression of who I am.

EXERCISE 6.4

Getting to Know Your Bad Habits
(pp. 241–242)

A-C. Students' negative habits and their effects will vary.

D-E. Answers will vary but should demonstrate that students have made a systematic effort to observe the circumstances surrounding the habit.

F. Answers will vary but should include a description of a positive replacement habit and positive, encouraging self-talk.

Exploring Further

Without calling on students to discuss the specific habit they wrote about, ask for volunteers to describe the unpleasant feelings that drive them to their habit, as well as the rewarding feelings that the habit brings. What experiences do students have in common? Where do they differ?

Personal Journal 6.3

Habit Change Chart (p. 244)

The habit(s) being tracked here should reflect the habit(s) described in Exercise 6.4. For example, a student who identifies procrastination as his worst habit in Exercise 6.4 might choose to modify and track his habit of surfing the Internet at work.

✓ **SECTION 6.1
SELF-CHECK** (p. 245)

1. Self-discipline is the process of teaching yourself to do what is necessary to reach your goals, without becoming sidetracked by bad habits.

2. Persistence is one of the key elements of self-discipline. It allows you to put in effort, again and again, until you reach your goal. You need persistence to keep going instead of giving up.

3. The three steps to changing bad habits are 1. wanting to change, 2. understanding the habit, and 3. replacing the bad habit with a good habit.

Artificial Intelligence (p. 247)

Answers will vary but could recognize that computers that can reason would also be able to make decisions and solve problems in a wide range of situations, not just in one pre-programmed way. Therefore, AI computers could be used in challenging environments, such as outer space or urban traffic jams. A computer used in outer space, for example, could navigate unfamiliar territory, record information not originally sought, or even repair itself if it were damaged.

EXERCISE 6.5

How Critical Is Your Thinking?
(pp. 248–250)

A-B. Students' responses and scores will vary.

C-D. Habits or attitudes will vary. Applications should help students understand how they can improve their critical thinking skills.

PROFESSIONAL DEVELOPMENT

Sought: Multitaskers (p. 253)

Answers will vary. Some students may suggest doing projects in stages, completing one stage of a project before shifting focus to another project. Other students may suggest combining similar tasks, such as keyboarding or photocopying, for different projects.

EXERCISE 6.6

Developing Your Critical Thinking
(pp. 256–257)

A. Answers will vary but should show analytic thinking and an understanding of each critical thinking standard.

B. Students' responses will vary.

C. Answers will vary but may recognize that politicians, especially when campaigning, are trying to sell themselves and their ideas to the people who would vote for them. In this case, they may use advertising slogans rather than critical thinking skills to present their ideas.

Sample Answers

A. Explain what is wrong with each statement, then rewrite each one to correct the flaw.

1. **Clarity**
Unclear: All are invited to partake in refreshments in the parking lot after the festivities of the football game have reached their conclusion.
Why It's Unclear: <u>This statement is wordy, complicated, and confusing.</u>
Clear: <u>Join us for pizza and cookies in the parking lot after the football game.</u>

2. **Precision**
Imprecise: Internet companies are out to scam people.
Why It's Imprecise: <u>This statement indiscriminately lumps all Internet companies together.</u>
Precise: <u>Internet companies that sell get-rich-quick schemes are out to scam people.</u>

3. **Accuracy**
Inaccurate: Drug testing doesn't work.
Why It's Inaccurate: <u>If the goal of drug testing is to detect drugs, then drug testing does work.</u>
Accurate: <u>Although drug testing is not 100 percent accurate, it is generally effective at detecting drug use.</u>

4. **Relevance**
Irrelevant: Steve is not well liked; that's why he's flunking all his classes.
Why It's Irrelevant: <u>Steve's popularity has nothing to do with his GPA.</u>
Relevant: <u>Steve never studies; that's why he's flunking all his classes.</u>

5. **Depth**
Shallow: Our government only passes good laws.
Why It's Shallow: <u>This statement is extremely simplistic.</u>
Deep: <u>Recently passed environmental laws have had positive effects, but loopholes in these laws have allowed corporations to commit repeated violations.</u>

6. Breadth

Narrow: The painting looks like chickens ran across it. No one could like such a thing.
Why It's Narrow: <u>This is an opinion being stated as if it were a fact.</u>
Broad: <u>This painting is considered pivotal in John Smith's development as an artist, but to me it is unappealing.</u>

7. Logic

Illogical: Jane, who lives in a rundown neighborhood, steals from her friends. All people who live in rundown areas steal from others.
Why It's Illogical: <u>It's wrong to base generalizations on a single example.</u>
Logical: <u>Jane, unemployed and penniless, was driven by desperation to steal food from the supermarket.</u>

Pros and Cons (p. 262)

Students' responses will vary. Suggest that students review some of the goals they established in Chapter 3.

Exploring Further

Formulate a two-option (yes/no) decision that the class can consider together. For example, you might select a decision relevant to contemporary politics (such as whether a certain law should be passed or a certain military action should be taken) or to student life (such as whether tuition fees should be raised or certain required classes made optional). As a class, fill out the pros and cons sheet provided in reproducible master form on page 287. Encourage students to think of as many pros and cons as possible before making their choice.

EXERCISE 6.7

Using the Decision-Making Process
(pp. 264–266)

A. Students' responses will vary but could include: Should I buy a new car? Should I repair the old car? Should I move closer to my new job so the commute is not so far?

Can I use mass transit to get work? Should I look for a different job?

B. Students' responses will vary but could include moving closer to work, taking mass transit, riding a bicycle, carpooling or vanpooling, or buying a moped.

C. Answers will vary but could include talking to the mechanic about the advisability of repairing the old car, consulting a second mechanic for another estimate, talking to people at the new job about their commutes, looking at real estate ads or talking to a realtor about moving closer to the job, and looking at ads for new or used cars and/or visiting car lots.

D-E. Students' responses will vary depending on their goals and values.

F. Answers will vary but should include actions that lead toward the decision described in question E.

G. Responses will vary, but students should reflect on the positive and negative effects their chosen option would create.

Exploring Further

Since all students are presented with the same scenario in this Exercise, it is a good opportunity for a class discussion comparing students' decisions and decision-making styles. First ask students to describe their final decision as described in question E. Then, going back to question A, have students with a variety of different final decisions trace the steps to their decision. Encourage students to offer differing opinions and to explain why they answered the way they did.

 SECTION 6.2
SELF-CHECK (p. 266)

1. Critical thinking is active, self-reflective thinking.

2. Critical thinking is necessary for making important decisions that will affect your life, for solving problems and overcoming

obstacles, and for developing skills and personal qualities that are central to success, including self-awareness, self-honesty, self-motivation, open-mindedness, and empathy.

3. Regret is the feeling of wishing you had decided something differently.

Additional Activities

These additional activities are exclusive to this Instructor's Resource Manual. They are designed to meet the special needs of your students. The activities can be used as in-class activities or as take-home assignments. They can be assigned to individual students, pairs of students, or groups of students.

Critical Thinking

MISTAKES AND EXPERIENCE   Oscar Wilde once wrote, "Experience is simply the name we give our mistakes." Write this quote on the board. Have students consider what they think this quote might mean and discuss their answers in a class forum. To give further direction to the discussion, you might ask students whether they find this quote helpful, discouraging, or amusing. Encourage students to come up with specific examples to demonstrate whether there is always something to be learned from making a mistake.

COPING SKILLS   *Coping* can be defined as the capacity to deal with stressful or otherwise difficult situations, events, people, things, etc. How people cope with difficult situations begins with their attitude. People with effective coping skills tend to believe that they have some control over how they react to a problematic situation. Those with lesser coping skills, by contrast, are more likely to blame the situation on bad luck or the incompetence of others. Ask students to come up with situations that might require coping skills. Examples might include getting lost, being laid off from a job, a romantic rejection, the loss of a loved one, or even a terrorist attack.

Write a few of these examples on the board and ask students to suggest what kind of coping skills might be helpful for each scenario. If desired, ask students to write a short story or create a role-play of the scenario.

Application

PHYSICAL AND MENTAL SELF-DISCIPLINE   There is a growing number of organizations in North America that teach martial arts to young people in low-income, high-crime communities. Many martial arts practitioners believe that the regular practice of activities requiring a high degree of physical and mental self-control can help people develop greater self-discipline. (Note that the words *kung fu* literally mean "progress achieved through discipline.") Ask students to think about and discuss ways in which martial arts training might help young people cope with their environment and channel their frustrations in a positive direction. How might physical self-discipline help develop mental self-discipline? Besides martial arts, what other kinds of physical activities would help develop self-discipline? Why? Would students be interested in practicing kung fu or another martial art? Ask students who have had practice with martial arts to share insights from their experiences.

CREATIVE THINKING   This activity functions well as a warm-up to a discussion of decision making. Explain that creative thinking involves looking at a problem in new, unusual ways. It is an enormous asset in decision making and problem solving, and it is also part of critical thinking, since it helps one to evaluate a situation from many different perspectives. Ask small groups of students to perform one of the following creative thinking activities:

- Ask students to draw a simple shape, such as a circle, curving line, or triangle, on the board or a piece of paper. Give them five to ten minutes to list all the things the shape or picture could represent.

- Bring in a group of common objects, such as a paper clip, a basketball, a pencil, a newspaper, a soft drink container, or a paper bag. Ask each student group to choose one of these objects. Give the students five to ten minutes to list all of the potential uses for that object.

After the five to ten minutes are up, ask students to share the results of their brainstorming.

To expand this activity, ask students to imagine that they were stranded on an island with this same object, either by itself or in quantity. How could they use this object to help them survive? Use the opportunity to emphasize that everyone has a great deal of creativity waiting to be tapped. Then ask how creative thinking could be helpful in decision making. Guide students to the idea that creativity helps decision makers generate options that are not obvious at first glance.

Internet Activity

LOGIC IN CRITICAL THINKING   In Chapter 6 students learn about the seven critical thinking standards. This exercise is designed to teach students more about the importance of logic, one of the seven standards. Ask students to locate the Web site of San Jose State University and find the faculty Web page discussing "Fallacious Appeals." Fallacious appeals are irrelevant or emotionally loaded arguments. (Examples: "I'm buying a Bumpster mountain bike. My critical thinking instructor says they're the best, and she is so logical!" "Gosh, officer, I know I made an illegal left turn, but there ought to be special laws for those of us proud to be American and driving American cars on American streets.") Ask students to read the descriptions of the different kinds of fallacious appeals and to complete the related online exercises. An answer key for the exercises is also found on the Web site.

ASSESS

Review and Activities Answers

Review Questions (p. 268)

1. Persistence and self-determination are both elements of self-discipline, but persistence is the ability to go on despite opposition, setbacks, and occasional doubts, while self-determination is the ability to determine the path your life travels.

2. Many people resist change because it can be scary. Some people fear that change will bring bad things or that they will make the wrong choices or expose themselves to failure and ridicule. Some people resist change because they do not want to give up the rewards from staying the way they are, such as not having to face problems.

3. The three stages people go through before beginning to take action to break a habit are: 1. the precontemplation stage, in which they still have no intention of changing; 2. the contemplation stage, in which they begin thinking about changing; and 3. the preparation stage, in which they edge closer to making serious efforts to change.

4. Positive self-talk helps you change a bad habit because it provides psychological support, helping you paint a new picture of yourself acting and behaving in a positive way. You can use positive self-talk to persuade your subconscious mind that the change has already taken place.

5. The framing effect is the decision-making bias that results from the way a decision, question, or problem is worded. It can affect the decision-making process because the way a decision is defined will affect the options you generate and the choice you make.

6. People sometimes feel regret over decisions they have made because they wish they had made a different decision. No matter how

carefully you weigh and choose an option, there are usually other options that were also attractive.

Critical Thinking (p. 268)

7. Answers will vary. Many students will recognize that the threat of being fired may reinforce the importance of changing and therefore make it easier to change. However, being robbed of autonomy by being forced to do something is likely to undermine one's motivation to change.

8. Answers will vary. In the first case, answers may recognize that a child who is given no limits would have difficulty developing self-discipline because he or she would have very little experience with holding him- or herself to any kind of standards. In the second case, answers may acknowledge that a child who is given too many limits would have difficulty developing self-discipline because he or she wouldn't know how to impose discipline on him- or herself—he or she would only know how to obey discipline from an outside source.

Application (p. 268)

9. Surveys will vary. Students may want to apply the three-step format to the interviewees' answers.

10. Students' decisions will vary but will probably reflect the types of activities associated with that stage of life. For example, ages 11–15 might include choosing to live with one parent or another or to try out for a school sport or other school activity; ages 15–21 might include whether or not to go to college or how to pay for college; ages 21–30 might include taking a particular job, moving, or getting married; and age 30 onward might include deciding to marry, remarry, divorce, move, make a job or career change, or go back to school.

Internet Activities (p. 269)

11. Analysis of the articles will vary but should examine all seven standards: clarity, precision, accuracy, relevance, depth, breadth, and logic.

12. Answers will vary. For Persisting, summaries of behavior of students who lack this habit will probably include giving up easily when the answer to a problem isn't immediately known, and writing any answer to get the task over with as quickly as possible. Students may also cite difficulty staying focused and tuning out distractions, and having a limited repertoire of problem-solving strategies. Answers may suggest that students could become better learners by not giving up easily and by developing a system, structure, or strategy to solve a problem. For example, a student having trouble learning a concept in chemistry could attempt several different ways of understanding it, such as looking for more than one description of the concept in different textbooks or reference books, talking to other students in the class, talking to the instructor, and getting help from a tutor.

For Managing Impulsivity, summaries of behavior of students who lack this habit will probably include blurting the first answer that comes to mind, starting to work without fully understanding the directions, lacking an organized plan or strategy for approaching a problem, and making immediate value judgments about an idea. Answers may suggest that students could become better learners by being more deliberate, clarifying and understanding directions, and developing a strategy for approaching a problem before beginning an assignment.

Real-Life Success Story "Should I Make a Change?" (p. 269)

Letters will vary but should display an understanding of factors discussed in the chapter: the importance of self-direction and persistence, the fear associated with change, hidden resistance to change, and the benefits of making proactive changes and decisions.

CLOSE

Culminating Activity

Ask students to research (in books, libraries, and on the Internet) different ways in which people demonstrate great self-discipline, both in their culture and in other cultures around the world. Examples could include anything from training for a marathon to studying for a certain exam to fasting for health or for a religious occasion. Encourage students to share what they have discovered with other members of the class in a short presentation. They might construct a mural, write a report, make a short videotape, or create a Web page that explains and demonstrates what they found.

Personal Success Portfolio

Lead this activity using one of suggestions given on pages 9 and 10.

Additional materials that you may wish students to include in their Personal Success Portfolio for Chapter 6 include:

- an action plan to increase the student's self-discipline in a specific area (such as studying, diet, exercise, etc.)
- a list of impulses that the student will be alert for in the future
- an index card containing three large words in three different colors: Stop (red), Think (yellow), Decide (green)
- a list of individually tailored affirmations the student can use to help him- or herself make positive changes
- a list of insights the student has gained into the decision-making process and his or her decision-making style
- a list of questions the student can use to determine whether a statement follows the standards of critical thinking (questions are presented under each standard on pages 251–255)

ADDITIONAL RESOURCES

The following books offer information on self-discipline, habit change, critical thinking, and decision making.

Books

Bassham, Gregory, William Irwin, Henry Nardone, and James M. Wallace. *Critical Thinking: A Student's Introduction.* New York: McGraw-Hill Higher Education, 2002.

Baumeister, Roy F., Todd F. Heatherton, and Dianne M. Tice. *Losing Control: How and Why People Fail at Self-Regulation.* San Diego: Academic Press, 1994.

Bransford, John D. and Barry S. Stein. *The Ideal Problem Solver: A Guide for Improving Thinking, Learning, and Creativity.* 2nd ed. New York: W. H. Freeman and Company, 1993.

Claiborn, James and Cherry Pedrick. *The Habit Change Workbook.* Oakland: New Harbinger Publications, 2001.

Hammond, John S., Ralph L. Keeney, and Howard Raiffa. *Smart Choices: A Practical Guide to Making Better Life Decisions.* New York: Broadway Books, 1999.

Kern, Harris and Karen Willi. *Discipline: Training the Mind to Manage Your Life.* Bloomington: 1st Books Library, 2003.

Lewis, H.W. *Why Flip a Coin? The Art and Science of Good Decisions.* Hoboken, NJ: John Wiley and Sons, 1997.

Pirozzi, Richard. *Critical Reading, Critical Thinking: A Contemporary Issues Approach.* 2nd ed. New York: Longman, 2003.

Plous, Scott. *The Psychology of Judgment and Decision Making.* New York: McGraw-Hill, 1993.

Timm, Paul R. and Michael G. Crisp, eds. *Successful Self-Management: A Psychologically Sound Approach to Personal Effectiveness.* Los Altos, CA: Crisp Publications, 1988.

Weinstein, Bruce D. *What Should I Do? 4 Simple Steps to Making Better Decisions in Everyday Life.* New York: Perigee Books, 2000.

Young, Jeffrey E. and Janet S. Klosko. *Reinventing Your Life: The Breakthrough Program to End Negative Behavior and Feel Great Again.* New York: Plume, 1994.

CHAPTER **7**

Self-Motivation

OVERVIEW

In Chapter 7 students read about motivation and how it drives them to reach their goals and realize their full potential. In Section 7.1 they explore the different types of motivation and learn why internal motivation is the most lasting form of motivation. They also learn how their needs and wants drive their behavior. In Section 7.2 they work on overcoming the fears that can drain their motivation and learn to use visualization to boost their motivation and self-expectancy.

OBJECTIVES

After they complete this chapter, students should be able to:

- Contrast intrinsic motivation with extrinsic motivation.
- Describe how to distinguish needs from wants.
- Explain why needs motivate their behavior.
- Cite ways to overcome fear of failure.
- Cite ways to overcome fear of success.
- Describe visualization and how it can boost motivation.

Copyright © Glencoe/McGraw-Hill

OUTLINE

Chapter Topics

UNDERSTANDING MOTIVATION
The Power of Motivation
     Positive and Negative Motivation
     Sources of Motivation
     Understanding Incentives
Needs and Motivation
     Needs and Wants
     A Hierarchy of Needs

RECHARGING YOUR MOTIVATION
Motivation and Emotion
     The Importance of Desire
Overcoming Fear of Failure
     Accept Your Fear
     Expand Your Comfort Zone
     Rethink Failure
     Failure Is Part of Success
Overcoming Fear of Success
     Fighting Your Fears
Visualization
     Visualization and Success
     The Power of Imagination
     Steps to Visualization

Chapter Activities

EXERCISE 7.1 **What Motivates You?** (pp. 277–279)
EXERCISE 7.2 **Are Your Needs Being Met?** (pp. 286–287)
EXERCISE 7.3 **Expanding Your Comfort Zone** (pp. 293–294)
EXERCISE 7.4 **Visualizing Success** (pp. 301–302)

Personal Journal 7.1   **Generating Positive Motivation** (p. 274)
Personal Journal 7.2   **Confronting Fear of Success** (p. 297)

Chapter Features

INTERNET ACTION   **Collaborative Learning Motivates** (p. 283)
Applying Psychology   **Beliefs That Make Smart People Dumb** (p. 285)
PROFESSIONAL DEVELOPMENT   **What's Your Goal-Setting Style?** (p. 289)

FOCUS

Introducing the Chapter

Write *motivation* on the board and ask a volunteer to give a definition (the force that moves us to action). Ask, "How do you think jumping from a burning building and climbing to the top of Mount McKinley represent different types of motivation (negative and positive)?" and, "How do you think being motivated by wanting to feel good about yourself is different from being motivated by wanting to fit in socially (intrinsic and extrinsic)?" Discuss students' responses and explain that in this chapter they will be learning about different types of motivation and how they can apply them to their own lives.

Real-Life Success Story "How Can I Succeed?" (p. 270)

Ask a volunteer to read the first part of the Real-Life Success Story, "How Can I Succeed?" to the class. Then ask, "Why would Elijah be afraid of succeeding?" Discuss their responses and then have another volunteer read the remainder of the story. Ask students how they might advise Elijah. What would they do if they were in his shoes?

Opening Quote (p. 271)

"To succeed, you need to find something to hold on to, something to motivate you, something to inspire you."

Write the quote on the board or make a transparency of it using the reproducible master on page 289. Ask students what they think this statement means. What does "something to hold on to" mean? Why, do you think, do you need motivation and inspiration to succeed?

Tony Dorsett played football for the University of Pittsburgh where he was the first player in NCAA history to rush for more than 1,000 yards in each of four seasons. He won the Heisman Trophy in 1976 and is second only to Walter Payton for yards rushed (12,379) in a

career. Ask students what might have motivated Tony Dorsett. What motivates others to reach unprecedented achievements?

INSTRUCT

Teaching Tips

The following topics are discussed in this chapter. You may want to expand on them in large or small class groups.

The Power of Motivation (pp. 272–279)

To help explain the different types and sources of motivation, write the following definitions on the board:

Positive (type of motivation): motivation to do something because it will move us toward a goal

Negative (type of motivation): motivation to do something in order to avoid negative consequences

Extrinsic (source of motivation): motivation that comes from outside

Intrinsic (source of motivation): motivation that comes from inside

Explain that **positive** and **negative** are different types of motivation, and **extrinsic** and **intrinsic** are different sources of motivation. Point out that intrinsic motivation is always positive. As a class, brainstorm specific examples of each kind of motivation.

Needs and Motivation (pp. 280–287)

Before reviewing this section, have the class brainstorm different needs. (For example, to feel accepted, to have enough food, to feel useful, and to have medical care.) Write these on the board. Then have students review Maslow's hierarchy of needs and decide how to categorize the needs you brainstormed. Make sure that students have brainstormed at least one need for each of Maslow's categories.

Motivation and Emotion (pp. 288–289)

Ask a student to read the paragraph containing the key term *desire*. Ask students to explain what they think the author means by, "Desire is the emotional state between where you are and where you want to be." Ask them to compare the definition of desire (a conscious drive to attain a satisfying goal) to the definition of persistence (the ability to go on despite opposition, setbacks, and occasional doubts). What do these two qualities have to do with one another? Help students see that both desire and persistence are necessary for achievement of a goal.

Overcoming Fear of Failure (pp. 290–294)

Have students look at this section. Point out that the headings describe the different actions you can take to overcome the fear of failure:

- accept your fear
- expand your comfort zone
- rethink failure
- recognize that failure is part of success

As a class, discuss how these steps can help a person to overcome a fear of failure.

Overcoming Fear of Success
(pp. 295–297)

Divide the class into seven small groups, assigning each group one of the fears of success (such as "Even if I succeed, I still won't be happy," "I won't be able to live up to the expectations," etc.) Have each group write a role-play between two or three people discussing this fear and how to combat it. Allow students to present their role-plays to the class.

Visualization (pp. 298–302)

Review with students the steps to visualization described on page 300. Then have each student think of a goal he or she is striving for right now and write the steps to visualizing that goal. Make sure the steps include being relaxed, focusing on one image at a time, taking each step needed to achieve the desired outcome, and proceeding without anxiety. Have students add their visualizations to their Personal Success Portfolios.

In-Chapter Answers and Notes

FIGURE 7.1

Positive and Negative Motivation
(p. 273)
When we are negatively motivated, we are driven by unpleasant thoughts and feelings such as fear, worry, and self-doubt. These thoughts and feelings can lead to low self-esteem.

`Personal Journal 7.1`

Generating Positive Motivation
(p. 274)
Responses will vary but should reflect positive thoughts and feelings.

Sample Answers

Transform each negative motivation into a positive motivation.

I have to work hard on my résumé, or else I won't get any interviews.
<u>Working hard on my résumé will help prepare me for interviews by reminding me of my abilities and accomplishments.</u>
I'm gathering references because no one will hire me without them.
<u>By gathering references, I'm building a support network to help me reach my career goals.</u>
I'm applying for lots of jobs because I don't want to feel like I missed an opportunity.
<u>The more jobs I apply for, the more opportunities I'll have.</u>
I need to practice interview techniques so I don't bungle it on the big day.
<u>By practicing interview techniques, I will be better prepared for my interview and feel more confident.</u>
I have to follow up on the interview, or else they'll think I don't want the job.
<u>By following up on the interview, I can convey that I really want this job.</u>

Exploring Further

Explain to students that they can use the technique of transforming negative motivation into positive motivation to boost their own motivation. Ask students to write down one of their personal goals and to identify three or more of their reasons for pursuing that goal. Do any of these reasons reflect negative motivation? If so, ask students to rethink these reasons and rewrite them to reflect positive motivation, using their completed Personal Journal as a guide.

EXERCISE 7.1

What Motivates You? (pp. 277–279)

A-B. Students' responses and scores will vary.

C. Students' motivation will vary. Students should be open to the results of the questionnaire. If they disagree with the results, they should back their reasons with critical thinking and examples.

D. Responses will vary but should recognize that intrinsic motivation fuels people's interests and passions, driving them to do things that they enjoy and that allow them to grow as individuals. This means that people who are intrinsically motivated seek interesting activities and challenging ones—ones that help them expand their skills. Extrinsic motivation, by contrast, prompts people to do things not because they really want to but because these things are a means to an end. People who are extrinsically motivated would not want to try challenging things, because there is the possibility that they might fail and therefore not obtain social approval.

Exploring Further

Display a transparency of the reproducible master on page 291, "Intrinsic and Extrinsic Goals." Ask students to brainstorm specific examples of each of the intrinsic and extrinsic goals listed.

FIGURE 7.2

Hierarchy of Needs (p. 281)

Answers will vary but could mention that a parent might give up some lower-level need, such as a physical need, in order to provide greater security for his or her child. A soldier might give up his or her security, and even his or her life, in order to fight for an ideal (i.e., to attain self-actualization).

Exploring Further

Point out to students that it is not uncommon for people to sacrifice physical needs in order to pursue higher needs. For example, even when food is plentiful, many people throughout the world participate in the practice of fasting (giving up food). This is done for many different reasons, including self-discipline, religious beliefs, and protest. People such as relief workers, missionaries, explorers, and artists may place themselves in unsafe situations or give up certain basic needs in order to do something for others. Ask students to think about why a person might ignore, or at least appear to ignore, a lower need such as food or security to fulfill a self-actualizing need such as searching for wisdom, justice, aesthetics, or spiritual fulfillment. Encourage students to discuss their responses in class.

 INTERNET ACTION

Collaborative Learning Motivates (p. 283)

Students' responses will vary but should reflect whether the student is primarily an interpersonal or intrapersonal learner.

Exploring Further

Ask students to think about past collaborative or group learning experiences. Were they helpful, unhelpful, or neutral? Why? Do students believe that certain subjects lend themselves to collaborative learning better than others? Why or why not? Encourage comments and discussion.

Applying Psychology

BELIEFS THAT MAKE SMART PEOPLE DUMB (p. 285)
Students' responses will vary but should recognize that intelligence is a potential that can be developed. By putting in the extra effort for a class, you really *can* improve your intelligence in that area.

EXERCISE 7.2

Are Your Needs Being Met?
(pp. 286–287)

A. Students' responses and scores will vary.

B. Responses will vary but should reflect the highest score among relatedness, competence, and autonomy.

C. Students' needs will vary, but should be consistent with their scores on the questionnaire. Students should demonstrate an understanding of each of the different needs and how these needs can be satisfied (or not satisfied). If a student's need for relatedness is not being satisfied, for example, he or she might lack satisfying intimate relationships, be estranged from a family member(s), or lack activity partners who share his or her interests.

✓ SECTION 7.1
SELF-CHECK (p. 287)

1. Intrinsic motivation is motivation that comes from inside.

2. Needs represent things we must have in order to function. Wants represent things we can survive and thrive without.

3. The five levels of the hierarchy of needs are physical needs, security needs, social needs, esteem needs, and self-actualization needs.

PROFESSIONAL DEVELOPMENT

What's Your Goal-Setting Style? (p. 289)
Students' responses will vary but should demonstrate an understanding of the difference between performance goals (goals that involve measuring up to a standard and winning the approval of others) and learning goals (goals that involve building new skills, understanding new things, and finding new ways of dealing with problems.)

FIGURE 7.3

Expanding the Comfort Zone (p. 291)
It is better to expand the comfort zone in small steps than in giant leaps because taking small steps allows you to try new things without becoming too stressed and discouraged by obstacles or difficulties.

EXERCISE 7.3

Expanding Your Comfort Zone
(pp. 293–294)

A. Students' responses will vary.

B. Students' responses will vary but should recognize that the threat of failure often keeps people from trying new things.

C. Students' responses will vary but should reflect the students' level of desire, as well as their level of self-expectancy.

D. Students' responses will vary but should recognize that the possibility of future regret might help motivate a person to keep trying.

E. Goals will vary but should represent realistic steps rather than overly ambitious leaps.

Personal Journal 7.2

Confronting Fear of Success (p. 297)
Students' responses will vary. Positive feelings should reflect pleasure and pride at the accomplishment. Negative feelings should reflect fears such as "Even if I succeed, I still won't be

happy," "I won't be able to live up to the expectations," "The minute I achieve success, I'll probably blow it," and so on.

Sample Answers

Write down three positive feelings and three negative feelings that you might experience in each of the following situations.

Your manager recognizes you in front of your coworkers for outstanding work.
Positive Feelings
delight
happiness
anticipation
Negative Feelings
embarrassment at being center of attention
guilt

You and two friends take an advanced course. You are the only student who receives an A.
Positive Feelings
success
surprise
relief
Negative Feelings
isolation
worry what others might think
self-consciousness at being singled out

You submit several humorous articles to a local newspaper. The editor offers you a column.
Positive Feelings
pleasure
amazement
pride
Negative Feelings
anxiety
fear of failure
worry that editor made a mistake

EXERCISE 7.4

Visualizing Success (pp. 301–302)
A-B. Situations and visualizations will vary.
C. Responses will vary, but students should recognize a greater sense of confidence.

D. Visualizations of the future will vary but should be realistic and reflect the self-awareness gained over the course of the book.
E. Students' responses will vary but should recognize that repeated visualization can help boost motivation.

 **SECTION 7.2**
SELF-CHECK (p. 302)

1. Desire is the emotional state between where you are and where you want to be. Desire is important for success because to attain success, you need to want to change and improve yourself.
2. Failure is an unwanted outcome.
3. Visualization works like positive self-talk, by harnessing the power of the subconscious mind.

Additional Activities

These additional activities are exclusive to this Instructor's Resource Manual. They are designed to meet the special needs of your students. The activities can be used as in-class activities or as take-home assignments. They can be assigned to individual students, pairs of students, or groups of students.

Critical Thinking

FEAR OF SUCCESS AND SELF-SABOTAGE
Some people repeatedly set themselves up for failure. For example, they may set goals they cannot possibly achieve or pursue relationships with people who are emotionally unavailable. This ensures failure and disappointment. This kind of behavior is known as *self-sabotage*. Self-sabotage results from the internal struggle between a person's desire for something and that person's feeling that he or she should not, cannot, or does not deserve to have that thing. In a class discussion, ask students to think of examples of self-sabotaging behavior that people use in order to make themselves fail. Students should consider various areas such as career progress, academic

success, and relationships. Then ask them to think of possible strategies for overcoming these kinds of self-sabotaging behaviors.

GOALS AND MOTIVATION   Ask students to think about what they would do if they discovered that achieving a certain goal required more effort than originally expected. To give them some ideas, you can suggest the examples of getting a degree, breaking into the music or movie business, or starting a business. Break the class into small groups and ask each group to choose one goal and come up with scenarios in which obstacles to achieving that goal might arise. Have the students think about what might make them modify the goal or their methods of achieving it. Ask them to also think about what kinds of obstacles might force a person to give up a goal altogether, and why.

WORK MOTIVATION   Motivation researchers Richard Hackman and Greg Oldham believe that some jobs are inherently more motivating than others. They believe that the most motivating jobs have five important qualities: skill variety, task identity, task significance, job feedback, and autonomy. Explain these five factors to students with the aid of the reproducible master on page 295, "Work Motivation." Ask students to write for five to ten minutes on a piece of paper or in their journals about whether these five factors are present in their work on the job or at school. Do they get to build skills? Do they feel they are accomplishing an identifiable, important project? Do they learn and grow by doing? Do they have autonomy? Ask students to share their thoughts.

Application

GOAL COLLAGE   In the end-of-chapter Application activities for Chapter 2, students were asked to create a personality collage using pictures that represent aspects of themselves. Now ask students to create a goal collage with photos, diagrams, symbols, words, objects, and any other items that represent the students' goals and have motivational value for them. Break the class into small groups and ask students to share their collages with the other members of their group. The other students in each group should try to guess what significance the text, images, and objects in the collage might have. What does each student's goal collage say about him or her? Reunite the class and ask each group to mention what they found to be the most inspiring and creative aspects of each member's collage.

Remind students that to reach their goals they need to know them by heart and be truly committed to them. Recommend that they post their goal collage in a prominent place so it can serve as a visual reminder of their goals. The more often students remind themselves of their goals, the more their goals become an automatic part of their thinking.

Internet Activities

HIERARCHY OF NEEDS   Ask students to go to the Chapter 7 section of the book Web site at **www.mhhe.com/psychofsuccess** and click on the link to the self-evaluation on the subject of Maslow's self-actualizing principles. After they have completed the self-evaluation, students should select two to three of these self-actualizing principles and discuss ways in which they could use them to improve specific areas of their lives.

NAMING YOUR FEARS   Direct students to the book Web site and have them follow the link to the "Fear Inventory Checklist." Ask students to read the checklist and write down all of the items on the list that they fear. What do they think contributed to these fears? Why? Follow up this activity by asking students whether they believe that identifying or giving a name to a fear is important in controlling or conquering that fear.

ASSESS

Review and Activities Answers

Review Questions (p. 304)

1. Positive motivation is the drive to do something because it will move us toward a goal or because we associate it with positive thoughts and feelings. For example, we might be positively motivated to work hard on a term paper because it gives us a feeling of accomplishment or because we have a natural curiosity about the topic. Negative motivation, by contrast, is the drive to do something in order to avoid negative consequences. If we are negatively motivated, we might work hard on a term paper because we are afraid of getting a low grade or disappointing the teacher.

2. Intrinsic motivation is positive motivation that fuels your interests and passions. It drives you to do things that you enjoy and that allow you to grow as a person. Extrinsic motivation is motivation that comes from external sources, such as avoiding trouble, punishment, shame, or guilt. Intrinsic motivation is healthier because it promotes higher self-esteem and guides a person toward success and happiness.

3. The hierarchy of needs is shaped like a pyramid and has five horizontal levels. The first (bottom) level of needs is physical needs. The second level is security needs; the third level is social needs; the fourth level is esteem needs; and the fifth (top) level is self-actualization needs.

4. Relatedness is fulfilling relationships with others. Competence is the ability to do something well. Autonomy is freedom of choice, independence, and the chance to exercise independent judgment.

5. Low self-esteem is the major reason people fear success; they feel that they do not deserve success and are not worth the effort to succeed.

6. Visualization helps you prepare for any kind of challenge. This improves performance and helps you succeed in difficult situations, overcome obstacles, and improve your self-esteem.

Critical Thinking (p. 304)

7. Answers will vary, but most students will recognize that many of the contestants for reality shows are extrinsically motivated because the objectives for the shows are usually to look good, fit in socially, please others, and/or earn a material reward.

8. Situations and fears will vary. Solutions for handling fear could include accepting your fear, expanding your comfort zone, and rethinking failure.

Application (p. 304)

9. Charts will vary.

Sample Answers

Physical Needs
eat meals
buy groceries
see the doctor

Security Needs
lock the house
park in lighted parking lots
participate in neighborhood watch group

Social Needs
meet friends for dinner
call parents
participate in neighborhood watch group

Esteem Needs
attend school
join a gym
work at a job for pay

Self-Actualization Needs
attend school
save enough money to take a trip overseas
work at a job for pay

10. Visualizations will vary but should include each step necessary for success, from entering the room to turning in the test. At each step the friend should imagine herself feeling calm, prepared, and confident.

Internet Activities (p. 305)

11. The four criteria used by the authors of this study to test whether belongingness is really a need were: 1. whether it is universal in the sense of applying to all people; 2. whether it affects a broad range of behaviors; 3. whether it leads to ill effects when thwarted, and 4. whether it elicits goal-oriented behavior designed to satisfy it. People only need a certain relatively small number of close relationships. They state, "Having two as opposed to no close relationships may make a world of difference to the person's health and happiness; having eight as opposed to six may have very little consequence." People who lack belongingness are likely to suffer mental and physical illness and are highly prone to a broad range of behavioral problems.

12. Fears and research will vary but should address the following issues: causes, symptoms, how many people suffer from it, and how to cope with it.

Real-Life Success Story "How Can I Succeed?" (p. 305)

Completed stories will vary but should explain that positive self-talk could help Elijah see himself as a successful college student who is able to succeed academically while retaining his current friends and making new ones.

CLOSE

Culminating Activity

Open a class discussion by asking students whether they have ever gotten "stuck," or stopped making progress, while trying to achieve a certain goal. Did they later become "unstuck," or did they give up their goal? Broaden the discussion to address what a person can do to renew his or her motivation when progress stops or slows. Discuss how the idea of perspective is important when evaluating goals, successes, and failures. What may seem like a failure today may not seem like a failure a year or a decade from now.

As a second part to this activity, ask students to complete the exercise "Recharging Motivation" provided in reproducible master form on page 296. This exercise contains three vignettes about people who have gotten stuck on the way to reaching a goal. Ask students to work together in groups. Students should read each story and generate ideas for how each character could make renewed progress toward his or her goal. Then bring the class back together and have groups share their ideas.

Personal Success Portfolio

Lead this activity using one of the suggestions given on pages 9 and 10.

Additional materials that you may wish students to include in their Portfolios for Chapter 7 include:

- a motivational goal collage
- an action plan for fulfilling their needs for esteem and self-actualization
- a short essay describing the kinds of incentives the student has been offered at home, school, or work, and whether these incentives increased his or her motivation
- a list of affirmations the student can use to combat fear of success
- a list of three or four "Keys to Success" from the chapter that the student wants to remember for the future
- a description of a specific visualization exercise the student could use to boost his or her self-confidence in a certain area

ADDITIONAL RESOURCES

The following books offer theoretical and practical perspectives on motivation, advice for overcoming fears, and guidelines for effective visualization.

Books

Bourne, Edmund. *Healing Fear: New Approaches to Controlling Anxiety.* Berkeley: Publishers' Group West, 1998.

Clarkson, Petruska. *How to Overcome Your Secret Fear of Failure: Recognizing and Beating Your Achilles Syndrome.* London: Vega Books, 2003.

Deci, Edward L., with Richard Flaste. *Why We Do What We Do: Understanding Self-Motivation.* New York: Penguin Books, 1995.

Dweck, Carol S. *Self-Theories: Their Role in Motivation, Personality, and Development.* Philadelphia: Psychology Press, 2000.

Franken, Robert E. *Human Motivation.* 5th ed. Belmont, CA: Wadsworth Publishing, 2001.

Gawain, Shakti. *Creative Visualization.* 25th anniversary edition. Novato, CA: New World Library, 2002.

Gawain, Shakti. *The Creative Visualization Workbook.* 2nd ed. Novato, CA: New World Library, 1995.

Green, Joey. *The Road to Success is Paved with Failure: How Hundreds of Famous People Triumphed Over Inauspicious Beginnings, Crushing Rejection, Humiliating Defeats and Other Speed Bumps Along Life's Highway.* New York: Little, Brown and Company, 2001.

Greene, Don. *Fight Your Fear and Win: Seven Skills for Performing Your Best Under Pressure—At Work, in Sports, on Stage.* New York: Broadway Books, 2001.

Jeffers, Susan J. *Feel the Fear and Do It Anyway.* New York: Fawcett Books, 1992.

Kasser, T. and R. M. Ryan. "A Dark Side of the American Dream: Correlates of Financial Success as a Central Life Aspiration." *Journal of Personality and Social Psychology* 65, 410–422.

Lewis, Robert T. *Taking Chances: The Psychology of Losing and How to Profit from It.* Gretna, LA: Wellness Institute, 2000.

Mager, Robert F. *Goal Analysis: How to Clarify Your Goals So You Can Actually Achieve Them.* 3rd ed. Atlanta: Center for Effective Performance, 1997.

Maslow, Abraham. *Motivation and Personality.* 3rd ed. New York: Harper, 1987.

Ryan, R. M., and Edward L. Deci. "Self-Determination Theory and the Facilitation of Intrinsic Motivation, Social Development, and Well-Being." *American Psychologist* 55 (2000), 68–78.

Sheldon, Kennon M. and Tim Kasser. "Goals, Congruence, and Positive Well-Being: New Empirical Support for Humanistic Theories." *Journal of Humanistic Psychology*, January 2001, vol. 41, no. 1, pp. 30–50.

Tesser, Abraham, Diederik A. Stapel, and Joanne V. Wood, eds. *Self and Motivation: Emerging Psychological Perspectives.* Washington, D.C.: American Psychological Association, 2002.

Managing Your Resources

OVERVIEW

In Chapter 8 students read about two valuable but limited resources—time and money. Students learn that in order to reach their goals they need to manage their time and money efficiently. In Section 8.1 they examine how to make the most of their time. They learn that planning ahead enables them to accomplish more and to focus on their top priorities. In Section 8.2 students learn how to make their money work for them. They examine their spending habits, learn to make a budget, and develop a plan to align their finances with their goals and values.

OBJECTIVES

After they complete this chapter, students should be able to:

- Outline the three steps in time management and in money management.
- Describe the three categories of time and the three categories of expenses.
- Explain how to make a to-do list and a schedule.
- Define procrastination and explain its causes.
- Describe the criteria for an effective budget.
- Cite ways to reduce excess spending.

OUTLINE

Chapter Topics

TIME MANAGEMENT
Taking Control of Your Time
        Steps to Time Management
        Step 1: Analyze How You Use Your Time
        Step 2: Prioritize Your Activities
        Step 3: Create a Plan for Your Time
Tackling Procrastination
        Why We Procrastinate

MONEY MANAGEMENT
Money Matters
        Wealth and Well-Being
        Your Money and You
Managing Your Finances
        Step 1: Analyze How You Use Your Money
        Step 2: Prioritize Your Expenses
        Step 3: Create a Plan for Your Money
Stretching Your Resources
        Spend, Spend, Spend
        Drop the Shopping Habit
        Using Credit Wisely
        Keep it in Perspective

Chapter Activities

Chapter Features

FOCUS

Introducing the Chapter

Ask students to write down three to five habits they have that may keep them from getting things done on time (for example, talking on the phone too long). Then ask them to write down three to five habits they have that may keep them from having enough money to pay their expenses (for example, using the ATM too often). Have volunteers share their lists and write their ideas on the board. Then explain that in this chapter they will be reading about how to reevaluate these types of habits and manage their time and money more efficiently.

Real-Life Success Story "Can I Have a Career and a Social Life, Too?" (p. 306)

Have a volunteer read the first part of the Real-Life Success Story. Then ask, "Do you think Anna made a mistake by going out with her coworkers Friday night? Why or why not?" Have another volunteer read the second part of the story and then ask, "Do you now think Anna made a mistake in the way she spent her time this weekend? What could she have done to make Monday a more successful work day?"

Opening Quote (p. 307)

"You are good when you strive to give of yourself. Yet you are not evil when you seek gain for yourself."

Write the quote on the board or make a transparency of the reproducible master on page 297. Ask students what they think this statement means. What does "give of yourself" mean? Do they agree with this statement?

Ask students to think of people who give of themselves. Do these people also seek gain for themselves? Discuss with students why these two actions are not mutually exclusive.

INSTRUCT

Teaching Tips

The following topics are discussed in this chapter. You may want to expand on them in large or small class groups.

Taking Control of Your Time (pp. 308–321)

Have students think back over the past week and make a list of their activities, such as "went to school, worked, bought groceries, went out with friends," and so on. Then explain that time management involves taking control of your time, and that the first step in taking control of your time is to analyze how you use your time. Point out that you can analyze your use of time by assigning each of your activities to one of three categories: committed time, maintenance time, and discretionary time. Review these categories and allow students to sort their activities. Ask volunteers to share how much of their time is spent on each of the different categories.

When you assign Exercise 8.3, emphasize the importance of using the practice schedule in question C for the entire week. Explain that trying different time-management strategies will help students become more organized and self-aware.

Tackling Procrastination (pp. 322–325)

Ask a volunteer to define *procrastination* (the habit of putting off tasks until the last minute) and write the definition on the board. Have the class brainstorm different activities that people put off doing (homework, breaking up with a boyfriend/girlfriend, paying bills, etc.) and write them on the board. Then discuss why they think people procrastinate on these particular things and what damage this procrastination does. Conclude with a general discussion about how procrastination can affect students' ability to reach their goals.

Exploring Further

Remind students that perfectionism is a major cause of procrastination. Ask students to recall the definition of *vicious cycle* (a chain of events in which one negative event causes another negative event). Then point out that perfectionism is a kind of self-defeating attitude that can cause a vicious cycle. Ask students to explain why this might be the case. Project a transparency of the reproducible master on page 299, "Perfectionism: A Vicious Cycle."

Money Matters (pp. 326–328)

Ask students to write a paragraph describing how they feel about money. Then ask, "Does the way you feel about money affect they way you handle money?" Point out that the most useful attitude toward money is a practical one. By viewing money as a tool, we can be more objective about it. We can think, "I control my money. It does not control me." Why do students think so many people worry about money and feel controlled by it?

Managing Your Finances (pp. 328–337)

Ask students to raise their hands if they have a budget. Explain that creating a budget, which is a plan for your money, is the third step in managing your finances. (The first two are analyzing how you use your money and prioritizing your expenses.) Then ask volunteers to explain how they made their budget, whether or not it is important to them, and whether or not they stick to it. Also ask for volunteers who do not have a budget to explain how they manage their spending and whether they feel in control of their finances. As a class, discuss how budgeting can help you achieve your goals.

Stretching Your Resources (pp. 338–342)

Ask for a volunteer to explain the basic recipe for financial fitness. (Spend less than you earn.) Then ask, "What can happen if you do not follow this basic recipe?" (You either have no savings because you spend all you earn or you are in debt because you spend more than you earn.) Have students brainstorm ways to spend less and to earn more and discuss their ideas. How many of them are truly realistic? How many people would be willing to follow through with the realistic suggestions?

In-Chapter Answers and Notes

EXERCISE 8.1

Time-Demand Survey (pp. 311–312)

A. Students' time logs will vary.

B-C. Total number of hours and percentages will vary. If the total number of hours is over 168, the student is overcommitted. Check written totals against the pie-chart graphic to make sure students have filled in the chart correctly.

D. Students' responses will vary, but they may recognize that they are not spending their time to their greatest advantage.

Personal Journal 8.1

Prioritizing Your Life (p. 314)

Answers will vary, although certain tasks, such as paying the overdue credit card bill, are clearly more important and urgent than certain other tasks, such as seeing a movie.

Sample Answers

Important/Urgent
fix flat tire
pay overdue credit card bill
study for Friday's exam

Important/Not Urgent
do grocery shopping
do laundry
start looking for summer job

Not Important/Urgent
return call from best friend
drop off dry cleaning

Not Important/Not Urgent
see movie
file old papers and bills

Examining Your Priorities (pp. 316–317)

A. Students' areas and changes will vary.

B. Students' responses will vary but should explain why these activities are not the students' top priorities (i.e., why they are not important or urgent).

C. Students' areas and changes will vary.

D. Students' responses will vary but should explain why these activities are priorities for them (i.e., why they are important).

E. Answers will vary but should describe realistic changes.

Exploring Further

After a week has passed, revisit this activity and ask for a show of hands to indicate how many students made the change they described in question E. Ask students who did make the change to describe the change and their reasons for making it. Did it work out as planned? Were they realistic in their assessment of how much time each activity takes? Ask students who did not make the change to try to explain what might have held them back (habit, forgetfulness, lack of planning). Do they still want to make the change? If so, when will they do it?

Personal Journal 8.2

What's Your Prime Time? (p. 319)

Students' responses will vary. This activity should help them identify the time of day at which their mental and physical capacity is at its peak.

EXERCISE 8.3

Time-Management Practice (pp. 320–321)

A-B. To-do lists and the prioritization of tasks will vary.

C. Weekly schedules will vary, but tasks should be organized in order of importance from most to least important.

D. Students' responses will vary, but should show evidence of a genuine attempt to implement the schedule. Some students may acknowledge the difficulty in producing a realistic schedule or in following a set plan.

Exploring Further

After students have made their schedules, ask them to examine them in light of their prime time (peak-capacity hours). Are their most difficult tasks scheduled for their prime time? For example, if a student tends to be a night owl, has he or she scheduled high-importance tasks, such as studying, for the evening hours? If a student is a morning person, has he or she scheduled classes, work, and other important activities for the morning hours? Have students work in pairs (night people with night people and morning people with morning people) to analyze one another's schedules and suggest changes that could make them more productive.

INTERNET ACTION

E-Mail Efficiency (p. 323)

Students' strategies will vary. Examples include choosing to read e-mails only on certain days or at certain times and being very selective about who receives your e-mail address.

EXERCISE 8.4

Do You Procrastinate? (pp. 324–325)

A-B. Students' responses and scores will vary.

C. Students' answers will vary. However, people tend to put off tasks that are unenjoyable (such as chores) or unpleasant in some way. For example, a student may put off bringing up a problem with a roommate because of a lack of assertiveness or an aversion to conflict.

D. Actions will vary but should be realistic and time-limited (e.g., tackling one specific task on a large project.)

Exploring Further

Ask students to share their answers to question C. Do any students in the class procrastinate in the same areas? Why? Ask students who do *not* procrastinate on those areas to explain why they do not. As a class, brainstorm a list of excuses for procrastinating. Encourage students to give specific examples from their current situation. Then display a transparency of the reproducible master on page 300, "Procrastination Excuses," and ask students to work in small groups to think of effective rebuttals to each of these excuses.

SECTION 8.1
SELF-CHECK (p. 325)

1. The three categories of time are committed time, maintenance time, and discretionary time.
2. Benefits of making to-do lists are that they keep you from worrying about forgetting a task or getting sidetracked; help you separate things that matter from things that don't matter; motivate you to get started and complete your assignments on time; and give you a sense of achievement when you check off finished tasks.
3. Procrastination is the habit of putting off tasks until the last minute.

Personal Journal 8.3

How Do You See Money? (p. 327)
Students' responses will vary, but this activity should help students recognize their attitudes and identify their feelings about money.

Sample Answers

To me, money is <u>a source of inequality among people; a necessary evil</u>
My financial goals are <u>to pay off my credit card debt and save up enough to take a European vacation</u>

If I had a $100 bill in my wallet, I <u>would probably go to a store and spend half of it, then save the rest for routine expenses</u>
When I think about paying bills, I feel <u>resentful and somewhat panicked</u>
One thing I don't understand about money is <u>why some things cost so much and others cost so little</u>
To me, planning for retirement is <u>the last thing I think about</u>
I worry about having enough money for <u>ever being able to travel or take a day off</u>
Money helps me enjoy <u>my home, which I enjoy decorating; food; books and entertainment</u>
I don't need money to enjoy <u>nature, gardening, my family, the beach</u>

PROFESSIONAL DEVELOPMENT

**Teen Spending:
A Good Thing?** (p. 329)
Opinions will vary, but students should recognize that young people who have maintained a budget or been involved in their families' financial decisions are more likely to have realistic expectations.

Exploring Further

Your class probably has students with a wide variety of work experiences. Ask students who have entered the workforce to explain what problems they faced and how they coped when they first became financially independent. Were they prepared for all the new expenses they faced? Did they have a realistic idea of how much was required to pay for necessities such as rent, food, and transportation? Ask students who have not yet become financially independent to estimate how much they would need to earn each month in order to cover all their expenses. Make a list of all the expenses that a single person would face each month. (Refer to the expenses listed in Exercise 8.6 on pages 335–337 for ideas.) Point out that most young people forget to consider periodic expenses such as car registration, dental visits, dry cleaning, gifts, and household supplies when they are figuring out how much money they will need to live independently. Ask students to describe a time when an unanticipated expense caused financial problems for them. Students might describe a pricey car repair, an emergency veterinary procedure for a pet, a home-repair disaster, or another similar unlucky event.

EXERCISE 8.5

Expense Log (pp. 331–332)

A. Expense logs will vary but should be accurate and show an understanding of the different types of expenses.

B. Percentages and charts will vary. Check written totals against the pie-chart graphic to make sure students have filled in the chart correctly.

C. Students' responses will vary, but they may recognize that they are not spending their money to their greatest advantage.

FIGURE 8.1

Where the Money Goes (p. 333)

Answers will vary but could include that many American families own two or three cars, that Americans tend to drive alone rather than carpooling or taking public transportation, and that Americans often travel long distances to work or school.

Exploring Further

Ask students how far they commute to school, what form of transportation they use, and what they spend on transportation each month. Students who have cars should calculate how much it costs each month to operate their vehicles. This total should include any loan payments, state registration fees, insurance, repairs, maintenance, and fuel. How much are they paying per mile? Would they save money or lose money if they were to switch to public transportation? (Note: the

Internal Revenue service allows 36 cents per mile for vehicle expenses.) Students who do not have cars should calculate how much it would cost to buy, finance, and operate a car in their price range. Are students surprised by all the costs associated with operating a car?

EXERCISE 8.6

Budget Worksheet (pp. 335–337)

A. Students' projected and actual amounts will vary but should be realistic and comprehensive.

B. Students' responses will vary. If budgeted expenses are greater than income, students may try to find expenses to cut back on. If budgeted expenses are less than income, students may choose to increase savings.

C. Students' responses will vary but should recognize the importance of savings.

D. Answers will vary but should reflect the fact that it is difficult to project one's expenses down to the penny. If students dramatically exceed their budget for the month, they should explain how and why this happened.

Exploring Further

Ask students, "What if your actual expenses are *less* than your projected expenses? What should you do then?" Some students may believe that they can revise their budget upwards or spend the excess. Point out, however, that some months bring lower-than-average expenses, while other months bring higher-than-average expenses. By saving the extra one month, they will be able to take care of unanticipated and one-time expenses in later months.

Applying Psychology

THE LURE OF ADVERTISING (p. 338)
Answers will vary, but students should recognize that advertising affects everyone's buying decisions in some way.

Exploring Further

People are constantly bombarded with advertisements for the latest trendy items and "must-haves." To be smart and savvy consumers, students need to be aware of tactics used by advertisers to sway people into buying their products. In the so-called bandwagon technique, for example, an advertiser states or implies that "everyone" is embracing a certain trend, triggering the consumer's desire to fit in and to have what everyone else has. Ask students to use the Internet to research advertising techniques. What does each technique consist of and how does it work?

Alternatively, bring in several consumer magazines and ask students to do the same. Select several advertisements and ask students how the merchants are trying to tap into consumers' psychological needs in order to sell their products. For example, are they trying to sell clothing by implying that a certain kind of garment will make the consumer popular and loved?

Ask students what words they often see used in advertisements (such as "new," "number one," and so on). Make a transparency of the reproducible master on page 302, "Persuasive Words Used in Advertising" and ask for students' reactions. Can they recall seeing any of these words on billboards or television advertisements? Why do they think these words would be persuasive? Ask students to work in small groups to create an advertisement that tries to sell a very simple, everyday commodity—such as pencils, car tires, jeans, or bottled water—by tapping into people's psychological needs. Ask students to use as many of the most popular advertising words as possible. Have groups present their advertisements to the class.

Personal Journal 8.4

Look Before You Leap (p. 340)
Students' responses will vary.

Sample Answers

Describe four purchases you have made over the past year or two that you now wish you hadn't.

Purchase
Silk throw pillow
Why You Made Purchase
Liked retro pattern and style
Why You Wish You Hadn't
Don't need it; is dry-clean only; don't like it that much any more

Purchase
Digital camera
Why You Made Purchase
To take photos for school project
Why You Wish You Hadn't
Haven't used it since then; should have waited and bought higher-tech model

Purchase
Lunch at fast-food burger place
Why You Made Purchase
Didn't have lunch that day and was starving
Why You Wish You Hadn't
Was unhealthful and expensive; felt unwell afterwards

Purchase
Clothes at garage sale
Why You Made Purchase
Bargain!
Why You Wish You Hadn't
None of the clothes actually fit

Exploring Further

Ask students to bring in and show to the class one of the objects they described in this Personal Journal. When did they buy the object? Why? How much did it cost? At the time, why did they need or want it? What does this object tell them about their spending habits? Encourage students to have fun with this activity but also to use it to examine their spending habits.

1. A budget is a money management plan that specifies how you will spend your money during a particular period.

2. Impulse buying means spending money on the spur of the moment without planning.

3. Pros of credit include: it allows you to receive a product or service now and pay for it later; using credit cards is safer than carrying cash; and a credit card bill provides a useful record of your purchases. Cons of credit include: credit cards make it easy to overspend and accumulate debt, and if you don't pay off your bill every month, you owe finance charges in addition to the amount of your purchases.

Additional Activities

These additional activities are exclusive to this Instructor Resource Manual. They are designed to meet the special needs of your students. The activities can be used as in-class activities or as take-home assignments. They can be assigned to individual students, pairs of students, or groups of students.

Critical Thinking

CONSUMPTION AND THE ENVIRONMENT
Read students this quote from *Power Therapy* by Michael Aleksiuk: "Though there are exceptions, as a rule the more money an individual earns and spends, the more that individual contributes to the depletion of resources and destruction of the environment. Together with overpopulation, it's the fact that money symbolizes achievement that's causing our environmental problems." Divide students into groups of three to five people and have them discuss their responses to this statement— whether they agree or disagree, and why or why not. Ask the groups to think of real-life examples that both support and contradict Aleksiuk's statement.

SCHEDULING TOOLS In this chapter, students learn about some of the different tools that help people keep track of their schedules, such as written lists, appointment books, PDAs, and computer programs. In a class discussion, ask students to name the advantages and possible disadvantages of each method. Write each one down on the board or a transparency. Ask students whether they believe that a person could become too dependent on technology tools, such as computer programs. Could too much reliance on these tools make a person unproductive? Why or why not?

Application

RESISTING IMPULSE BUYING Ask students to go to a store of their choice (preferably one that contains a wide variety of products, such as Wal-Mart, Target, or a grocery store) and take notes on items they have a desire to buy. Ask them to note the price, the store location, the placement of the product (on a high shelf, in an end-of-aisle display, on a freestanding rack, etc.), and any other reason why they are drawn to an item. For example, is the packaging or slogan attractive or appealing? Does it smell nice? Does it seem like a great bargain? Is it situated by the check stand? Students should record whether they bought each object and why. Have students summarize their actions and thoughts on their "impulse buying" in a one-page report. Ask them to suggest how product/label design and location/placement of items can make people want to buy things they don't need.

MAKING A PLAN Have students imagine that you have assigned them a research paper that will be due in one month. Ask them to create a schedule for themselves for the project in the format of their choice (calendar, time line, etc.), beginning from that day's date. Their schedules should include all of the steps necessary to the success of their paper, such as research, writing, revising, and proofreading.

Ask students to share their schedules with one another and note any similarities and differences. Do students think that starting a large project by making a schedule would help them overcome procrastination? Why or why not?

SLOWING DOWN   Ask students who drive a car to take public transportation to a place they would normally drive, such as school, work, or a friend's house. Ask students who take public transportation to walk or bicycle to a similar destination instead. What is different about the route when they walk or ride? What things do they notice for the first time? Do they find the slower pace relaxing? Why or why not?

Internet Activities

CONSUMER RESEARCH   Explain to students that there are many Web sites that provide a forum for people to compare, review, and contrast all kinds of goods and services. Some of these Web sites are also e-commerce Web sites (such as Amazon.com), whereas others are specifically dedicated to sharing information (such as epinions.com). Ask students to pick a specific type of product (such as a two-door compact car, a four-megapixel digital camera, a travel guidebook for England, a semi-gloss paint, etc.) and compare the products available by searching the Internet for sites that offer reviews, customer satisfaction ratings, service ratings, and price comparisons. Have students write a one-page summary of which product they would buy as a result of their research, which sites they found to be helpful (and unhelpful), and whether they would do online consumer research again.

A WIRED EXISTENCE   Have students imagine that they are going to be confined to their homes for the next six months. They will, however, be given a large computer system with a fast connection to the Internet. Ask students to research what kinds of tasks it might be possible for them to do using only

the Internet. For example, they could use the Internet to do some banking, to write letters, to take online school courses, to order food and groceries, to get flowers or birthday presents delivered, to buy clothing, and to have prescriptions filled. What kinds of jobs would students be able to do via telecommuting? What kind of social life would they have? Are there any services, such as medical services, that they would be unable to obtain? Have students discuss their scenarios in class.

ASSESS

Review and Activities Answers

Review Questions (p. 344)

1. Committed time is the fixed amount of time you devote to goal-related activities. Discretionary time is the flexible amount of time you can use for any purpose.

2. Benefits of making to-do lists are that they keep you from worrying about forgetting a task or getting sidetracked; help you separate things that matter from things that don't matter; motivate you to get started and complete your assignments on time; and give you a sense of achievement when you check off finished tasks.

3. Because time, like all resources, is limited, prioritizing your activities allows you to figure out which activities deserve the biggest share of your time.

4. Emotions affect people's relationship with money because how we feel about money affects what we do with money. For example, people who view money as a security blanket are afraid to spend it. However, people who are objective about money are better able to make wise decisions about how to use it.

5. Analyzing your spending habits is important because it helps you understand where your money goes, which is the first step in managing your finances.

6. Pros of credit include: it allows you to receive a product or service now and pay for it later; using credit cards is safer than carrying cash; and a credit card bill provides a useful record of your purchases. Cons of credit include: credit cards make it easy to overspend and accumulate debt, and if you don't pay off your credit card bill every month, you owe finance charges in addition to the amount of your purchases.

Critical Thinking (p. 344)

7. Answers will vary, but students should recognize that spending a relatively brief amount of time making to-do lists and schedules saves time in the long run. Students should also recognize that organizing your time effectively allows you to shift your focus to activities that have meaning for you, which helps you achieve your goals.

8. Answers will vary, but should show evidence of self-awareness and critical thinking.

Application (p. 344)

9. Interviews will vary. Students are likely to encounter people with a wide range of approaches to money management. The average person saves very little of his or her income, so students will most likely encounter people who have little or no provision for savings.

10. Students' responses will vary, but most students will recognize that doing something—anything—toward a goal makes the goal seem more attainable and helps boost enthusiasm for the goal.

Internet Activities (p. 345)

11. Answers will vary by state, county, and city. Make sure students have arranged the spreadsheet from most expensive to least expensive.

12. Answers will vary depending on the cards chosen. Some students may choose a card with a higher APR but no annual fee if they plan on paying off the balance every month. Others may choose a card with a low introductory rate if they want to pay off a high-interest credit card by transferring the balance to a new card. Others may choose the lowest APR possible.

Real-Life Success Story "Can I Have a Career and a Social Life, Too?" (p. 345)

Letters will vary but should explain that a to-do list will enable Anna to see which activities are most urgent and important and that a schedule will help her organize her time so that she can complete the important activities on her to-do list and still build in time for leisure activities.

CLOSE

Culminating Activity

Give students examples of real-life material goals that necessitate a large one-time cost, such as cosmetic dental work ($2,500 due at time of service), a down payment on a vehicle ($2,000), or a cruise vacation ($3,000). Have students suggest other examples. Assign students to pairs or groups and ask each team to select one such expense and to develop a plan to save for their goal. Using one of the team members' actual budgets, teams should choose different savings amounts per month and calculate how long it would take the student to save up enough money to achieve that financial goal. Have teams present their goals and financial calculations to the rest of the class. Ask students if they are surprised, pleasantly or unpleasantly, by the amount of time it would take to save the required amount. If saving proves difficult, would students consider altering their budget? If so, how? If not, why not? Would they change the goal instead? If so, how? If not, why not?

Personal Success Portfolio

Lead this activity using one of suggestions given on pages 9 and 10.

Additional materials that you may wish students to include in their Personal Success Portfolio for Chapter 8 include:

- a list of the student's top three long-term goals along with a detailed explanation of how much time and money each one will require
- a short research report on the benefits of adequate sleep, along with an action plan for getting more and better sleep
- a review of an article or Web site that offers a specific approach to getting organized
- a list of simple questions the student can ask him- or herself to determine whether something is important and urgent (such as, "Does this relate to my goals?" or "Does this have to be done right now?")
- an article from a personal finance magazine that offers advice the student finds useful

ADDITIONAL RESOURCES

The following books and periodicals offer information on various aspects of time and money management, including procrastination, budgeting, and personal organization.

Books

Burka, Jane B., and Lenora M. Yuen. *Procrastination: Why You Do It, What to Do About It*. Reading, MA: Addison-Wesley, 1984.

Carlson, Richard and Joseph Bailey. *Slowing Down to the Speed of Life: How To Create A More Peaceful, Simpler Life From the Inside Out*. New York: HarperCollins, 1998.

Covey, Stephen R. *First Things First*. New York: Simon & Schuster, 1994.

Covey, Stephen R. *The Seven Habits of Highly Effective People: Restoring the Character Ethic*. New York; Simon & Schuster, 1989.

Dacyczyn, Amy. *The Complete Tightwad Gazette*. New York: Random House, 1999.

Ellis, Dave. *Creating Your Future: Five Steps to the Life of Your Dreams*. Boston: Houghton Miffin, 1998.

Emmett, Rita. *The Procrastinator's Handbook: Mastering the Art of Doing It Now*. New York: Walker & Company, 2000.

Fiore, Neil. *The Now Habit*. New York: Jeremy P. Tarcher, 1989.

Gleeson, Kerry. *The Personal Efficiency Program: How to Get Organized to Do More Work in Less Time*. 2nd ed. Hoboken, NJ: John Wiley and Sons, 2000.

Glickman, Marshall. *The Mindful Money Guide: Creating Harmony Between Your Values and Your Finances*. New York: Ballantine Books, 1999.

Keyes, Ralph. *Timelock: How Life Got So Hectic and What You Can Do About It*. New York: HarperCollins, 1991.

Lakein, Alan. *How to Get Control of Your Time and Your Life*. 2nd ed. New York: New American Library, 1996.

Lawrence, Judy. *The Budget Kit: The Common Cents Money Management Workbook*. Chicago: Dearborn Trade Publishing, 2000.

Morgenstern, Julie. *Time Management from the Inside Out: The Foolproof System for Taking Control of Your Schedule and Your Life*. New York: Henry Holt, 2000.

Orman, Suze. *Nine Steps to Financial Freedom: Practical and Spiritual Steps So You Can Stop Worrying*. New York: Crown Publishing, 2000.

Robinson, Marc. *Essential Finance Guide*. New York: DK Publishing, 2001.

Sapadin, Linda. *It's About Time! The Six Styles of Procrastination and How to Overcome Them*. New York: Penguin, 1996.

Scharf-Hunt, Diana, and Pam Hait. *Studying Smart: Time Management for College Students*. New York: HarperPerennial, 1990.

Tracy, Brian. *Eat That Frog! 21 Great Ways to Stop Procrastinating and Get More Done in Less Time*. San Francisco: Berrett-Koehler, 2001.

Winston, Stephanie. *Getting Organized: The Easy Way to Put Your Life in Order*. New York: W.W. Norton, 1978.

Periodicals

Bloomberg Personal Finance

Money

Kiplinger's Personal Finance

Simple Living Oasis

Smart Money

The Wall Street Journal

Communication and Relationships

OVERVIEW

Throughout this book students have been learning about themselves and what they want out of life. In this final chapter they read about how to improve their relationships with others. In Section 9.1 they focus on interpersonal communication. They explore the communication process, learn how to become effective speakers and active listeners, and examine how to use their communication skills to resolve conflicts with others. In Section 9.2 they explore the nature of relationships, learning how they form and develop and what skills they can use to strengthen them.

OBJECTIVES

After they complete this chapter, students should be able to:

■ Describe the six elements of communication.

■ Summarize the forms and functions of nonverbal communication.

■ List several skills necessary for effective speaking and active listening.

■ Explain the relationship between stereotypes, prejudice, and empathy.

■ Define intimacy and explain how to develop it in a relationship.

■ Cite the characteristics of satisfying intimate relationships.

■ Explain how to handle conflict effectively.

OUTLINE

Chapter Topics

EFFECTIVE COMMUNICATION
A Look at Communication
       Interpersonal Communication
       Elements of Communication
       Communication Breakdown
Nonverbal Communication
       Functions and Forms of Nonverbal Communication
       Interpreting Nonverbal Cues
Improving Your Communication Skills
       Becoming an Effective Speaker
       Becoming an Active Listener

HEALTHY RELATIONSHIPS
A Look at Relationships
       Group Relationships
       Conformity and Diversity
       Rejecting Stereotypes and Prejudice
       Developing Empathy
Interpersonal Relationships
       Intimacy and Self-Disclosure
       Successful Intimate Relationships
       Handling Relationship Conflict

Chapter Activities

EXERCISE 9.1 **How Much Do You Know About Communication?** (pp. 350–351)
EXERCISE 9.2 **Analyzing Communication** (pp. 355–356)
EXERCISE 9.3 **Body Language Log** (pp. 362–363)
EXERCISE 9.4 **Giving Feedback** (pp. 368–369)
EXERCISE 9.5 **Your Close Relationships** (pp. 380–381)

Personal Journal 9.1 **"I" Statements** (p. 365)
Personal Journal 9.2 **Understanding Diversity** (p. 373)
Personal Journal 9.3 **Circles of Yourself** (p. 375)
Personal Journal 9.4 **Dealing With Conflict** (p. 385)

Chapter Features

Applying Psychology **GENDER AND STRESS** (p. 359)
PROFESSIONAL DEVELOPMENT **Getting Your Résumé Right** (p. 367)
INTERNET ACTION **E-Mail Empathy** (p. 379)

FOCUS

Introducing the Chapter

Have students reread the beginning of Chapter 1, particularly the section entitled "Ingredients of Success." Ask a volunteer to explain how positive relationships affect success. ("No one ever succeeds without the help, ideas, and emotional support of others. The happiest and most fulfilled people are usually those who make time for other people in their lives instead of focusing all their energy on piling up accomplishments.") Explain that in this chapter students will read about how to cultivate positive relationships. Ask students what attributes they think a "positive" relationship has. Make a list and keep it for reference for the Chapter 9 Culminating Activity.

Real-Life Success Story "How Do I Stand Up for Myself?"

(p. 346)

Ask a volunteer to read the Real-Life Success Story. Then ask the following questions: Is Jose handling the situation the right way by being silent, or would it be a better idea for him to bring up the situation with his boss? Why? Does Jose have any other options in this situation? Ask students to suggest ways he could handle his situation. Should he go along with what his coworkers say, or should he do something different? Also, ask for volunteers to describe experiences from their own lives that mirror Jose's. For example, have any of the students had experience with a difficult, highly critical supervisor? What did they do in the situation, and was it effective?

Opening Quote (p. 347)

"The most important single ingredient in the formula of success is knowing how to get along with people."

Write the quote on the board or make a transparency of it using the reproducible master on page 303. Ask students what they think the statement means. What exactly does it mean to "get along with people"? Do they agree that knowing how to get along with people is the most important ingredient of success? Why does Roosevelt say "*knowing how* to get along with people" rather than simply "getting along with people"?

Ask students to think about people who they feel are good at getting along with others. Ask, "What qualities do these people have that make them easy to be around?" As a class, create a list of these qualities and write them on the board.

INSTRUCT

Teaching Tips

The following topics are discussed in this chapter. You may want to expand on them in large or small class groups.

A Look at Communication (pp. 348–356)
Have students work in pairs to create two role-plays. The first role-play should illustrate the six elements of communication: sender, message, receiver, channel, feedback, and context. The second role-play should demonstrate how one of the types of barriers (physical, emotional, or language and cultural) interferes with the communication process.

Nonverbal Communication (pp. 357–363)
Begin by having students tell you what you are trying to convey when you demonstrate the following actions: shrugging your shoulders and turning your palms upward (I don't know); smiling and waving (hi, good to see you); raising and shaking your fists (anger about something). Explain that these were all nonverbal signals, and ask students what nonverbal means. Tell them that the definition of *verbal* is "of or associated with words" and that *nonverbal*, therefore, means "without words." Finally, write the definition of *nonverbal communication* on the board (the process of giving or exchanging information without words).

Ask students to cite specific examples. Elicit examples of nonverbal cues besides body language, such as style of dress, tone and pitch of voice, and even smell.

Improving Your Communication Skills
(pp. 363–369)
Have students work together in small groups. Ask them to think about what makes a person an effective speaker or a good listener. Have each group make two lists: one listing the characteristics of an effective speaker, and the other listing the characteristics of an active listener. After about 10 minutes, come back together again as a class and allow groups to share their lists. Ask students to describe people they know who are effective speakers and/or active listeners. Are these people good at getting along with others?

A Look at Relationships (pp. 370–377)
Write the definition of *group* on the board (a set of people, usually three or more, who influence each other) and ask students to make a list of every group to which they belong. Their groups could include a family group, a school or student body, an ethnic group, a religious group, a social club, or a work group. Then ask, "What are some of the benefits people receive from belonging to a group? What are some problems that come with belonging to a group?" Have students cite specifics from their own experience. As a class, discuss their answers.

Interpersonal Relationships
(pp. 378–386)
Have students work in pairs to write a role-play that describes the resolution of a conflict between two friends, family members, or coworkers. Students' role-plays should include a clear explanation of the origin and nature of the conflict. Allow students to perform their role-plays, then discuss what actions they took to help resolve the conflict. Would these strategies be effective in real life? Why or why not?

In-Chapter Answers and Notes

EXERCISE 9.1

How Much Do You Know About Communication? (pp. 350–351)
A–B. Responses will vary, but students will probably be surprised that all of the statements are true.

C. Students' answers will vary but should recognize that showing respect is reflected in other good communication strategies, such as being an attentive listener and responding with positive comments.

D. Students' responses will vary but should be at least somewhat consistent with their score in question A.

FIGURE 9.1

Elements of Communication (p. 352)
Answers will vary but could mention mass communication, such as television, radio, and advertising. Many written communications, such as memos or letters, and sometimes e-mail, also prevent immediate feedback.

EXERCISE 9.2

Analyzing Communication
(pp. 355–356)
A. Students' observations will vary but should demonstrate an understanding of the six elements of communication, the difference between verbal and nonverbal communication, and the possible effects of the three barriers.

B. Students' responses will vary as in question A, above.

Sample Answers

A. Observe a conversation between two people you've never met. Note all six elements of communication: the identity or role of the sender, the content of the message, the channel of the message, the identity or role of the receiver, the content of the feedback, and the context of the conversation.

Sender: father
Message: Yelling: "You were supposed to call me if your plane was going to be late!"
Channel: face-to-face conversation
Receiver: teenage daughter
Feedback: Pouting, acknowledgement, explanation: "I couldn't get through."
Context: airport gate at midnight

Could you figure out the relationship between the sender and the receiver? If so, how? If not, why not? (Consider both verbal and nonverbal information.) The receiver referred to the sender as "dad," and their body language showed that they were on intimate terms.

Did any physical, emotional, or cultural barriers affect the conversation? Explain.
Yes. The father was so distressed that he was not listening to his daughter's reasons for not calling (the flight was delayed in progress and she could not use her cell phone on the plane). It was also very noisy by the gate. The father might have been less emotional and accusatory if he had realized that he was talking so loudly.

B.   Now describe the same elements for a conversation in which you were involved.

Sender: coworker
Message: "You're not going to believe this! They just moved our presentation up by an hour and I'm worried I might not have enough time to finish. Do you possibly have some time this morning to help me assemble the folders? I'm really freaking out."
Channel: phone conversation
Receiver: myself
Feedback: concern, assent, humor
Context: my desk, 8:30 AM

What was the relationship between you and the other person, and how do you think it influenced the conversation? For example, how did it affect the words you chose, your tone of voice, and so on? We were coworkers and that person was my superior, but we had a good relationship. I knew he had a tendency to get stressed out easily, so I tried to joke a little bit to calm him down.

Did any physical, emotional, or cultural barriers affect the conversation? Explain.
Since we weren't face-to-face, I couldn't

immediately see what he needed to be done, but I could tell from the tone of his voice how anxious he was, so I agreed to do it.

Exploring Further

Ask students to recall a conversation or part of a conversation that they had while experiencing a strong negative emotion such as anger, guilt, shame, distress, or sadness. Then ask them to consider the following questions: How did your emotions affect what you said and how you said it? How did your emotions affect the way you reacted to the other person's words? Ask students to write a short paragraph answering these questions, then discuss students' answers as a class. If desired, ask students to contrast these experiences with similar experiences involving a strong positive emotion.

Applying Psychology

GENDER AND STRESS (p. 359)
Answers will vary but could suggest that because women try to "befriend" others, they may also resolve conflict more readily. Other answers might suggest that, because of this same tendency, women might be more likely to sacrifice their own needs in order to resolve a conflict harmoniously.

Exploring Further

Ask students to research the concepts of "tend and befriend" and "fight or flight." (The tend-and-befriend response involves seeking social support from others, the fight-or-flight response involves withdrawing from others or provoking conflict with them.) Present students with an example of a stressful situation and ask them which response they would be more likely to use, and why. Is one of these responses to stress better than the other? Why or why not?

FIGURE 9.2

Influences on Nonverbal Communication (p. 361)

Answers will vary but should show an understanding of the fact that women are socialized to be less assertive and more submissive than men, which is reflected in their nonverbal behavior.

EXERCISE 9.3

Body Language Log (pp. 362–363)

A-D. Students' observations will vary but should reflect an understanding of how people use body language to express themselves and how the meaning of nonverbal signals is affected by cultural differences, gender differences, and individual differences.

Exploring Further

Arrange for a video camera and player to be available to the class during an earlier part of the course. Videotape (or ask a class member to videotape) a group discussion or even a one-on-one discussion. Try to be as unobtrusive as possible so that people react not to the camera, but to one another. When you get to this section of the course, play the tape back for the class without sound. Ask each student to observe him- or herself using the same criteria used in Exercise 9.3. Next, play the tape a second time, asking students to observe and make notes on another individual. Finally, play the tape a third time, with sound. Have students discuss their observations and the difference that sound made to their interpretations, if any. (Note: If it is not possible to videotape the class, bring in a recording of a television show or film and perform the second and third parts of the exercise, asking students to concentrate on the nonverbal behavior of one individual, first without and then with sound.)

Personal Journal 9.1

"I" Statements (p. 365)

"I" statements will vary but should be worded as, "I feel…about…because…" or "I feel… when you…because…."

Sample Answers

Change each of the following "you" statements into an "I" statement.

You always interrupt when I'm talking.
I feel unhappy when you interrupt me, because I feel that you are being disrespectful.
You just have to criticize, don't you.
I feel humiliated when you criticize me, because I feel like you don't think very much of me.
You're late again, as usual.
I feel unhappy about your being late so often, because I think you don't value my time.
You need to help out more around the house.
I feel frustrated when you don't help around the house, because it seems like you don't want to share responsibility for taking care of our home.
You get on my nerves when you act so babyish.
I feel annoyed when you pout if you don't get your way, because I feel like you are trying to manipulate me.

PROFESSIONAL DEVELOPMENT

Getting Your Résumé Right (p. 367)

Answers will vary but should recognize that the people who read résumés are very busy and want to view the qualifications of the candidates as quickly as possible.

Exploring Further

Ask students to draft an up-to-date, one-page résumé using the guidelines presented in the feature. Request that students bring a copy of their résumé to class. Have students pass their résumés to their neighbor on the right or left. Then group students into teams and instruct them to review all the résumés they have and to select the one that demonstrates the strongest communication skills. After this is done, regroup as a class and ask students to discuss features of the résumés they liked the best. As a class, make a list of strategies for demonstrating good communication skills on a résumé. (Note: Emphasize that this activity is about helping everyone write the best possible résumé, not about criticizing or finding fault with any particular résumé. By the time the class has reached Chapter 9, students should have developed respect and understanding for one another. If the class is not as cohesive as you might wish, you could instruct students to omit their names on their résumés.)

EXERCISE 9.4

Giving Feedback (pp. 368–369)
Students' responses will vary but should include paraphrasing and reflecting in statements worded as, "It sounds like you feel (emotional content of the message) because (factual content of the message)." For example, the first active listening response could be: "It sounds like you feel that Mr. Havivi doesn't trust you because he watches you so closely when you're doing the receipts."

Exploring Further

This in-class activity is designed to help students review their knowledge of active listening skills. Make a transparency of the reproducible master on page 308, "Listening Do's and Don'ts." Ask students to work in pairs or small teams to decide whether each item on this list represents a good listening practice or a poor listening practice. Check the answers together as a class. If you wish, make a transparency of the reproducible master on page 309, which contains the correct answers.

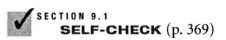

1. Communication is the process of giving or exchanging messages.
2. The three barriers to good communication are physical barriers, emotional barriers, and language and cultural barriers.
4. EAR stands for the three active listening skills of encouraging, attending, and responding.

Personal Journal 9.2

Understanding Diversity (p. 373)
Responses will vary, but this activity should help students recognize their personal experience with diversity.

Exploring Further

Ask students to describe a situation in which social or cultural diversity might lead to conflicts. For example, how might misunderstandings arise between students who are of different cultures or subcultures (such as between Caucasian American students and African American students, or between Mexican students and Mexican American students)? How might misunderstandings arise when members of one culture (such as the dominant Caucasian American culture) look at the music or lyrics produced by members of another culture (such as hip-hop culture)?

Personal Journal 9.3

Circles of Yourself (p. 375)
Students' responses will vary, but could mention religious, ethnic, racial, cultural, or national groups, as well as groups that reflect physical or mental characteristics or personal interests.

INTERNET ACTION

E-Mail Empathy (p. 379)

Answers will vary but could include that written communication is usually more formal than oral communication and that written communication lacks the nonverbal cues that are present in oral communication.

EXERCISE 9.5

Your Close Relationships (pp. 380–381)

A-D. Students' responses will vary but should demonstrate a serious reflection on the relationships listed.

Sample Answers

A. Write down the names of up to six people with whom you have close relationships, and describe their relationship to you (e.g., wife, father, friend). Then describe what important thoughts and feelings you share with one another and what important thoughts and feelings you don't share (or haven't yet shared) with one another.

Name/Relationship
mother
We Share
everyday worries, joys
We Don't Share
deeper worries

Name/Relationship
boyfriend
We Share
thoughts about our lives and our future
We Don't Share
our feelings about having children

Name/Relationship
best friend
We Share
innermost thoughts
We Don't Share
how we feel about our other friends

Name/Relationship
older brother

We Share
family concerns
We Don't Share
discussions on ideas or romantic relationships

B. Are you satisfied with the level of intimacy in your relationships? Why or why not?

I am pretty happy with the intimacy in most of my relationships, but I would like to be able to talk about more subjects with my brother.

C. Would you like to share more with any of the people on your list? If so, what would you want to share and why? If not, why not?

I would probably share most with my best friend. I am very close to my mother, but I don't like to worry her by talking too much about my own problems. There are also some things that my brother and boyfriend wouldn't understand or be sensitive to, such as how I feel about my weight and physical appearance. I wish I could talk to them about these kinds of topics, but this isn't realistic.

D. Very few people reveal everything of themselves to another person. Are there any private thoughts or feelings that you would never share with anyone? Explain.

Yes. I think there are some thoughts which would only hurt or offend some people, and no good would be served by expressing those thoughts.

FIGURE 9.3

The Johari Window (p. 382)

Students' responses may vary, but most students will probably say that the Open Pane contains the most information because it is information known to both yourself and others.

Exploring Further

Make a transparency of Figure 9.3 using the reproducible master on page 307. Display the figure and ask students what they think the arrows (one pointing down and one pointing to the right) mean. Explain that these arrows indicate ways of expanding the amount of information contained in the open self. The open self contains information about a person that he or she knows about him- or herself and that he or she has no reason to hide from others. By self-disclosing (vertical arrow), a person increases the amount of information that others know about him or her. By soliciting feedback (horizontal arrow), a person increases the amount of information he or she knows about him- or herself. Ask students to think of questions they could ask others to expand their knowledge about themselves. Are there any areas of their lives in which they would rather *not* become more self-aware? Why or why not?

Dealing With Conflict (p. 385)

Students' responses will vary but may refer to some of the conflict-resolution strategies mentioned in the text.

SECTION 9.2
SELF-CHECK (p. 386)

1. Conformity is a change in behavior caused by a desire to follow the norms of a group.

2. A stereotype is a set of oversimplified *beliefs* about the attributes of a group of people. Prejudice is a negative *feeling* or attitude toward a group of people.

3. Four sources of conflict are needs, values, emotions, and power.

Additional Activities

These additional activities are exclusive to this Instructor's Resource Manual. They are designed to meet the special needs of your students. The activities can be used as in-class activities or as take-home assignments. They can be assigned to individual students, pairs of students, or groups of students.

Critical Thinking

SELF-DISCLOSURE Self-disclosure, the communication of one's real thoughts, desires, and feelings, is required for intimacy to develop in a relationship. Yet many people do not self-disclose, or are afraid to do so. Ask

students why this might be the case. Why does self-disclosure involve risk? Ask students to brainstorm a list of the possible negative outcomes of self-disclosure. Explain that major risks of self-disclosure are indifference, rejection, loss of control of a situation or person, and betrayal. In what specific situations might self-disclosure lead to a negative outcome? Why? Encourage students to use examples from their personal experience.

CONFORMITY One of the most famous studies in the history of psychology was conducted by Solomon Asch in the 1950s. Participants in Asch's experiments were shown one card with three lines of varying lengths (one short, one medium, and one long) and a second card that had a single line matching one of the other three in length (in other words, one line that was either short, medium, or long). Participants were asked to identify the line on the first card that matched the line on the second card. When respondents were interviewed alone, they gave the correct answer 99 percent of the time. This changed when they were interviewed in groups of seven. When Asch hired six people in each group to lie and give the wrong answer, he discovered that the seventh (unwitting) person in the group, after hearing the six wrong answers, often conformed and gave the wrong answer as well. On average, participants conformed 37 percent of the time.

Give students a brief summary of Asch's study, then ask them to explain why a person might conform in this situation. Explain that people sometimes conform to gain social acceptance and sometimes conform because they believe others know better. Do students believe they would conform in such a situation? What does this study tell them about the power of group norms?

UNCOVERING STEREOTYPES Visit www.tolerance.org, an educational Web project of the Southern Poverty Law Center. Locate the "Writing for Change" activities and print the worksheet titled "Uncovering

Impressions." Give students five minutes to complete each of the ten sentences in their own words, using the first thought that comes to mind. (Emphasize that this exercise is about examining stereotypes, not judging the groups mentioned in the exercise or singling out students who have stereotypes.) For each of the ten statements, ask a volunteer to reveal what he or she wrote. What stereotypes—positive or negative—do students' answers reveal? What is the likely origin of these stereotypes? Ask students to think about what other stereotypes they might have and to try to pinpoint the origin of these beliefs. Do students believe that it is possible to be entirely free of stereotypes? Why or why not? As a follow-up homework assignment, ask students to write a paragraph or more about how this exercise made them reexamine their stereotypes.

CHALLENGING ASSUMPTIONS This activity ties in to the previous activity, "Uncovering Stereotypes." Go to **www.tolerance.org** and print out the student activity worksheet titled "Challenging Your Assumptions." Ask students to identify the assumptions inherent in each statement regarding age, ability, appearance, ethnicity, gender, race, religion, sexual orientation, and socioeconomic power or status. (For example, the sentence "We need more manpower" reflects the norm that men are effective and powerful.) Then ask students to rewrite each sentence to remove the unjustified assumption.

Application

USING NONVERBAL COMMUNICATION
Have students divide into pairs. (If there is an uneven number of students, have one student complete the activity with you.) Each student should try to convey one of the following emotions, without first letting their partner know which one, by reciting the first seven letters of the alphabet.

love	fear
happiness	jealousy
hate	disappointment
pride	curiosity
sadness	pleasure
sympathy	disgust
anger	sarcasm
nervousness	urgency

The first student should ask his or her partner to close his or her eyes. The speaker should communicate the emotion through speed, pitch, volume, and tone. If the partner is unable to identify the emotion, have the students discuss what voice or listening elements might have helped. Variation for use with hearing impaired students: Rather than asking students to convey emotions using vocal aspects, ask them to use facial expressions, posture, and gestures.

COMMUNICATION AND INTERVIEW SUCCESS Revisit the Exploring Further activity suggested for the Professional Development feature "Image Consulting" on page 149 in Chapter 4. Did students mention good communication skills as an important element of a positive first impression? Ask students to think again about what would make a good impression on a job interviewer. Ask them to work in small groups and to make two lists: one of communication habits that would make a positive impression on an interviewer and the other of communication habits that would make a negative impression. Reunite the class and ask students to share their ideas. Display a transparency of the reproducible master on page 310, "Communication and Interview Success," and add any ideas that are not listed here. Emphasize to students that the communication skills required for interview success are the same skills required for career success—interviewers are looking for candidates who have the skills to do well on the job. If desired, ask students to create interview role-plays demonstrating good (and bad) communication habits.

Internet Activities

NONVERBAL COMMUNICATION AND ETHNICITY The nonverbal communication styles of Caucasian North Americans often differ from that those of African Americans, Latinos, Asian Americans, and Native Americans. For example, some African Americans and Latinos avoid making eye contact with the person to whom they are speaking, especially if this person is in a position of authority. Some Caucasian Americans take this as a sign of indifference or rudeness, but in fact this behavior simply represents a cultural difference in nonverbal communication. Explain these facts to students and ask them to conduct online research on the nonverbal behavior of a particular ethnic group in North America. For example, how does the nonverbal communication behavior of Native Americans differ from that of the dominant Caucasian culture? What misunderstandings or awkward situations might this create? Ask students to share the highlights of their research with the class. If desired, ask them to present short role-plays illustrating their findings.

RELATIONSHIP ADVICE The Internet is full of Web sites and articles offering advice on relationships, "rules" for good relationships, relationship self-quizzes, and other similar materials. Ask students to browse the World Wide Web and to select one relationship quiz and one relationship advice article. Students should take the quiz and read the article and then summarize the content. Do students think that the quiz and/or article have genuine, meaningful advice to offer? Why or why not? What are the possible dangers of seeking advice on serious topics on the Internet? How can students be sure that the advice they are receiving comes from a reputable source?

ASSESS

Review and Activities Answers

Review Questions (p. 388)

1. Emotions can create barriers to communication when they make it hard to pay attention to what someone is trying to communicate or when they make it hard to formulate a clear message.

2. Cultural awareness is the ability to recognize the ways cultures differ and how these differences affect cross-cultural interactions.

3. Examples will vary but might include some of the following: crossed arms can reflect defensiveness; hands on hips can show aggressiveness; looking down or away can demonstrate self-consciousness or guilt; and a smile, eye contact, upright posture, and a firm handshake can reflect self-confidence.

4. Paraphrasing and reflecting are both part of the active listening skill of responding. However, paraphrasing is restating the factual content of the message, while reflecting is restating the emotional content of the message.

5. Positive stereotypes can put pressure on members of a group to fit that stereotype. If they can't or don't want to conform, they may face criticism and develop low self-esteem. Positive stereotypes may also mask negative feelings about a group.

6. Self-disclosure is communicating your real thoughts, desires, and feelings. It is important in relationships because it demonstrates emotional openness and lets the other person know that you care about the relationship.

Critical Thinking (p. 388)

7. Answers will vary but should recognize that when we feel love and kindness toward

others, we have the open, empathetic attitude necessary to establish meaningful connections with other human beings. This helps to satisfy our need for relatedness, boosts our self-esteem, and provides a source of understanding and support. This, in turn, helps us develop inner happiness and peace.

8. Answers will vary but should recognize that people with large vocabularies have the tools to express their thoughts and feelings more effectively than people with smaller vocabularies do.

Application (p. 388)

9. Answers will vary. Allow students to demonstrate to the class some of the more unusual (but appropriate) displays of non-verbal communication they witnessed.

10. Answers will vary. Allow time for students to discuss their findings in small groups.

Internet Activities (p. 389)

11. Answers will vary. Two sources are John Gray's book *Men Are from Mars, Women Are from Venus* and Deborah Tannen's book *You Just Don't Understand.*

12. Answers will vary, but values featured include ambition, appreciation, civility, commitment, compassion, courage, and dependability.

Real-Life Success Story "How Do I Stand Up for Myself?" (p. 389)

Letters will vary but should include suggestions for specific "I" statements, an explanation of why assertiveness is important and necessary for self-esteem, and a suggestion to use one or more of the strategies for resolving conflict (move away from confrontation, listen actively, state your needs, generate options for resolving the conflict, be flexible and open-minded, and commit to a solution).

CLOSE

Culminating Activity

Remind students of the list of attributes of a positive relationship that they made at the beginning of the chapter (see "Introducing the Chapter" on page 161.) Review the list. Now that students have completed the chapter, ask whether they have anything to add (or subtract) from the list. Can the class agree on the two or three attributes that are most important in a satisfying relationship (romantic or otherwise)? Ask students how each attribute relates to communication.

To extend the activity, have students complete the activity sheet on page 311, "Improving Relationships Through Communication," and discuss their answers in class.

Personal Success Portfolio

Lead this activity using one of the suggestions given on pages 9 and 10.

Additional materials that you may wish students to include in their Personal Success Portfolio for Chapter 9 include:

- a paragraph describing the two or three communication skills the student most needs or wants to develop, and why
- an action plan for enlarging the student's vocabulary
- a review of a best-selling book on communication and/or relationships
- a brief report about nonverbal communication behavior in another culture
- an action plan for broadening the student's cultural awareness; the plan might include a bibliography, a listing of cultural activities, and a list of people the student will try to get to know better
- documentation of a person the student finds to be an effective speaker, including a description of the person's specific communication skills and practices and ways the student can use these in his or her own communication

ADDITIONAL RESOURCES

The following books and periodicals offer information on interpersonal communication, stereotypes and prejudices, empathy, interpersonal interaction, and conflict resolution.

Books

Adler, Ronald B. and Neil Towne. *Looking Out, Looking In: An Introduction to Interpersonal Communication.* 10th ed. New York: Holt, Rinehart, and Winston, 2002.

Adler, Ronald, Laurence B. Rosenfeld, and Neil Towne. *Interplay: the Process of Interpersonal Communication.* 5th ed. Ft. Worth: Harcourt Brace Jovanovich, 1992.

Blaine, Bruce Evan. *The Psychology of Diversity: Perceiving and Experiencing Social America.* New York: McGraw-Hill Higher Education, 2000.

Ciaramicoli, A. P., and Ketcham, K. *The Power of Empathy: A Practical Guide to Creating Intimacy, Self-Understanding, and Lasting Love in Your Life.* New York: E. P. Dutton, 2000.

Dana, Daniel. *Conflict Resolution.* New York: McGraw-Hill, 2000.

Fisher, Bruce and Nina Hart. *Loving Choices: An Experience in Growing Relationships.* 2nd ed. Atascadero, CA: Impact Publishers, 2000.

Gamble, Teri Kwal and Michael Gamble. *Communication Works.* 7th ed. New York: McGraw-Hill/Irwin, 2002.

Garner, Alan. *Conversationally Speaking: Tested New Ways to Increase Your Personal and Social Effectiveness.* 3rd ed. New York: McGraw-Hill, 1997.

Gilbert, Roberta M. *Extraordinary Relationships: A New Way of Thinking About Human Interactions.* Hoboken, NJ: John Wiley and Sons, 1992.

Hanna, Sharon L. *Person to Person: Positive Relationships Don't Just Happen.* 4th ed. Englewood Cliffs, NJ: Prentice Hall, 2002.

Jones, James M. *Prejudice and Racism.* 2nd ed. New York: McGraw-Hill Higher Education, 1997.

LeCompte, Andrew. *Creating Harmonious Relationships: A Practical Guide to the Power of True Empathy.* Portsmouth, NH: Atlantic Books, 2000.

Patterson, Kerry, Joseph Grenny, Ron McMillan, and Al Switzler. *Crucial Conversations: Tools for Talking When Stakes are High.* New York: McGraw-Hill, 2002.

Plous, Scott, ed. *Understanding Prejudice and Discrimination.* New York: McGraw-Hill Higher Education, 2003.

Rosenberg, Marshall B. *Nonviolent Communication: A Language of Compassion.* Encinitas, CA: PuddleDancer Press, 1999.

Tannen, Deborah. *That's Not What I Meant! How Conversational Style Makes or Breaks Your Relations With Others.* New York: Ballantine Books, 1986.

Tannen, Deborah. *You Just Don't Understand: Men and Women in Conversation.* New York: Quill, 2001.

Tatum, Beverly. *Why Are All the Black Kids Sitting Together in the Cafeteria?* Cambridge, MA: Perseus, 1997.

Periodicals

American Communication Journal   *Language*

Journal of Nonverbal Behavior   *Psychology Today*

PART 3
TESTS AND ANSWER KEYS

CHAPTER 1 QUIZ

A. MATCHING

Match each definition in the left column with the correct term in the right column. Write the letter of the term in the space provided.

_____ 1. The sense of being a unique, conscious being.

_____ 2. Anything that people think, feel, or do.

_____ 3. A set of norms that define how males and females are supposed to behave.

_____ 4. How a person chooses to define him- or herself to the world.

_____ 5. Lifetime fulfillment that comes from creating a sense of meaning in your work and personal life.

_____ 6. Mental processing of information in any form.

_____ 7. The scientific study of human behavior.

_____ 8. A subjective feeling that is accompanied by physical and behavioral changes.

_____ 9. The behaviors, ideas, attitudes, and traditions shared by a large social group and transmitted from one generation to the next.

_____ 10. A state of well-being that comes from having a positive evaluation of your life.

a. behavior
b. cognition
c. culture
d. emotion
e. gender role
f. happiness
g. identity
h. psychology
i. self
j. success

B. SHORT ANSWER

Write a paragraph in response to one of the following questions.

11a. What are the ingredients of lifelong success? How do they contribute to a person's success in life?

11b. What does it mean to have a complex self-image? Is it desirable to have a complex self-image? Explain your answer.

_____
_____
_____
_____
_____
_____

CHAPTER ① T E S T

A. COMPLETION

Complete the following sentences using the correct term from the list below.

success	role model	social role
self-image	self-direction	nervous system
happiness	self-presentation	psychology
identity		

1. Humans are biological beings, with a complex _____ that regulates thoughts, feelings, and actions.

2. A _____ is a person who has the qualities you would like to have.

3. Our _____ defines how we are supposed to act in a social position or setting.

4. In this book, _____ means a lifetime of personal fulfillment that comes from creating a sense of meaning in your work and life.

5. How we choose to define ourselves to the world makes up our

   _____.

6. _____ is one of the ingredients of success and is the ability to set a well-defined goal and work toward it.

7. Altering our behavior to make a good impression on others is known as

   _____.

8. The word _____ comes from two Greek words meaning "mind" or "self" and "science" or "study."

9. _____ is the natural experience of winning your self-respect and the respect of others.

10. Our _____ is all the beliefs we have about ourselves.

B. MULTIPLE CHOICE

Identify the letter of the choice that best completes the statement or answers the question.

11. All of the following have little effect on happiness EXCEPT _____.
   a. being married
   c. getting to know yourself better
   b. owning a BMW
   d. having a Ph.D.

12. _____ is the ability to use your knowledge and experience to make sound decisions.
- **a.** Courage
- **b.** Wisdom
- **c.** Optimism
- **d.** Work ethic

13. A major goal of psychology is to _____ human behavior. ✓
- **a.** describe
- **b.** explain
- **c.** change
- **d.** all of the above

14. The part of the brain that stores the emotions and sensations of which we are not quite aware is called the _____.
- **a.** nervous system
- **b.** conscious mind
- **c.** subconscious mind
- **d.** paraconscious mind

15. Cognition refers to the functions of processing information and includes activities such as _____.
- **a.** loving
- **b.** recognizing
- **c.** being angry
- **d.** all of the above

16. Your _____ is the sum of all the social roles you play and the social groups to which you belong.
- **a.** collective identity
- **b.** familial identity
- **c.** individual identity
- **d.** relational identity

17. Your _____ is made up of the personal characteristics that distinguish you from other people.
- **a.** collective identity
- **b.** familial identity
- **c.** individual identity
- **d.** relational identity

18. Your _____ refers to how you identify yourself in relation to the important people in your life, such as your parents, siblings, close friends, children, and partner.
- **a.** collective identity
- **b.** familial identity
- **c.** individual identity
- **d.** relational identity

19. Culture consists of the _____ shared by a large social group and transmitted from one generation to the next.
- **a.** behaviors
- **b.** ideas
- **c.** traditions
- **d.** all of the above

20. As children grow up and develop an identity, they are powerfully affected by _____, which tell them how males and females are supposed to behave.
- **a.** television commercials
- **b.** gender roles
- **c.** social roles
- **d.** cultural roles

C. SHORT ANSWER

Write a paragraph in response to each of the following questions.

21. Do you agree with this statement? "Happiness should not be confused with indulging yourself or seeking pleasure." Give your reasons.

_____

_____

_____

_____

_____

_____

_____

22. Name three positive personal qualities you especially admire in others and explain how they can contribute to personal happiness.

_____

_____

_____

_____

_____

_____

_____

_____

23. Explain the concept of self-image. How can a positive self-image contribute to personal success?

_____

_____

_____

_____

_____

_____

CHAPTER ② QUIZ

A. MATCHING

Match each definition in the left column with the correct term in the right column. Write the letter of the term in the space provided.

_____ 1. The principles you use to define acceptable behavior and decide what is right and wrong.

_____ 2. The ability to do something specific as a result of learning and practice.

_____ 3. The process of paying attention to yourself.

_____ 4. The process of recognizing, identifying, and accepting your emotions.

_____ 5. An understanding of facts or principles in a particular subject area.

_____ 6. A set of abilities that enables you to solve certain types of real-world problems.

_____ 7. The ability to see your strengths and weaknesses clearly and realistically.

_____ 8. The beliefs and principles you choose to live by.

_____ 9. Personal preferences for specific topics or activities.

_____ 10. The tendency to frequently think about and observe yourself.

a. emotional awareness

b. ethics

c. intelligence

d. interests

e. knowledge

f. self-awareness

g. self-consciousness

h. self-honesty

i. skill

j. values

B. SHORT ANSWER

Write a paragraph in response to one of the following questions.

11a. What are the benefits of self-awareness?

11b. Explain the relationship between knowledge, skills, and interests.

_____

_____

_____

_____

_____

_____

_____

CHAPTER ② T E S T

A. COMPLETION

Complete the following sentences using the correct term from the list below.

self-awareness	trait	self-honesty
skill	emotional awareness	knowledge
self-consciousness	intelligence	personality
interests		

1. With _____, you can see both what you have to offer and what you need to do to become the person you want to be.

2. A _____ is an individual's pattern of emotions (feelings), cognitions (thoughts), and actions.

3. Another useful way to understand skills is to see them as ways of using

   _____.

4. _____ is the process of paying attention to yourself—your thoughts, feelings, attitudes, motivations, and actions.

5. _____ involves observing yourself, recognizing a feeling as it happens, and seeing the links between your thoughts, feelings, and actions.

6. A _____ is a disposition to behave in a certain way regardless of the situation.

7. _____ is the ability to do something specific as a result of learning and practice.

8. _____ is an understanding of facts or principles in a particular subject area.

9. Psychologists often distinguish between private and public

   _____.

10. People who ignore their _____ often end up in careers they don't enjoy.

B. MULTIPLE CHOICE

Identify the letter of the choice that best completes the statement or answers the question.

11. _____ is the tendency to frequently think about and observe oneself.
    a. self-awareness
    b. self-absorption
    c. self-consciousness
    d. self-centeredness

12. The tendency to be aware of the aspects of yourself that are on display in social situations is called _____.

    a. self-consciousness

    b. private self-consciousness

    c. public self-consciousness

    d. social self-consciousness

13. Which of the following is NOT a benefit of self-awareness?

    a. It helps you appreciate your unique personality, skills, and interests.

    b. It helps you be swayed by what other people say or do.

    c. It helps you act in accordance with your personal values.

    d. It helps you identify what you are really feeling and thinking inside.

14. Which of the following questions should you ask yourself in order to become more emotionally aware?

    a. Can I put a specific name to this emotion?

    b. How is my body feeling?

    c. What happened right before I started to experience this emotion?

    d. all of the above

15. An aspiration, a hope, or a vision of the future is known as _____.

    a. a dream

    b. having a purpose

    c. having a goal

    d. being a visionary

16. Personality traits include all of the following except:

    a. beautiful

    b. cheerful

    c. loyal

    d. strong-minded

17. Skills are often expressed as _____.

    a. nouns

    b. adjectives

    c. gerunds

    d. verbs

18. A person who is able to follow complex lines of reasoning probably has _____ intelligence.

    a. naturalistic

    b. bodily/kinesthetic

    c. logical/mathematical

    d. verbal/linguistic

19. In order to develop your interpersonal intelligence, you could _____.

    a. attend concerts and musicals

    b. join a volunteer or service group

    c. visit a planetarium or aquarium

    d. all of the above

20. According to John Holland's personality type theory, _____ people are persuaders who enjoy using their verbal skills.

    a. investigative

    b. realistic

    c. conventional

    d. enterprising

C. SHORT ANSWER

Write a paragraph in response to each of the following questions.

21. How does having a dream affect the progress of your life?

_____

_____

_____

_____

_____

_____

_____

_____

22. Why do you think the word "pretty" is not listed in Exercise 2.3 as a personality trait?

_____

_____

_____

_____

_____

_____

_____

_____

23. What is the difference between transferable skills and job-specific skills? Is one type more important that the other? Why or why not?

_____

_____

_____

_____

_____

_____

_____

_____

CHAPTER ❸ Q U I Z

A. MATCHING

Match each definition in the left column with the correct term in the right column. Write the letter of the term in the space provided.

_____ 1. Being flexible and open to change.

_____ 2. Physical and psychological reactions to the demands of life.

_____ 3. Behaviors that help you deal productively with stress.

_____ 4. An outcome you want to achieve and toward which you direct your effort.

_____ 5. A strong feeling of displeasure, resentment, or hostility.

_____ 6. A goal with a specific plan of action to accomplish within the coming year.

_____ 7. Behavior intended to harm or injure a person or object.

_____ 8. Any barrier that prevents you from achieving your goals.

_____ 9. Standing up for your rights without threatening the self-esteem of the other person.

_____ 10. A goal you plan to achieve in the more distant future.

a. adapting

b. aggression

c. anger

d. assertiveness

e. coping skills

f. goal

g. long-term goal

h. obstacle

i. short-term goal

j. stress

B. SHORT ANSWER

Write a paragraph in response to one of the following questions.

11a. What is the first step toward conquering anger, and why is it the first step?

11b. What are goal cards, and how can using them help you reach your goals?

_____

_____

_____

_____

_____

_____

_____

_____

_____

_____

A. COMPLETION

Complete the following sentences with the correct term below.

assertiveness   anger   obstacle
denial   perfectionism   aggression
escape response   adapt   stress
goal

1. It is normal to experience _____ when faced with hassles, the small stressors of everyday life.

2. A(n) _____ is a signpost to the future, telling you which way to go.

3. Rather than resisting change, you can _____, or be flexible and open to change.

4. While _____ is a basic human emotion and a normal response to aggravating situations, it steals our energy and sidetracks us from achieving our goals.

5. A(n) _____ is any barrier that hinders us from achieving our goals.

6. When people respond to stressful situations with _____, they are refusing to accept painful thoughts and feelings.

7. Saying "no" to unreasonable requests and dealing with minor irritations before they become anger-provoking situations are two ways of demonstrating

_____.

8. The belief that you are only worthy as a person if you do everything perfectly is known

as _____.

9. A(n) _____ is a behavior that helps get your mind off your troubles and that can be either positive or negative.

10. Angry behavior intended to harm or injure a person or object is called

_____.

B. MULTIPLE CHOICE

Identify the letter of the choice that best completes the statement or answers the question.

11. The "A" in SMART goals stands for _____.
    a. assertive
    b. aggressive
    c. achievable
    d. artistic

12. Which of the following is NOT an obstacle to achieving a goal?
    a. choosing a goal to please yourself
    b. not really wanting it
    c. going it alone
    d. resisting change

13. Each person has his or her own _____, or causes of stress.
    a. eustress
    b. distresses
    c. internal naggers
    d. stressors

14. Good stress, the kind you feel when playing a sport or going on a date, is called _____.
    a. eustress
    b. distress
    c. stressors
    d. technostress

15. In the ABC model, the "B" stands for _____.
    a. bridge
    b. belief
    c. build
    d. beyond

16. When we experience stress, a response is triggered from the ANS, or the _____.
    a. autoimmune nervous system
    b. automatic nervous system
    c. autonomic nervous system
    d. autonomic nervous stressor

17. Behaviors that help you deal productively with stress are known as _____.
    a. escape responses
    b. relaxation responses
    c. stressor responses
    d. coping skills

18. All of the following can assist with stress management EXCEPT _____.
    a. physical exercise
    b. avoiding responsibilities
    c. engaging in hobbies
    d. keeping your sense of humor

19. Suppressed anger can lead to _____, a way of dealing with emotional conflict by indirectly expressing aggression toward others.
    a. depression
    b. sarcasm
    c. passive-aggression
    d. cynicism

20. Anger can be used constructively to _____.
    a. enhance your self-esteem
    b. enhance aggression tendencies
    c. further your ambitions
    d. further your self-awareness

C. SHORT ANSWER

Write a paragraph in response to each of the following questions.

21. What does the ABC model demonstrate? Explain how understanding this formula can help you deal with stress.

_____

_____

_____

_____

_____

_____

_____

22. Name the three core characteristics of people who handle stress effectively, and describe strategies for developing each one.

_____

_____

_____

_____

_____

_____

_____

23. Now that you have read this chapter, do you agree that setting goals is important? Why or why not?

_____

_____

_____

_____

_____

_____

CHAPTER 4 ❹ Q U I Z

A. MATCHING

Match each definition in the left column with the correct term in the right column. Write the letter of the term in the space provided.

_____ **1.** Recognition and acceptance of what is true about yourself.

_____ **2.** Confidence in and respect for yourself.

_____ **3.** A generalized feeling of worry and nervousness that does not have any specific cause.

_____ **4.** Anything completed through effort, skill, or persistence.

_____ **5.** The person we want to be or feel we ought to be.

_____ **6.** Any remark that contains a judgment, evaluation, or statement of fault.

_____ **7.** A positive self-statement that helps a person think of him- or herself in a positive, caring, and accepting way.

_____ **8.** Words and actions from other people that help a person feel valued, cared for, and connected to a community.

_____ **9.** The belief that you are able to achieve what you want in life.

_____ **10.** The practice of comparing your traits and accomplishments with those of others.

a. accomplishment

b. anxiety

c. affirmation

d. criticism

e. ideal self

f. self-acceptance

g. self-esteem

h. self-expectancy

i. social comparison

j. social support

B. SHORT ANSWER

Write a paragraph in response to one of the following questions.

11a. How can you overcome loneliness?

11b. How does self-acceptance relate to self-esteem?

_____

_____

_____

_____

_____

_____

CHAPTER ❹ T E S T

A. COMPLETION

Complete the following sentences using the correct term from the list below.

self-esteem	inner critic	self-expectancy
avoidance	self-acceptance	criticism
coping	social comparison	probing
label		

1. _____ reduces short-term discomfort, but leaves you with the feeling that you are incapable of dealing with the situation.

2. The voice that bombards you with constant negative self-talk is known as your _____.

3. When you have healthy _____, you appreciate your worth and importance, but you also realize that no one is any more or less worthy or important than you are.

4. When destructive criticism is vague and general, you can use a technique called _____ to get more specific information from the critic.

5. When you enjoy _____, you recognize that you are good enough just the way you are.

6. _____ means facing up to threatening situations, such as a problem in a relationship, a bad habit, or anything else that you are putting off because it is unpleasant or painful.

7. Many of us are addicted to _____, comparing our traits and accomplishments with those of other people.

8. _____ is not about what you really can accomplish but what you think you can accomplish.

9. A(n) _____ is a simplistic statement that we use to define who we are.

10. Some _____ is constructive, designed to help us improve ourselves, but it can also be destructive and cripple our self-esteem.

B. MULTIPLE CHOICE

Identify the letter of the choice that best completes the statement or answers the question.

11. Children and adolescents who receive _____ usually develop healthy self-esteem.
    - **a.** conditional positive regard
    - **b.** conditional negative regard
    - **c.** unconditional positive regard
    - **d.** unconditional negative regard

12. Parents who give their children _____ give love and acceptance on the condition that they behave in a certain way.
    - **a.** conditional positive regard
    - **b.** conditional negative regard
    - **c.** unconditional positive regard
    - **d.** unconditional negative regard

13. Sadness about being alone is usually called _____.
    - **a.** anxiety
    - **b.** loneliness
    - **c.** avoidance
    - **d.** negative self-acceptance

14. Social support comes in two basic forms: _____.
    - **a.** emotional and instrumental
    - **b.** emotional and monetary
    - **c.** conditional and unconditional
    - **d.** conditional and emotional

15. It's not what you can't do that holds you back—it's _____.
    - **a.** people who don't believe in you
    - **b.** a lack of monetary resources
    - **c.** what you *think* you can't do
    - **d.** your personal physical limitations

16. The person you might realistically become in the future is your _____.
    - **a.** ideal self
    - **b.** possible self
    - **c.** real self
    - **d.** composite self

17. The person you want to be or feel you ought to be is known as your _____.
    - **a.** ideal self
    - **b.** possible self
    - **c.** real self
    - **d.** composite self

18. _____ is (are) a tool for developing newer, healthier visions of ourselves.
    - **a.** Criticisms
    - **b.** Negative self-talk
    - **c.** Self-talk
    - **d.** Affirmations

19. The first step in responding to both constructive and destructive criticism is to _____.
    - **a.** assert yourself
    - **b.** listen carefully
    - **c.** restate the criticism
    - **d.** probe

20. Which of the following reactions to criticism is the most effective?
    - **a.** Directly confront the critic.
    - **b.** Acknowledge the criticism as true and apologize.
    - **c.** Agree with the specific part of the criticism you can acknowledge to be true.
    - **d.** Pretend to acknowledge the criticism and then get even.

C. SHORT ANSWER

Write a paragraph in response to each of the following questions.

21. What is self-expectancy, and why is it important?

_____

_____

_____

_____

_____

_____

_____

22. How can you mend a negative self-image?

_____

_____

_____

_____

_____

_____

_____

_____

_____

23. Explain the difference between constructive criticism and destructive criticism. Give examples.

_____

_____

_____

_____

_____

_____

_____

_____

CHAPTER ❺ Q U I Z

A. MATCHING

Match each definition in the left column with the correct term in the right column. Write the letter of the term in the space provided.

_____ 1. Focusing on the flaws and problems in ourselves, other people, and the world around us.

_____ 2. Distress caused by contemplating worst-case scenarios.

_____ 3. An illness characterized by profound feelings of sadness, hopelessness, and helplessness.

_____ 4. A negative attitude about ourselves that dooms us to failure.

_____ 5. The tendency to expect the best possible outcome.

_____ 6. A distorted, self-destructive idea or assumption.

_____ 7. The tendency to expect the worst possible outcome.

_____ 8. Focusing on what is good about ourselves, other people, and the world around us.

_____ 9. The habit of condemning people or things because they are not the way we think they should be.

_____ 10. The sharing of distress, discomfort, or worry with another person.

a. complaint

b. depression

c. irrational belief

d. judgmentalism

e. negative thinking

f. optimism

g. pessimism

h. positive thinking

i. self-defeating attitude

j. worry

B. SHORT ANSWER

Write a paragraph in response to one of the following questions.

11a. Compare the effect of positive thinking on feelings and actions with the effect of a self-defeating attitude on feelings and actions.

11b. How does attitude affect health?

_____

_____

_____

_____

_____

_____

CHAPTER 5 T E S T

A. COMPLETION

Complete the following sentences using the correct term from the list below.

positive thinking	depression	optimism
self-defeating attitude	attitude	vicious cycle
negative thinking	cognitive distortion	pessimism
ABCDE method		

1. A(n) _____ is a belief or opinion that predisposes us to act in a certain way.

2. People with a negative self-image develop a(n) _____ in which they see themselves failing before they even try.

3. People with _____ focus their energy on making their goals happen, rather than on bracing for the worst.

4. Using the _____, we can challenge our irrational beliefs to create positive new emotional outcomes for ourselves.

5. _____ dampens our mood and blocks us from taking risks, making changes, and expressing our real selves.

6. People with _____ find signs of failure and disaster everywhere they go.

7. Self-defeating attitudes create a(n) _____, a chain of events in which one negative event causes another negative event.

8. _____ gives you the drive to work hard to make good things happen. It does not promise success, but there is no success without it.

9. A(n) _____ is a self-critical, illogical pattern of thought.

10. An illness characterized by profound feelings of sadness, hopelessness, and helplessness, _____ affects 20 million people each year in the United States and Canada.

B. MULTIPLE CHOICE

Identify the letter of the choice that best completes the statement or answers the question.

11. Which of the following is NOT a positive habit?
    a. Be judgmental.
    b. Don't worry.
    c. Choose your words.
    d. Look for the good.

12. Which of following is myth about worrying, not a reality?
    a. Caring and worrying are not the same.
    b. Worrying helps me deal with my problems.
    c. Worrying drains your energy.
    d. None of the above.

13. Positive thinkers are healthier than negative thinkers because _____.
    a. they are less vulnerable to depression
    b. they are more likely to practice positive health behaviors
    c. positive thoughts and feelings stimulate endorphins
    d. all of the above

14. According to the Food Guide Pyramid, a person should eat up to five servings of _____ every day.
    a. fats, oils, and sweets
    b. meat, beans, eggs, and nuts
    c. vegetables and fruits
    d. milk, yogurt, and cheese

15. Strategies for good health include all of the following EXCEPT _____.
    a. try to be physically active for at least 20 minutes each week
    b. vary your activities
    c. set SMART exercise goals for yourself
    d. eat when you are hungry and stop when you are nearly full

16. Self-defeating attitudes are based on _____.
    a. facts
    b. negative, distorted perceptions of ourselves
    c. negative, realistic perceptions of ourselves
    d. positive, distorted perceptions of ourselves

17. Drawing broad negative conclusions based on limited evidence is a cognitive distortion called _____.
    a. filtering
    b. emotional reasoning
    c. overgeneralizing
    d. catastrophizing

18. Dramatically exaggerating the negative consequences of events is known as _____.
    a. filtering
    b. emotional reasoning
    c. overgeneralizing
    d. catastrophizing

19. Albert Ellis calls distorted, self-destructive assumptions _____.
    a. helpless thinking
    b. irrational beliefs
    c. self-blame
    d. none of the above

20. The C in the ABCDE method refers to _____.
    a. character
    b. challenge
    c. criticize
    d. consequences

C. SHORT ANSWER

Write a paragraph in response to each of the following questions.

21. Give an example of a self-defeating attitude and how you could overcome it.

_____

_____

_____

_____

_____

_____

_____

_____

22. Name the six important positive habits of thought and action. Choose one of the habits that you have and explain how you know you have it. Choose one that you do not have and explain what you need to do to cultivate it.

_____

_____

_____

_____

_____

_____

_____

_____

23. What is an irrational belief? How does the ABCDE method help you overcome irrational beliefs?

_____

_____

_____

_____

_____

_____

_____

MIDTERM EXAM

SHORT ANSWER

Write a paragraph in response to each of the following questions.

1. How can being self-aware make it easier to choose a satisfying job or career? Explain.

_____

_____

_____

_____

_____

_____

_____

2. Explain why it is important to have goals and describe the characteristics of a well-set goal.

_____

_____

_____

_____

_____

_____

_____

3. Define self-expectancy and self-acceptance and describe one specific strategy you can use to increase each quality.

_____

_____

_____

_____

_____

_____

_____

4. Consider this statement: "I should never make mistakes." What is this statement an example of, and what method can you use to change this kind of thinking? Explain.

_____

_____

_____

_____

_____

_____

_____

_____

_____

_____

_____

_____

5. Which strategies covered in Chapters 1 through 5 have been most helpful for you? Why?

_____

_____

_____

_____

_____

_____

_____

_____

_____

_____

_____

_____

_____

_____

CHAPTER 6 Q U I Z

A. MATCHING

Match each definition in the left column with the correct term in the right column. Write the letter of the term in the space provided.

_____ 1. The ability to go on despite opposition, setbacks, and occasional doubts.

_____ 2. A behavior that has become automatic through repetition.

_____ 3. Active, self-reflective thinking.

_____ 4. The process of teaching yourself to do what is necessary to reach your goals, without becoming sidetracked by bad habits.

_____ 5. Determining the path your life travels.

_____ 6. A reasoned choice among several options.

_____ 7. A sudden wish that can lead to unwise actions.

_____ 8. A logical series of steps to identify and evaluate options and to arrive at a good choice.

_____ 9. The ability to make independent, proactive decisions and to accept the consequences of them.

_____ 10. The logical effects of an action.

a. consequences

b. critical thinking

c. decision

d. decision-making process

e. habit

f. impulse

g. persistence

h. responsibility

i. self-determination

j. self-discipline

B. SHORT ANSWER

Write a paragraph in response to one of the following questions.

11a. What are the three steps to controlling impulses? Give an example.

11b. Are you a critical thinker? Why or why not? Explain.

_____

_____

_____

_____

_____

_____

_____

_____

CHAPTER **6** T E S T

A. COMPLETION

Complete the following sentences using the correct term from the list below.

self-discipline	habit	self-determination
impulse	persistence	regret
responsibility	mistake	critical thinking
decision		

1. People who believe that fate, luck, or some other force outside their control shapes the

   outcome of their lives are demonstrating a lack of _____.

2. People who have poor _____ control may end up with problems such as gambling, drug addiction, or compulsive spending.

3. People who have the quality of _____ put in effort, again and again, until they reach their goal.

4. A(n) _____ is an important opportunity to intervene in the flow of your life and create a new future for yourself.

5. People who are in control of their lives display _____, the ability to make independent decisions and to accept the consequences of them.

6. People who fear a(n) _____ have trouble making decisions for fear of doing the wrong thing.

7. People who feel _____ wish they had decided something differently.

8. You rely on _____ to get up when the alarm rings in the morning.

9. People who practice _____ are able to look at an issue from all sides before coming to a conclusion.

10. You know a(n) _____ is causing you problems if it is making you unhappy or draining your energy.

B. MULTIPLE CHOICE

Identify the letter of the choice that best completes the statement or answers the question.

11. The first step in controlling impulses is to _____.
    - **a.** think
    - **b.** decide
    - **c.** stop
    - **d.** relate

12. The two key ingredients of self-discipline are _____.
    a. persistence and responsibility
    b. persistence and self-awareness
    c. self-awareness and self-control
    d. persistence and self-determination

13. In the concept of embracing change, hidden resistance refers to _____.
    a. physical factors   **c.** environmental factors
    b. psychological factors   **d.** sociological factors

14. In the contemplation stage in Step 1 of conquering bad habits, you _____ the behavior.
    a. still have no intention of changing
    b. begin thinking about changing
    c. edge closer to making a serious effort to change
    d. decide it is time to change

15. The critical thinking standard of _____ means that the fact or idea has a direct connection to the subject being discussed.
    a. logic   **c.** accuracy
    b. clarity   **d.** relevance

16. The critical thinking standard of _____ means that a given statement has factual truth.
    a. logic   **c.** accuracy
    b. clarity   **d.** relevance

17. The critical thinking standard of _____ means that a thought digs below the surface to consider the substance of the issue.
    a. depth   **c.** relevance
    b. breadth   **d.** logic

18. The first step in the decision-making process is to _____.
    a. act
    b. gather information
    c. define the decision you need to make
    d. assess the consequences of each option relative to your values and goals

19. The final step in the decision-making process is to _____.
    a. define the decision   **c.** assess each option
    b. evaluate your progress   **d.** act

20. Listing all possible options is the _____ step in the decision-making process.
    a. second   **c.** sixth
    b. third   **d.** seventh

C. SHORT ANSWER

Write a paragraph in response to each of the following questions.

21. How does self-discipline help you achieve your goals? Give one specific example of how self-discipline could or does help you achieve your goals.

_____

_____

_____

_____

_____

_____

_____

22. How can positive self-talk help you change a bad habit? How does this work psychologically?

_____

_____

_____

_____

_____

_____

_____

_____

_____

23. Think about a major decision you have made in the past several years. Explain the process you used to make the decision and compare it to the decision-making process described in the text.

_____

_____

_____

_____

_____

_____

_____

CHAPTER ❼   Q U I Z

A. MATCHING

Match each definition in the left column with the correct term in the right column. Write the letter of the term in the space provided.

_____ 1. Freedom of choice, independence, and the chance to exercise independent judgment.

_____ 2. A conscious drive to attain a satisfying goal.

_____ 3. An unwanted outcome.

_____ 4. The force that moves us to action.

_____ 5. The process of creating detailed mental pictures of the behavior you wish to carry out.

_____ 6. A reward offered in order to motivate a person to do something.

_____ 7. The creative power of the mind.

_____ 8. Something we can survive and thrive without.

_____ 9. An unpleasant feeling of anxiety caused by the anticipation of danger.

_____ 10. Something we must have in order to survive and thrive.

a. autonomy

b. desire

c. failure

d. fear

e. imagination

f. incentive

g. motivation

h. need

i. visualization

j. want

B. SHORT ANSWER

Write a paragraph in response to one of the following questions.

11a. Define *positive motivation, negative motivation, extrinsic motivation,* and *intrinsic motivation* and explain how they are alike and how they are different.

11b. Define *relatedness, competence,* and *autonomy,* and explain where they belong on the hierarchy of needs.

_____

_____

_____

_____

_____

_____

_____

CHAPTER 7 · T E S T

A. COMPLETION

Complete the following sentences using the correct term from the list below.

motivation	autonomy	hierarchy of needs
comfort zone	relatedness	failure
competence	visualization	self-actualization
imagination		

1. _____ is feedback that lets you know where you need to work to improve.

2. _____ means reaching one's full potential and achieving long-term personal growth.

3. When we lack _____, we feel like powerless participants in a game controlled by others.

4. _____ is the force that moves us to action.

5. Each time you accept a new challenge, you expand the _____.

6. _____ helps you stay positive by allowing you to create a mental image of you achieving your goals.

7. The _____ depicts the five central human needs.

8. The need for _____ can be fulfilled through romance, friendship, family ties, or the camaraderie of school or the workplace.

9. Napoleon once said, "_____ rules the world."

10. The ability to reach our goals and cope with the challenges of life is key to self-esteem.

    Because of this, we all have a deep need to feel a sense of _____ in the important areas of our lives.

B. MULTIPLE CHOICE

Identify the letter of the choice that best completes the statement or answers the question.

11. When we are driven away from failure, we experience _____.
    - **a.** positive motivation
    - **b.** negative motivation
    - **c.** intrinsic motivation
    - **d.** extrinsic motivation

12. When we are driven to do things that we enjoy and that allow us to grow as a person, we experience _____.

    a. positive motivation

    b. negative motivation

    c. intrinsic motivation

    d. extrinsic motivation

13. When we are driven to do things not because we really want to but because they are a means to an end, we experience _____.

    a. positive motivation

    b. negative motivation

    c. intrinsic motivation

    d. extrinsic motivation

14. When we are driven toward success, we experience _____.

    a. positive motivation

    b. negative motivation

    c. intrinsic motivation

    d. extrinsic motivation

15. The need to be free from physical harm is a(n) _____ need.

    a. esteem

    b. social

    c. security

    d. physical

16. The need to feel valuable and worthwhile as an individual is a(n) _____ need.

    a. esteem

    b. social

    c. security

    d. physical

17. Fear is _____.

    a. the opposite of desire

    b. caused by the anticipation of danger

    c. an unpleasant feeling

    d. all of the above

18. Intrinsic goals include all of the following EXCEPT _____.

    a. receiving recognition from the community

    b. building meaningful relationships

    c. growing as a person

    d. giving to the community

19. It doesn't matter how many times you have failed in the past. It only matters that _____.

    a. you know when to quit

    b. others don't see you as a failure

    c. you are willing to try again

    d. you quit with grace and poise

20. The key to visualization is focusing on _____.

    a. one image at a time

    b. the outcome you want to achieve

    c. your fears and anxieties

    d. none of the above

C. SHORT ANSWER

Write a paragraph in response to each of the following questions.

21. What are incentives? When are they successful? When do they fail? Give examples.

_____

_____

_____

_____

_____

_____

_____

_____

22. Explain Maslow's hierarchy of needs. Name the five levels in order and describe each one.

_____

_____

_____

_____

_____

_____

_____

_____

23. What is the difference between the fear of failure and the fear of success? Describe one way to overcome each type of fear.

_____

_____

_____

_____

_____

_____

_____

_____

CHAPTER 8 **QUIZ**

A. MATCHING

Match each definition in the left column with the correct term in the right column. Write the letter of the term in the space provided.

_____ 1. The intelligent use of money to achieve your goals.

_____ 2. The habit of putting off tasks until the last minute.

_____ 3. A sum of money a person can use before having to pay back the lender.

_____ 4. The planned, efficient use of time.

_____ 5. A checklist of tasks to be completed.

_____ 6. A convenient medium of exchange used to pay for goods and services.

_____ 7. A plan that specifies how you will spend your money during a particular period.

_____ 8. All the money you receive during a fixed period of time.

_____ 9. A chart showing dates and times when tasks must be completed.

_____ 10. Monetary resources.

a. budget

b. credit

c. finances

d. income

e. money

f. money management

g. procrastination

h. schedule

i. time management

j. to-do list

B. SHORT ANSWER

Write a paragraph in response to one of the following questions.

11a. How can you manage your time, and what are the benefits of doing so?

11b. What is the basic recipe for financial fitness? What can happen if you do not follow this basic recipe?

_____

_____

_____

_____

_____

_____

CHAPTER 8 T E S T

A. COMPLETION

Complete the following sentences using the correct term from the list below.

time management   money   to-do list
budget   schedule   impulse buying
procrastination   credit   money management
credit record

1. Basic _____ involves three steps: 1. Analyze how you use your money; 2. Prioritize your expenses; and 3. Create a plan for your money.

2. Advantages to using a _____ include not having to worry about forgetting a task or getting sidetracked.

3. _____ can stem from self-handicapping, perfectionism, or a lack of self-motivation.

4. The third step in money management is to make a _____.

5. When you use _____, you are really taking out a loan.

6. To establish a good _____, it's important to pay all bills promptly, avoid large debts, and not bounce checks.

7. Basic _____ involves figuring out where your time goes, determining where you want it to go, and creating a plan to make that happen.

8. While we all having feelings about _____, the most useful attitude toward it is a practical one. Look at it as a tool.

9. Many people overspend because they engage in _____ and recreational shopping.

10. Writing all your activities and do-by dates on a _____ provides a graphical reminder of what you have coming up over the following week.

B. MULTIPLE CHOICE

Identify the letter of the choice that best completes the statement or answers the question.

11. The time you spend taking care of yourself and your surroundings is called _____.
    a. committed time   c. priority time
    b. maintenance time   d. discretionary time

12. The time that you can use to do whatever you wish is called _____.
    a. committed time
    b. maintenance time
    c. priority time
    d. discretionary time

13. The time you devote to school, work, family, volunteering, and other activities that relate to your short-term and long-term goals is called _____.
    a. committed time
    b. maintenance time
    c. priority time
    d. discretionary time

14. The 80/20 rule states that _____.
    a. the relationship between input and output, or effort and results, is not balanced
    b. most people spend 80 percent of their time on activities that produce 20 percent of their progress
    c. we get 80 percent of our work done during 20 percent of our working hours
    d. all of the above

15. Creating obstacles to your success in order to have an easy excuse for doing poorly is known as _____.
    a. self-denial
    b. self-acrimony
    c. self-handicapping
    d. self-serving

16. One way to analyze your spending is to assign expenses to the categories of _____.
    a. fixed, flexible, or designated
    b. committed, flexible, or discretionary
    c. committed fixed, committed flexible, or designated
    d. committed fixed, committed flexible, or discretionary

17. When making a budget, most people look at _____ as their fixed period of time.
    a. one year
    b. a fiscal quarter
    c. a month
    d. none of the above

18. An effective budget meets all of the following criteria EXCEPT _____.
    a. it is realistic and accurate
    b. it centers around your goals and values
    c. it provides for savings
    d. it is balanced, with income equal to or less than expenses

19. Which of the following is NOT a question to ask yourself before buying anything?
    a. Do I really want this item?
    b. Do I really need this item?
    c. Have I allowed for this item in my budget?
    d. Is this the best time to buy?

20. You probably overuse credit if you use it to _____.
    a. buy items that cost less than $5.00
    b. pay overdue bills
    c. pay for a vacation
    d. all of the above

C. SHORT ANSWER

Write a paragraph in response to each of the following questions.

21. Explain the steps you can take and the tools you can use to take control of your time.

_____

_____

_____

_____

_____

_____

_____

_____

_____

22. What is procrastination and what are three sources for it? How does procrastination affect a person's ability to achieve his or her goals?

_____

_____

_____

_____

_____

_____

_____

_____

_____

23. What is the relationship between wealth and well-being? Why should you concern yourself with money management?

_____

_____

_____

_____

_____

_____

_____

_____

CHAPTER 9 QUIZ

A. MATCHING

Match each definition in the left column with the correct term in the right column. Write the letter of the term in the space provided.

_____ 1. Disagreement that occurs when individuals or groups clash over needs, values, emotions, or power.

_____ 2. The process of giving or exchanging messages without words.

_____ 3. Listening with understanding and paying close attention to what is being said.

_____ 4. A meaningful connection with another human being.

_____ 5. A set of oversimplified beliefs about the attributes of a groups and its members.

_____ 6. A relationship between two people.

_____ 7. One-on-one, usually face-to-face communication.

_____ 8. Facial expressions, posture, and gestures.

_____ 9. A negative feeling or attitude toward a group that results from oversimplified beliefs about that group.

_____ 10. The process of giving or exchanging messages.

a. active listening

b. body language

c. communication

d. conflict

e. interpersonal communication

f. interpersonal relationship

g. nonverbal communication

h. prejudice

i. relationship

j. stereotype

B. SHORT ANSWER

Write a paragraph in response to one of the following questions.

11a. Name and describe the six elements of communication.
11b. What is the relationship between communication and conflict? Explain.

_____

_____

_____

_____

_____

_____

_____

CHAPTER **9**   T E S T

A. COMPLETION

Complete the following sentences using the correct term from the list below.

communication   relationships   channel
groups   context   empathy
nonverbal communication   interpersonal relationships   active listening
self-disclosure

1. The _____ is the medium in which a message is delivered.

2. _____ requires three skills: encouraging, attending, and responding.

3. People need _____ because they satisfy our basic need to belong.

4. The most important function of _____ is to create and maintain bonds between people.

5. _____ means seeing life through other people's eyes—experiencing their pain, curiosity, hopes, and fears.

6. People with healthy _____ are happier and suffer less stress and illness than people who have destructive relationships or who suffer loneliness.

7. _____ means letting other people see the real you.

8. _____ is the time and place of communication.

9. Healthy _____ require self-awareness, empathy, and good communication.

10. The most frequent functions of _____ are managing conversations, providing feedback, and clarifying verbal messages.

MULTIPLE CHOICE

Identify the letter of the choice that best completes the statement or answers the question.

11. The most obvious roadblocks to communication are _____, which include background noise, being too warm or too cool, an unpleasant tone of voice, and even the speaker's appearance.
    a. physical barriers   **c.** language and cultural barriers
    b. emotional barriers   **d.** psychosomatic barriers

12. One example of _____ is the misunderstanding that would arise if you nodded your head to signal "yes" to a person from Bulgaria.
    a. physical barriers
    b. emotional barriers
    c. language and cultural barriers
    d. psychosomatic barriers

13. The acronym EAR stands for _____.
    a. Eagerly Attend and Respond
    b. Enthusiasm, Attention, and Respect
    c. Encouraging, Attending, and Responding
    d. Easy, Appropriate, and Ready

14. Paraphrasing is _____.
    a. restating the factual content of the message
    b. one way of giving constructive feedback
    c. a way to show that you are an active listener.
    d. all of the above

15. Reflecting is _____.
    a. restating the factual content of the message
    b. restating the emotional content of the message
    c. a strategy for becoming an effective speaker
    d. all of the above

16. The flip side of conformity is _____.
    a. groupthink
    b. diversity
    c. cohesiveness
    d. conflict

17. Which of the following may not be necessary in an intimate relationship?
    a. emotional support
    b. physical attraction
    c. sharing
    d. sociability

18. Empathy is _____.
    a. awareness of and sensitivity to the feelings, thoughts, and experiences of others
    b. a sense of closeness, caring, and mutual acceptance
    c. communicating your real thoughts, desires, and feelings
    d. none of the above

19. Intimacy is _____.
    a. awareness of and sensitivity to the feelings, thoughts, and experiences of others
    b. a sense of closeness, caring, and mutual acceptance
    c. communicating your real thoughts, desires, and feelings
    d. none of the above

20. Which of the following is NOT a strategy for resolving conflict?
    a. use self-expectancy
    b. listen actively
    c. state your needs
    d. be flexible and open-minded

C. SHORT ANSWER

Write a paragraph in response to each of the following questions.

21. Define interpersonal communication, and describe the types of barriers that can affect it.

_____

_____

_____

_____

_____

_____

_____

_____

22. Name three characteristics of a good speaker, and explain two strategies that can help you develop these characteristics.

_____

_____

_____

_____

_____

_____

_____

_____

_____

23. What is intimacy? How can you develop it in a relationship? Give an example.

_____

_____

_____

_____

_____

_____

_____

FINAL EXAM

SHORT ANSWER

Write a paragraph in response to each of the following questions.

1. What are the seven ingredients of success, and which of these ingredients do you think is (or are) most important? Support your opinion with specific examples.

_____

_____

_____

_____

_____

_____

_____

2. Explain why the following statement is true: "Self-esteem is one of the most important basic qualities of a successful human being."

_____

_____

_____

_____

_____

_____

_____

3. What is the relationship between self-esteem and positive thinking? Give examples.

_____

_____

_____

_____

_____

_____

_____

4. Explain how self-discipline and self-motivation help you accomplish your goals.

_____

_____

_____

_____

_____

5. How does managing time and money help you attain success? Explain and give examples.

_____

_____

_____

_____

_____

_____

6. Describe good communication and explain why it is important in interpersonal relationships. Give as many reasons as you can.

_____

_____

_____

_____

_____

7. Which strategies covered in Chapters 6 through 9 have been most helpful for you? Why?

_____

_____

_____

_____

_____

ANSWER KEYS

Chapter 1 Answer Key

Chapter 1 Quiz

A. MATCHING

1. i
2. a
3. e
4. g
5. j
6. b
7. h
8. d
9. c
10. f

B. SHORT ANSWER

11a. The ingredients of success are self-aware-ness, which allows you to know what you want out of life; self-esteem, which helps you to keep going when others are criti-cal; positive thinking, which helps you to focus on future possibilities instead of setbacks from the past; self-discipline, which helps you to put your plans into action and to do what you need to do to reach your goals; self-motivation, which allows you to focus on goals that have personal meaning for you and stay moti-vated; and positive relationships, because no one ever succeeds without the help, ideas, and emotional support of others.

11b. Having a complex self-image means hav-ing a variety of positive ways of seeing yourself. People who have a complex self-image are less likely to suffer from psy-chological troubles such as stress, anxiety, and depression. When they suffer a set-back or difficulty in one area of their life, they can fall back on the knowledge that they have many other positive roles to play in life. Having a complex self-image, therefore, is desirable and positive.

Chapter 1 Test

A. COMPLETION

1. nervous system
2. role model
3. social role
4. success
5. identity
6. self-direction
7. self-presentation
8. psychology
9. Happiness
10. self-image

B. MULTIPLE CHOICE

11. c
12. b
13. d
14. c
15. b
16. a
17. c
18. d
19. d
20. b

C. SHORT ANSWER

21. Answers will vary but should recognize that indulging yourself and seeking pleas-ure do not necessarily contribute to a positive evaluation of your life or to the sense of well-being that comes from a positive self-evaluation.

22. Positive qualities will vary but should include three of the following: ability to love, vocation, courage, trust, optimism, future-mindedness, social skill, aesthetic sensibility, work ethic, honesty, emotional awareness, persistence, forgiveness, cre-ative thinking, spirituality, self-esteem, and wisdom. Answers should reflect the understanding that building these quali-ties can contribute to personal happiness because they help you remain physically and emotionally healthy, enjoy strong friendships and family relationships,

derive satisfaction from a committed romantic relationship, be an effective and loving parent, find satisfaction in work, and feel good about yourself.

23. Answers will vary but should recognize that our self is our sense of being a unique, conscious being. It is the inner core of our being. It contains all of the traits, thoughts, feelings, actions, values, and beliefs that answer the question, "Who am I?" Having a firm sense of self helps us understand the world and make plans and decisions. It motivates us to achieve our goals and to improve ourselves. Having a firm sense of self also helps us build and maintain relationships with others.

Chapter 2 Answer Key

Chapter 2 Quiz

A. MATCHING

1. b
2. i
3. f
4. a
5. e
6. c
7. h
8. j
9. d
10. g

B. SHORT ANSWER

11a. Answers will vary but should recognize that self-awareness has many benefits. It helps you identify what you are really feeling and thinking inside. It helps you act in accordance with your values, rather than being swayed by what other people say or do. It helps you appreciate your unique traits, skills, and interests. When you are self-aware, you can make the choices that are right for you.

11b. Answers will vary but should reflect that knowledge is the understanding of facts or principles in a particular subject area, while skills are the result of knowledge combined with experience. Skills and interests usually overlap significantly, because people are usually skilled at the things they are interested in and interested in the things they are skilled at.

Chapter 2 Test

A. COMPLETION

1. self-honesty
2. personality
3. intelligence
4. self-awareness
5. emotional awareness
6. trait
7. skill
8. knowledge
9. self-consciousness
10. interests

B. MULTIPLE CHOICE

11. c
12. c
13. b
14. d
15. a
16. a
17. d
18. c
19. b
20. d

C. SHORT ANSWER

21. Answers will vary but should reflect the understanding that having a dream gives a person's life meaning, helps him or her make choices, and helps him or her persevere in the face of obstacles or hardship. Living without a dream, by contrast, can leave a person feeling adrift and unmotivated.

22. Answers will vary but should recognize that "pretty" describes a physical feature, not a personality trait, which is a disposition to behave in a certain way regardless of the situation. The traits listed in Exercise 2.3 describe ways of behaving, not ways of appearing.

23. Answers will vary but should recognize that a job-specific skill is the ability to do a specific task or job, while a transferable skill is an ability that can be transferred across a variety of tasks and jobs. Although it's easy to think that job-specific skills are more important than transferable skills, transferable skills are the foundation of specific skills. Therefore, both types of skills are important.

Chapter 3 Answer Key

Chapter 3 Quiz

A. MATCHING

1. a
2. j
3. e
4. f
5. c
6. i
7. b
8. h
9. d
10. g

B. SHORT ANSWER

11a. The first step toward conquering anger is to figure out what makes you angry and why. Answers will vary as to why it is the first step, but should recognize that anger usually arises when you feel something might happen to frighten, hurt, or threaten you or make you feel powerless. By figuring out what is causing you to feel this way, you can address the real cause of the problem. This will help you better understand and control your anger.

11b. Answers will vary but should explain that goal cards are small cards on which you write your current short-term goals and the time frame for achieving each goal. By carrying these cards with you, you can review your goals as often as possible and adjust them as necessary. This helps keep you motivated and reminds you to stay focused. Model answers will also suggest that writing down your goals in clear statements and setting a time for achieving each goal helps to make the goal more concrete and therefore more attainable.

Chapter 3 Test

A. COMPLETION

1. stress
2. goal
3. adapt
4. anger
5. obstacle
6. denial
7. assertiveness
8. perfectionism
9. escape response
10. aggression

B. MULTIPLE CHOICE

11. c
12. a
13. d
14. a
15. b
16. c
17. d
18. b
19. c
20. d

C. SHORT ANSWER

21. Answers will vary but should recognize that the ABC stress diagram describes that an activating event, A (any stress-causing situation), plus your belief, B (how you evaluate the situation), leads to certain consequences, C (emotional and behavioral outcome). In other words, the diagram explains how negative beliefs can create stress and lead to unwanted consequences. Answers should also explain that understanding this diagram can help you manage stress by showing that if you can control how you evaluate or react to a stressful situation, you can influence the outcome and have a more positive experience.

22. The three core characteristics of people who handle stress effectively are: 1. Seeing problems not as catastrophes but as challenges; 2. Having a sense of mission or purpose in life that helps put setbacks in perspective; and 3. Having a feeling of control over their own lives. Answers will vary as to how to cultivate a given characteristic. To cultivate the outlook that problems are really challenges, a student might write about a problem as it arises and break it down into smaller problems that are easier to solve. As he or she solves problems this way, he or she would develop better coping strategies and suffer less stress.

23. Answers will vary but should recognize that setting goals helps you achieve your dreams. They help you establish a plan and direct your abilities in the service of what you want most.

Chapter 4 Answer Key

Chapter 4 Quiz

A. MATCHING

1. f
2. g
3. b
4. a
5. e
6. d
7. c
8. j
9. h
10. i

B. SHORT ANSWER

11a. Answers will vary but should recognize that overcoming loneliness requires building and strengthening your social support network. Instead of waiting for others to take an interest in you, the first step is to reach out to others. You can also explore your interests by joining a school group, neighborhood club, or volunteer project. Finally, you can work on communication and relationship skills.

11b. Answers will vary but should reflect that people who accept themselves as they truly are realize that they have many more strengths than weaknesses, and that their weaknesses do not diminish their value. They therefore have higher self-esteem. People who do not accept themselves concentrate more on their weaknesses than their strengths. They therefore have lower self-esteem.

Chapter 4 Test

A. COMPLETION

1. avoidance
2. inner critic
3. self-esteem
4. probing
5. self-acceptance
6. coping
7. social comparison
8. self-expectancy
9. label
10. criticism

B. MULTIPLE CHOICE

11. c
12. a
13. b

14. a
15. c
16. b
17. a
18. d
19. b
20. c

C. SHORT ANSWER

21. Answers will vary but should define self-expectancy as the belief that you are able to achieve what you want in life. Self-expectancy is important because believing that you can achieve your goals will help you obtain them. Whatever you spend the most energy thinking about is what will come to pass, whether it is something you fear or something you desire. People with low self-esteem expect to fail, be in financial peril, suffer poor health, and have troubled relationships, and this is usually what comes true for them. People with high self-expectancy and self-esteem expect to succeed, have financial security, enjoy good health, and have happy relationships—and this is what usually comes true for them, too.

22. Answers will vary but should recognize that the first step to mending a negative self-image is to accept that it is distorted. This means recognizing that the truth you feel about yourself is really a figment of your imagination, and that you see yourself as far less worthy than you really are. The next step is to take a personal inventory and reassess your strengths and weaknesses. After creating a personal inventory, you should have a much fairer and more accurate assessment of yourself. Reviewing this personal inventory will help you teach yourself to accept your flaws, affirm your positive qualities, and move on.

23. Answers will vary but should recognize that constructive criticism can help you improve yourself, that it addresses specific behavior, and that it does not attack you as a person. It also usually makes mention of your positive points and offers helpful suggestions for improvement. Destructive criticism, by contrast, can cripple your self-esteem. It is often general, addressing your attitude or some aspect of yourself rather than focusing on specific behavior. It is also usually entirely negative, without any helpful suggestion about how to do things differently. Examples will vary but may be similar to those given in the text.

Chapter 5 Answer Key

Chapter 5 Quiz

A. MATCHING

1. e
2. j
3. b
4. i
5. f
6. c
7. g
8. h
9. d
10. a

B. SHORT ANSWER

11a. Answers will vary but should reflect that both effects are cyclical. Positive thinking leads to positive feelings and actions, which lead to success, in turn leading to more positive thinking and feelings. A self-defeating attitude leads to self-defeating behavior, which leads to a negative outcome, which strengthens the self-defeating attitude.

11b. Answers will vary but should recognize that the body's immune system, which fights infection and disease, is weakened by negative thoughts and feelings. Negative thoughts and feelings cause our bodies to produce fewer antibodies that fight illness. Positive thoughts and feelings, on the other hand, stimulate the production of morphine-like proteins called endorphins that reduce feelings of pain and cause a person to feel better.

Chapter 5 Test

A. COMPLETION

1. attitude
2. self-defeating attitude
3. optimism
4. ABCDE method
5. negative thinking
6. pessimism
7. vicious cycle
8. positive thinking
9. cognitive distortion
10. depression

B. MULTIPLE CHOICE

11. a
12. b
13. d
14. c
15. c
16. b
17. c
18. d
19. b
20. d

C. SHORT ANSWER

21. Examples will vary but should recognize that overcoming a self-defeating attitude is a two-step process of self-awareness and positive self-talk. The first step is to become aware of your self-defeating attitudes. The second step is to replace them with positive self-statements.

22. The six habits are 1. Look for the good; 2. Choose your words; 3. Surround yourself with positive people; 4. Accept, don't judge; 5. Limit complaints; and 6. don't worry. Students' choices of habits and explanations will vary.

23. Answers will vary but should recognize that an irrational belief is a distorted, self-destructive idea or assumption that interferes with rational thinking. The ABCDE method is based on the idea that we are more affected by how we view events than by the events themselves. ABC stands for Activating event, Belief, and Consequences. D and E stand for Dispute and Exchange. We can change our irrational beliefs by disputing them, which means confronting them with the facts of the situation. For example, when we have a negative, irrational, exaggerated thought, we can dispute our negative beliefs by asking questions such as, "Why? Who says so? Am I focusing on the negative?" Then we can exchange, or substitute, that irrational thought for a new, positive emotional and behavioral outcome. For example, instead of thinking "I'm a total failure" because a presentation doesn't go right, we can exchange that thought for a more rational thought such as, "Next time I will be more organized so that my presentation goes better."

Midterm Exam Answer Key

1. Students should explain that self-awareness helps people choose satisfying jobs and careers because it enables them to discover their dreams, goals, personality traits, values, skills, and interests. People can then use this information about themselves to choose the jobs and careers that will prove the most interesting and satisfying to them.

2. Setting goals is important because goals give us direction and help us spend our time and effort on the activities that matter most. By setting long-term goals and then working backward to establish a series of related short-term goals, we can develop a step-by-step plan with

deadlines to achieve what we want in life. Well-set goals have all five SMART factors: they are specific, measurable, achievable, realistic, and time-related.

3. Self-expectancy is a person's belief that he or she is able to achieve what he or she wants in life (i.e., to do what is necessary to achieve his or her goals). Self-acceptance is the recognition and acceptance of what is true about oneself. One strategy to increase self-expectancy is to set, and accomplish, a series of increasingly different goals in a certain life area. One strategy to increase self-acceptance is to take an honest personal inventory and then to rethink the negative items on that inventory in a realistic and compassionate way.

4. "I should never make mistakes" is an example of an irrational belief, a distorted, self-destructive idea or assumption that interferes with one's thinking. Students should refer to the ABCDE method and explain how it helps people dispute (D) their irrational beliefs (B) with the reality of the situation, exchanging the negative cognitive and emotional consequences (C) of the belief(s) for more positive consequences (E).

5. Answers will vary but should show an understanding of the concepts presented in Chapters 1-5 and a genuine effort to relate these concepts to real-life applications.

Chapter 6 Answer Key

Chapter 6 Quiz

A. MATCHING

1. g
2. e
3. b
4. j
5. i
6. c
7. f
8. d
9. h
10. a

B. SHORT ANSWER

11a. The three steps in controlling impulses are: 1. Stop—Realize that you are about to act impulsively; 2. Think—What will I gain in the short term by acting on this impulse? What will I lose in the long term by acting on this impulse? 3. Decide—Given the short-term and long-term consequences, it is worth it? Examples will vary but should include an impulsive action, such as buying a pair of $100 shoes on credit because you don't have the money. For example, 1. Stop—Realize that buying these shoes on credit is an impulsive action. 2. Think—Consider that if I buy these shoes, I will be happy with the way I look Saturday night, but I'll have $100 less for the vacation I am planning. 3. Decide—Since I already have shoes that will be okay for Saturday, I would rather save for my vacation.

11b. Answers will vary but should demonstrate an understanding that a critical thinker is an active self-reflective thinker. Answers should also show understanding of the seven standards: clarity, precision, accuracy, relevance, depth, breadth, and logic.

Chapter 6 Test

A. COMPLETION

1. self-determination
2. impulse
3. persistence
4. decision
5. responsibility
6. mistake
7. regret
8. self-discipline
9. critical thinking
10. habit

B. MULTIPLE CHOICE

11. c
12. d
13. b
14. b
15. d
16. c
17. a
18. c
19. b
20. a

C. SHORT ANSWER

21. Answers will vary but should reflect an understanding that self-discipline helps you to achieve your goals by strengthening your ability to control your destiny, persist in the face of setbacks, weigh the long-term consequences of your actions, make positive changes, break bad habits, think critically, and make effective decisions. Students' examples will vary but could include regular study habits that enable them to maintain good grades or a regular exercise program that helps them to maintain a healthy weight.

22. Answers will vary but should recognize that when you are trying to change a bad habit, you need to change your subconscious mind, as well as your conscious mind. Changing only at the conscious level is just using willpower, and the change will only be temporary. Because self-talk has a powerful effect on your subconscious mind, you can use it to replace the information you have already stored in your subconscious mind with new thoughts. You can use positive self-talk to persuade your subconscious mind that a change in habit has already taken place. By thinking of yourself as someone who has a particular positive habit, you will start to see yourself this way, and this will help you substitute a good habit for a bad one.

23. Answers will vary but should reflect knowledge of the seven steps and awareness of the utility of a step-by-step decision-making process.

Chapter 7 Answer Key

Chapter 7 Quiz

A. MATCHING

1. a
2. b
3. c
4. g
5. i
6. f
7. e
8. j
9. d
10. h

B. SHORT ANSWER

11a. Positive motivation is the drive to do something because it will move us toward a goal. Negative motivation is the drive to do something in order to avoid negative consequences. Extrinsic motivation is motivation that comes from outside. Intrinsic motivation is motivation that comes from inside. Positive motivation and negative motivation often lead you to the same goal, while extrinsic motivation and intrinsic motivation usually lead to different goals.

11b. Relatedness refers to fulfilling relationships with others. The need for relatedness is a social need in Maslow's hierarchy of needs. Competence is the ability to do something well. The need for competence is part of the need for (self-)esteem, because we all need to feel that we can reach our goals and cope with the challenges of life. Autonomy is freedom of choice, independence, and the chance to exercise independent judgment. The need for autonomy is part of the need for self-actualization, because in order to achieve our full potential we need to have control over our own lives.

Chapter 7 Test

A. COMPLETION

1. failure
2. self-actualization
3. autonomy
4. motivation
5. comfort zone
6. visualization
7. hierarchy of needs
8. relatedness
9. imagination
10. competence

B. MULTIPLE CHOICE

11. b
12. c
13. d
14. a
15. c
16. a
17. d
18. a
19. c
20. a

C. SHORT ANSWER

21. Answers will vary but should recognize that incentives are rewards offered in order to motivate a person to do something. They are successful at motivating someone if they reinforce an intrinsic motivation that person already has. They are not successful when the incentive is that person's only basis for motivation. For example, an incentive is effective if a company offers a bonus to someone who likes his or her job, and the bonus makes working longer hours more attractive. The incentive is ineffective if the bonus is offered to an employee who doesn't like his or her job. He or she may try to work harder for a little while but will run out of enthusiasm fairly quickly.

22. Maslow's hierarchy of needs is a theory and a diagram that organizes people's five basic needs into a pyramid, from the most basic at the bottom to the most complex at the top. The first (bottom) level of needs is physical needs. These are the needs that support our biological health and survival, such as the need for food and water. The second level is security needs, the need to feel safe and secure, to be free from physical harm, and to live in a stable environment. The third level is social needs, the need to be with others and to feel that important others in our lives acknowledge, appreciate, and love us for who we truly are. The fourth level is esteem needs, the need to feel that we are valuable and worthwhile as individuals and that others see us as valuable and worthwhile as well. The fifth (top) level is self-actualization needs, the need to reach one's full potential and achieve long-term personal growth.

23. Answers will vary but should recognize that fear of failure is often based on irrational beliefs about the terrible consequences of doing (or not doing) certain things. Fear of failure may be based on fear of the unknown, fear of rejection, or the fear of being inadequate. Fear of success, however, is based on low self-esteem. You cannot see your potential and what you can do. Ways to overcome the fear of failure include accepting your fear, expanding your comfort zone, rethinking failure, and seeing failure as part of success. For example, by rethinking failure, you might view failure as a tool—as feedback—that lets you know where you need to improve. In order to overcome the fear of success, you need to examine

the thoughts and feelings that might be holding you back. For example, if you fear that as soon as you achieve success you'll blow it, you need to recognize that success is not an accident or a possession that can be taken away by someone else. You can work on building your self-esteem so that you don't see success as an accident, but rather as a result of your hard work and ability.

Chapter 8 Answer Key

Chapter 8 Quiz

A. MATCHING

1. f
2. g
3. b
4. i
5. j
6. e
7. a
8. d
9. h
10. c

B. SHORT ANSWER

11a. Answers will vary but should recognize that the three steps to time management are to 1. analyze how you use your time; 2. prioritize your activities; and 3. create a plan for your time. Answers should also explain that by managing your time and planning ahead, you can spend most of your time doing what you value most, not just taking care of the latest crisis. Managing your time allows you to make the most of your time, which, in turn, helps to improve your mood, decrease your stress level, and create a satisfying balance between work and life.

11b. Answers will vary but should recognize that the basic recipe for financial fitness is: Spend less than you earn. If you do not following this basic recipe, you will either have no savings because you spend all you earn, or you will be in debt because you spend more than you earn.

Chapter 8 Test

A. COMPLETION

1. money management
2. to-do list
3. procrastination
4. budget
5. credit
6. credit record
7. time management
8. money
9. impulse buying
10. schedule

B. MULTIPLE CHOICE

11. b
12. d
13. a
14. d
15. c
16. d
17. c
18. d
19. a
20. d

C. SHORT ANSWER

21. The three steps to time management are to: 1. analyze how you use your time; 2. prioritize your activities; and 3. create a plan for your time. When analyzing your time, you can assign each of your daily and weekly activities to one of three different categories: committed time, which is the time you devote to school, work, family, volunteering, and other activities that relate to your short-term and long-term goals; maintenance time, which is the time you spend taking care of yourself and your surroundings; and discretionary time, which is the time you can use to do whatever you wish. When you prioritize

your time, you arrange your tasks and activities in order of importance. If your time is overcommitted, it is usually discretionary time that can be cut first. In order to make a plan for your time, you can make a to-do list and a schedule. A to-do list is a personal checklist of tasks and activities you need to complete over the course of a certain period. Once your to-do list is complete, you can create a schedule, a chart that shows dates and times when tasks must be completed.

22. Procrastination is the habit of putting off tasks until the last minute. One source of procrastination is self-handicapping, or creating obstacles to your own success in order to have an easy excuse for doing poorly. Two other sources are perfectionism and a lack of self-motivation. Procrastination can erode your self-determination and self-esteem, hindering your ability to achieve your goals.

23. Answers may vary but should recognize that while money can help us reach our goals, it doesn't buy happiness. Once our basic needs are met, more money cannot bring us happiness, and although money does allow for certain luxuries, it does not eliminate life's challenges. Answers should also recognize that by managing your money wisely, you can avoid financial worries and setbacks and make sure that you have the financial freedom to pursue your dreams.

Chapter 9 Answer Key

Chapter 9 Quiz

A. MATCHING
1. d
2. g
3. a
4. i
5. j
6. f
7. e
8. b
9. h
10. c

B. SHORT ANSWER
11a. The six elements of communication are sender, message, receiver, channel, feedback, and context. The sender is the person who translates a thought or feeling into a message and then sends this message to another person. The message is the sender's expression of a thought or feeling. The channel is the medium in which the message is delivered. The receiver is the person who takes in, or receives, the sender's message. Feedback is the receiver's response to a message. Context is the time and place of communication.

11b. Answers will vary but should recognize that because effective communication is the foundation of successful relationships, it can help to resolve conflicts. Good communication helps resolve conflicts, while poor communication both creates conflicts and makes them worse.

Chapter 9 Test

A. COMPLETION
1. channel
2. active listening
3. groups
4. communication
5. empathy
6. interpersonal relationships
7. self-disclosure
8. context
9. relationships
10. nonverbal communication

B. MULTIPLE CHOICE
11. a
12. c
13. c

14. d
15. b
16. b
17. b
18. a
19. b
20. a

C. SHORT ANSWER

21. Answers will vary but should recognize that interpersonal communication is one-on-one, usually face-to-face communication. The three types of barriers discussed in the text are physical barriers, emotional barriers, and language and cultural barriers. Physical barriers, such as background noise or the speaker's appearance, can make it difficult for the listener to hear or pay attention to the speaker. Emotional barriers are created when strong emotions such as sadness or excitement make it difficult to pay attention, or when conflicting emotions make messages confusing. Language and cultural barriers occur when people from differing cultural groups or geographic areas use words, concepts, and/or nonverbal cues that are unfamiliar or potentially offensive to the other person.

22. Answers will vary, but should include some of the characteristics mentioned in the text: speaking clearly, using a large and expressive vocabulary, telling the truth, welcoming feedback, and showing respect for others' feelings and points of view. Strategies to build these skills include building your vocabulary by reading widely and using the dictionary; being direct and honest, making eye contact, and avoiding conflicting messages; paying attention to the other person's reactions, both verbal and nonverbal, to show that you welcome feedback; and making a conscious effort to understand other people's points of view, even if you don't agree with them.

23. Answers will vary but should define intimacy as a sense of closeness, caring, and mutual acceptance that comes from sharing one's true inner self with another person. The primary way to build intimacy is self-disclosure, communicating your real thoughts, desires, and feelings. For example, a person might build intimacy with another by revealing his or her fears, dreams, hopes, or private feelings about something or someone.

Final Exam Answer Key

1. The seven ingredients of success (presented initially in Chapter 1) are self-awareness, self-direction, self-esteem, positive thinking, self-discipline, self-motivation, and positive relationships. Students' opinions will vary but should demonstrate critical thinking and be supported with thoughtful examples from their experience. Students may single out one particular quality or a group of qualities with particular importance for them.

2. This statement, "Self-esteem is one of the most important basic qualities of a successful human being," is the first sentence of Chapter 4. Answers will vary but should mention some or all of the benefits of self-esteem discussed in Chapter 4: Self-esteem motivates people to work hard to succeed; to take necessary risks; to rebound from setbacks and failures; to accept their strengths and weaknesses; to express their true thoughts and feelings; to establish emotional connections to other people; to be able to give and receive compliments; to give and receive affection; to try out new ideas and experiences; to express their creativity; to stand up for themselves (assertiveness); to handle stress and anger calmly, and to think positively and see the future with optimism.

3. Answers will vary, although students should understand that positive thinking is inherently related to self-esteem because it involves focusing on what is good about oneself. Many of the distorted thought patterns that characterize negative thinking—cognitive distortions such as personalizing and self-blame as well as irrational beliefs such as "I must succeed at everything"—are self-attacking and erode self-expectancy and self-acceptance. There are many other specific links between positive thinking and self-esteem. For example, positive thinkers tend to choose positive friends, who are more likely to provide the emotional and instrumental support that is crucial for self-esteem.

4. Both self-discipline and self-motivation are crucial to accomplishing goals, but in different ways. Without motivation, the force that moves a person to action, a person would not take action toward his or her goals, or even set goals in the first place. Motivation, however, may not always be enough. A person also needs self-discipline, the ability to teach oneself to do what is necessary to reach important goals. Self-discipline allows one to overcome bad habits, make difficult changes, and use critical thinking and decision-making skills. If a person has self-discipline, he or she can continue making progress toward his or her goals despite flagging motivation, setbacks, fears, or other obstacles.

5. Managing time and money is crucial to success, no matter how success is defined. Managing time helps people dedicate maximum time, energy, and effort to their top priorities. Likewise, managing money helps people align their spending with their goals and values. It also helps them save for their long-term goals. Students' examples will vary.

6. Good communication consists of effective speaking (speaking clearly, using a large and expressive vocabulary, using positive body language, telling the truth, welcoming verbal and nonverbal feedback, and showing respect for others) and active listening (encouraging, attending, and responding through paraphrasing and reflecting). Because communication is the way people develop and maintain bonds with one another, good communication is key to good relationships. Good communication helps people show respect and empathy, express feelings in "I"-statements, build intimacy through self-disclosure, resolve conflicts, and be assertive when necessary.

7. Answers will vary but should show an understanding of the concepts presented in Chapters 1–5 and a genuine effort to relate these concepts to real-life applications.

PART 4
REPRODUCIBLE MASTERS

PERSONAL SUCCESS PORTFOLIO

My Long-Term and Short-Term Goals (p. 95)

Goal #1	Goal #2	Goal #3

Short-Term Goals	Short-Term Goals	Short-Term Goals
_____	_____	_____
_____	_____	_____
_____	_____	_____
_____	_____	_____

Internal Obstacles I Know How to Face (p. 102) _____

_____

External Obstacles I Know How to Face (p. 102) _____

_____

My Personal Stressors (pp. 114–115)   **My Stress Relievers** (pp. 114–115)

_____   _____

_____   _____

_____   _____

My Personal Anger Triggers (p. 120)   **My Anger Strategies** (pp. 121–122)

_____   _____

_____   _____

_____   _____

PERSONAL SUCCESS PORTFOLIO

Three Actions I Will Take to Build My Social Support Network (p. 139)

_____

_____

_____

Goals I Will Accomplish to Raise My Self-Expectancy (p. 145)

Goal #1 _____

Goal #2 _____

Goal #3 _____

Goal #4 _____

Goal #5 _____

Goal #6 _____

Three Problems I Will Face (pp. 146–147)

_____

_____

_____

Three Affirmations I Will Use to Disarm the Inner Critic (p. 163)

_____

_____

_____

SELF-ESTEEM DECLARATION

I like and value myself as I am now, with whatever weaknesses I have.

Signed (YOUR NAME) _____

(PLACE AND DATE) _____

PERSONAL SUCCESS PORTFOLIO

Six Positive Habits I Will Adopt (pp. 186–191)

To look for the good, I will _____

_____

To choose positive words, I will _____

_____

To surround myself With positive people, I will _____

_____

To be more accepting, I will _____

_____

To limit complaints, I will _____

_____

To reduce worrying, I will _____

_____

Four Actions I Will Take for My Health (p. 198)

_____

_____

_____

_____

Five Questions I Will Use to Dispute My Irrational Beliefs (p. 215)

_____ ?

_____ ?

_____ ?

_____ ?

_____ ?

PERSONAL SUCCESS PORTFOLIO

Areas in Which I Will Build Self-Discipline

_____

_____

_____

Impulses I Will Resist (p. 228–232)

_____

_____

_____

Changes I Will Make (p. 235)

_____

_____

_____

Critical Thinking Habits I Will Adopt (pp. 248–250)

_____

_____

_____

_____

_____

Decision-Making Practices I Will Adopt (pp. 258–266)

_____

_____

_____

_____

_____

_____

PERSONAL SUCCESS PORTFOLIO

Intrinsic Goals I Will Strive to Accomplish (pp. 275–276)

_____

_____

_____

Actions I Will Take to Better Meet My Needs (pp. 280–287)

Physical Needs _____

_____

Security Needs _____

_____

Social Needs _____

_____

Esteem Needs _____

_____

Self-Actualization Needs _____

_____

What I Will Say to Myself to Overcome Fear of Failure (pp. 290–292)

_____

_____

_____

What I Will Say to Myself to Overcome Fear of Success (pp. 295–297)

_____

_____

_____

What I See When I Visualize Myself in the Future (pp. 301–302)

_____

_____

_____

PERSONAL SUCCESS PORTFOLIO

Activities That Are Most Important to Me (p. 310)

_____

_____

_____

Activities That Are Urgent But Not Important (pp. 313–314)

_____

_____

Actions I Will Take to Get More and Better-Quality Sleep (pp. 310, 313)

_____

_____

Actions I Will Take to Beat Procrastination (pp. 322–323, 325)

_____

_____

_____

How I Want to Spend My Money (pp. 333–334)

_____

_____

_____

_____

How I Don't Want to Spend My Money (pp. 339–340)

_____

_____

Actions I Will Take to Reduce My Spending (pp. 338–342)

_____

_____

_____

PERSONAL SUCCESS PORTFOLIO

Strategies I Will Use to Overcome Communication Barriers (pp. 353–354)

_____

_____

_____

Strategies I Will Use to Improve My Speaking Skills (pp. 363–365)

_____

_____

_____

_____

Strategies I Will Use to Improve My Listening Skills (pp. 366–367)

_____

_____

_____

_____

Ways I Will Show Empathy to Others (pp. 376–377)

_____

_____

_____

_____

Things I Will Dare to Self-Disclose (pp. 381–382)

_____

_____

_____

Ways I Will Handle Conflict Better (pp. 384–386)

_____

_____

_____

Chapter 1 Quotes

"*What lies behind us and what lies before us are small matters compared to what lies within us.*"

RALPH WALDO EMERSON

PHILOSOPHER

"*Life isn't about finding yourself. Life is about creating yourself.*"

GEORGE BERNARD SHAW

PLAYWRIGHT

"*Life is a series of collisions with the future; it is not a sum of what we have been but what we yearn to be.*"

JOSE ORTEGA Y GASSET

PHILOSOPHER

"*Personal change, growth, development, identity formation—these tasks that once were thought to belong to childhood and adolescence alone now are recognized as part of adult life as well.*"

LILLIAN BRESLOW RUBIN

PSYCHOLOGIST

Chapter 1 Keys to Success

Money and fame don't equal success. (p. 4)

Success is a journey, not a destination. (p. 7)

Use positive thinking to reach your goals. (p. 8)

Always make time for relationships. (p. 8)

Adults need role models, too. (p. 10)

Create your own opportunities for happiness. (p. 13)

Try new ways of thinking and doing. (p. 16)

Psychology helps you understand yourself. (p. 17)

Thoughts, feelings, and actions are all connected. (p. 20)

Pay attention to what is happening inside you and why. (p. 23)

A sense of self helps you understand the world and make plans and decisions. (p. 25)

A healthy self-image is positive but realistic. (p. 27)

It's healthy to find balance in your life. (p. 27)

No one sees you the way you see yourself. (p. 31)

Gender roles can be limiting. (p. 38)

Don't put limits on what you can become. (p. 40)

Thoughts, Feelings, and Actions

FIGURE 1.1

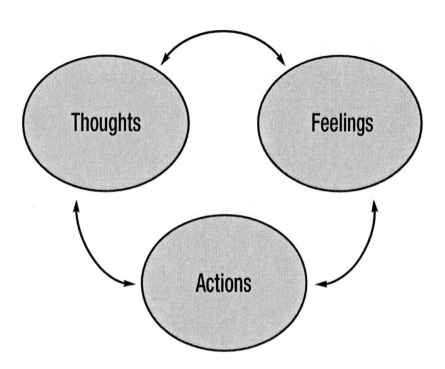

It's All Connected Thoughts, feelings, and actions all affect one another, even when we are unaware of it. *What might happen in a situation in which your thoughts and feelings are in conflict with one another?*

Positive and Negative Emotions

FIGURE 1.2

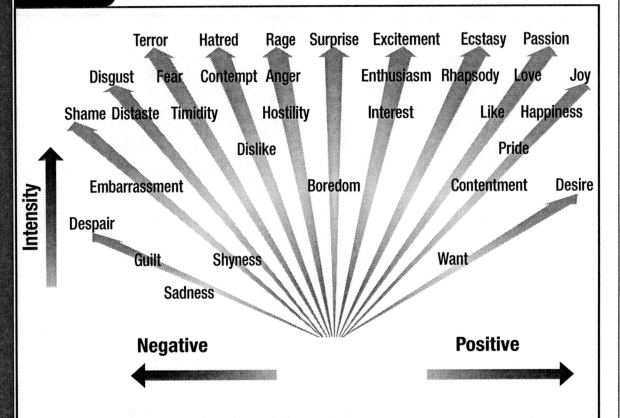

Terror Hatred Rage Surprise Excitement Ecstasy Passion

Disgust Fear Contempt Anger Enthusiasm Rhapsody Love Joy

Shame Distaste Timidity Hostility Interest Like Happiness

Dislike Pride

Embarrassment Boredom Contentment Desire

Despair

Guilt Shyness Want

Sadness

Intensity

Negative

Positive

The Range of Emotions Emotions can be extremely negative, such as guilt and despair, or extremely positive, such as happiness and joy. They can also be more neutral, such as boredom and surprise. *Describe an experience that provoked an intense feeling of joy.*

Predicting Thoughts, Feelings, and Actions

What would your first thought(s), feeling(s), and action(s) be in the following situations?

1. Gripping a hot pan

2. Seeing a great bargain at a store

3. Overhearing a funny comment

4. Smelling something burning

5. Seeing a friend crossing the street toward you

6. Seeing a nickel lying on the ground

7. Hitting your head on a cabinet door

8. Hearing an ambulance approach while you are driving

9. Stepping on a tack while barefoot

10. Seeing a ball sailing through the air toward you

16 Qualities That Foster Success and Happiness

- **Ability to love** the ability to feel, express, and receive love, affection, warmth, and compassion and to act in a giving way

- **Vocation** the ability to feel interest and excitement in something and to turn this into your life's work

- **Courage** the ability to take risks and challenge yourself

- **Trust** confidence in other people and their motives

- **Optimism** hope that things will turn out for the best

- **Future-mindedness** a focus on the possibilities of the future, rather than on the mistakes or disappointments of the past

- **Social skill** the ability to understand others, get along with others, and build fulfilling relationships

- **Aesthetic sensibility** the ability to appreciate and delight in the beauty of art, music, and nature

- **Work ethic** commitment to honoring obligations, being dependable and responsible, getting things done, and being productive

- **Honesty** thinking, speaking, and acting in a forthright way with yourself and others

- **Emotional awareness** the ability to experience and express a wide range of emotions

- **Persistence** the ability to persevere in the face of setbacks and adversity, to keep on track toward goals, and to handle stress

- **Forgiveness** generosity of spirit, and the ability to avoid grudges and blame

- **Creative thinking** the willingness to consider new opinions, beliefs, and points of view and to try out new ways of thinking and doing

- **Spirituality** the search for a greater good, purpose, or meaning to human existence

- **Self-esteem** a positive feeling of your own value, which includes self-respect as well as respect for the rights, feelings, and wishes of others

- **Wisdom** the ability to use your knowledge and experience to make sound decisions

24 Strengths of Character

- active open-mindedness
- awe/appreciation of beauty
- citizenship/teamwork
- creativity/ingenuity
- curiosity/interest
- equity/fairness
- forgiveness/mercy
- gratitude
- hope/optimism
- industry/perseverance
- integrity/honesty/authenticity
- intimacy/attachment (love)
- kindness/generosity
- leadership
- love of learning
- modesty/humility
- perspective (wisdom)
- playfulness/humor
- prudence/caution
- self-control/self-regulation
- social intelligence
- spirituality
- valor (bravery/courage)
- vitality/zest/enthusiasm

SOURCE: CHRISTOPHER PETERSON AND MARTIN E. P. SELIGMAN. *THE VIA CLASSIFICATION OF STRENGTHS.* (CINCINNATI, OH: VALUES IN ACTION INSTITUTE, 2004).

Chapter 2 Quotes

"*Few people even scratch the surface, much less exhaust the contemplation of their own experience.*"

RANDOLPH BOURNE

ESSAYIST

"*Hold fast to dreams, for if dreams die, life is a broken winged bird that cannot fly.*"

LANGSTON HUGHES

POET

"*Don't be afraid of the space between your dreams and reality. If you can dream it, you can make it so.*"

BELVA DAVIS

JOURNALIST

"*People travel to wonder at the height of mountains, at the huge waves of the sea, at the long courses of rivers, at the vast compass of the ocean, at the circular motion of the stars, and they pass themselves by without wondering.*"

SAINT AUGUSTINE

THEOLOGIAN

"*I think that self-awareness is probably the most important thing toward being a champion.*"

BILLIE JEAN KING

ATHLETE

Chapter 2 Keys to Success

Self-honesty helps you get in touch with your dreams, values, and interests. (p. 47)

Too much self-consciousness can produce anxiety. (p. 48)

Develop the courage to face painful emotions. (p. 51)

Look for the exact words to express what you feel. (p. 51)

Dreams give your life purpose. (p. 53)

Life asks something of everyone. (p. 53)

A dream can be anything you want it to be. (p. 54)

Aim to satisfy yourself, not someone else. (p. 54)

It's important to determine your own values. (p. 57)

Values are beliefs, not absolutes. (p. 58)

Values guide your choices in life. (p. 61)

Look for opportunities to express your values in a positive way. (p. 61)

Use your personality traits to help you succeed. (p. 63)

Find a variety of ways to describe yourself. (p. 66)

Transferable skills are the foundation of job-specific skills. (p. 68)

Pinpointing your strongest intelligences helps you discover what you do best. (p. 72)

You can strengthen your intelligences through learning and practice. (p. 76)

Skills and interests go hand in hand. (p. 77)

Let your skills and interests guide your career choices. (p. 79)

Work can and should be something you enjoy. (p. 80)

Consider your personality when choosing a career. (p. 81)

Skills, Interests, and Career Fields

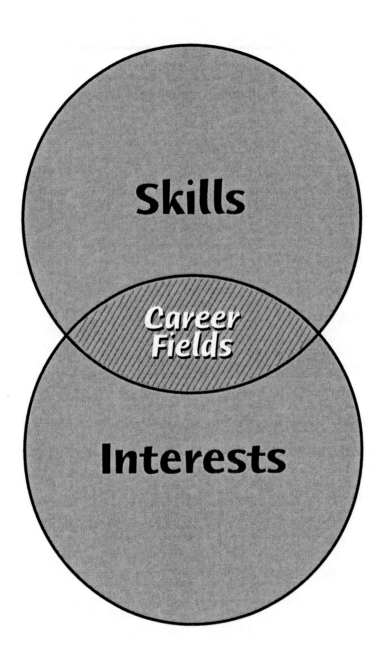

Workplace Skills

Basic Skills

▸ Reading
▸ Writing
▸ Mathematics
▸ Speaking
▸ Listening

Thinking Skills

▸ Critical thinking
▸ Creative thinking
▸ Decision making
▸ Problem solving
▸ Knowing how to learn
▸ Reasoning
▸ Visualizing

Personal Qualities

▸ Responsibility
▸ Dependability
▸ Self-esteem
▸ Sociability
▸ Integrity
▸ Self-management

Interpersonal Qualities

▸ Being a good team member
▸ Leadership

Resources

▸ Managing time
▸ Managing money
▸ Managing space and facilities
▸ Managing human resources
▸ Working with cultural diversity

Information

▸ Acquiring information
▸ Organizing information
▸ Maintaining information
▸ Evaluating information
▸ Using computers to process information

Systems

▸ Maintaining systems
▸ Improving systems
▸ Understanding systems

Technology

▸ Selecting and applying technology
▸ Maintaining technology
▸ Using both sides of the brain

Feeling Words

FIGURE 2.1

I FEEL GOOD

admired	delighted	inquisitive	satisfied
adored	devoted	intelligent	secure
amused	earnest	interested	self-accepting
appreciated	ecstatic	joyful	self-assured
attractive	effective	knowledgeable	sincere
brave	elated	loving	skillful
capable	encouraged	optimistic	tender
cheerful	excited	passionate	thrilled
competent	fascinated	pleased	useful
confident	flattered	proud	valued
contented	graceful	rambunctious	vindicated
courageous	grateful	resourceful	warm
creative	heroic	resilient	whole
curious	hopeful	respected	worthy
daring	important	romantic	zealous

I FEEL BAD

afraid	devalued	incompetent	self-doubting
agitated	devastated	jealous	shaken
aloof	disappointed	jittery	silly
angry	discouraged	lonely	skeptical
anxious	embarrassed	lost	snubbed
ashamed	empty	mediocre	sorrowful
awkward	fearful	neglected	suspicious
betrayed	foolish	nervous	tense
burdened	frightened	out of control	terrified
cheated	guilty	panicky	ugly
clumsy	heartbroken	pessimistic	uptight
cranky	helpless	put down	useless
defensive	hostile	rejected	weary
dejected	humiliated	self-critical	worried
deserted	ignored	self-destructive	worthless

Emotional Awareness To become more emotionally aware, practice asking yourself these three questions: How is my body feeling? What happened right before I started to experience this emotion? Can I put a specific name to this emotion? *Why would developing a vocabulary of feeling words help you become more aware of your emotions?*

Expanding Your Intelligences

FIGURE 2.2

Intelligence	Strategies
Verbal/Linguistic	• Join a book club or take a writing course. • Read anything and everything. • Use a new word in your conversation every day.
Logical/Mathematical	• Work on puzzles and brain teasers. • Visit a science center, planetarium, or aquarium. • Practice calculating problems in your head.
Visual/Spatial	• Work on jigsaw puzzles or visual puzzles. • Visit art museums and galleries. • Take a class in visual arts, such as photography.
Bodily/Kinesthetic	• Join a gym or a sports team. • Learn dance, yoga, t'ai chi, or martial arts. • Enroll in an aerobics or weight-training class.
Musical	• Attend concerts and musicals. • Take a class in music appreciation or performance. • Explore unfamiliar styles of music.
Interpersonal	• Join a volunteer or service group. • Learn about body language and communication. • Introduce yourself to new people often.
Intrapersonal	• Develop a meditative hobby, such as gardening. • Keep a journal of your thoughts and feelings. • Consult a counselor or therapist.
Naturalistic	• Explore the flora and fauna of your region. • Look for patterns in nature or architecture. • Start a collection of objects.

Learning + Practice = Progress Exploring new activities and meeting new people help you build your intelligences and discover new interests. *Select the intelligence you would most like to develop, and describe three specific actions you could take to do this.*

Skills Inventory

Below are descriptions of twenty-four transferable skills covering all the main skill areas. Read each statement and indicate how true it is for you by putting a check mark in the appropriate box.

Academic Skills

☐ I can understand written information in many different forms, such as text, tables, lists, figures, and diagrams.

☐ I can use different reading strategies, such as skimming for highlights, reading for detail, and reading for meaning.

☐ When I write and speak, I can express facts and ideas clearly and in an organized way.

☐ I can use correct spelling, punctuation, grammar, and sentence and paragraph structure.

☐ When I write and speak, I can tailor my words to my purpose and my audience.

☐ I can pay full attention to what another person is saying, and can interpret nonverbal cues such as body language.

☐ I can solve math problems through different methods such as arithmetic, algebra, and geometry.

Thinking Skills

☐ I can gather information on a particular question or issue through observation, discussion, or research.

☐ I can organize, analyze, and evaluate the information I find.

☐ I can anticipate and identify problems and their causes.

☐ I can develop and evaluate solutions using reason, logic, and creativity.

☐ I can make decisions by considering relevant information, risks and benefits, and short- and long-term consequences.

☐ I can organize my work to perform at my best and reach my goals.

☐ I can establish plans and priorities and adjust them as necessary.

☐ I am open to new information, ideas, or strategies that might help me achieve my goals.

Social Skills

☐ I can interact with others in a friendly, courteous, and tactful way.

☐ I can demonstrate respect for individual and cultural differences and for other people's attitudes and feelings.

☐ I can inspire others to achieve their goals and develop as individuals.

☐ I can serve as a mentor, coach, and role model.

☐ I can change my behavior to adjust to other people, to changing situations, or to new work demands.

☐ I can cooperate and work with others by sharing knowledge, skills, resources, responsibility, and recognition.

☐ I can help individuals or groups resolve their differences and come to agreements.

☐ I can solve conflicts in a positive and creative way.

Sensation Seeking Questionnaire

Read each statement and indicate which one is more like you by circling a *or* b.

---

1. a. I would like a job that requires a lot of traveling.

 b. I would prefer a job in one location.

---

2. a. I am invigorated by a brisk, cold day.

 b. I can't wait to get indoors on a cold day.

---

3. a. I get bored seeing the same old faces.

 b. I like the comfortable familiarity of everyday friends.

---

4. a. I would prefer living in an ideal society in which everyone is safe, secure, and happy.

 b. I would have preferred living in the unsettled days of our history.

---

5. a. I sometimes like to do things that are a little frightening.

 b. A sensible person avoids activities that are dangerous.

---

6. a. I would not like to be hypnotized.

 b. I would like to have the experience of being hypnotized.

---

7. a. The most important goal of life is to live it to the fullest and to experience as much as possible.

 b. The most important goal of life is to find peace and happiness.

---

8. a. I would like to try parachute jumping.

 b. I would never want to try jumping out of a plane, with or without a parachute.

---

9. a. I enter cold water gradually, giving myself time to get used to it.

 b. I like to dive or jump right into the ocean or a cold pool.

---

10. a. When I go on a vacation, I prefer the comfort of a good room and bed.

 b. When I go on a vacation, I prefer the change of camping out.

---

11. a. I prefer people who are emotionally expressive, even if they are a bit unstable.

 b. I prefer people who are calm and even-tempered.

---

12. a. A good painting should shock or jolt the senses.

 b. A good painting should give one a feeling of peace and security.

---

13. a. People who ride motorcycles must have some kind of unconscious need to hurt themselves.

 b. I would like to drive or ride a motorcycle.

SOURCE: ADAPTED FROM MARVIN ZUCKERMAN, BEHAVIORAL EXPRESSION AND BIOSOCIAL EXPRESSION OF SENSATION SEEKING. (CAMBRIDGE, ENGLAND: CAMBRIDGE UNIVERSITY PRESS, 1994).

Scoring: Give yourself one point for each of the following responses: 1a, 2a, 3a, 4b, 5a, 6b, 7a, 8a, 9b, 10b, 11a, 12a, 13b. What is your score? _____

0–5 Very low to low need for sensation
6–9 Average need for sensation
10–13 High to very high need for sensation

Keirsey Personality Types

Artisan

- You seek sensation, trust in spontaneity, and hunger for impact on others.
- You enjoy working with any and all kinds of equipment, implements, machines, and instruments, from bulldozers to paintbrushes.
- You enjoy crafts of many kinds—athletic, culinary, literary, martial, mechanical, rhetorical, theatrical, political, or industrial.
- You have an affinity to other artisans such as Wolfgang Amadeus Mozart, Steven Spielberg, Elvis Presley, Michael Jordan, Barbra Streisand, and Amelia Earhart.
- You would probably enjoy a career as an artist, musician, actor, chef, craftsperson, or mechanic.

Guardian

- You seek security and hunger for membership in a social group.
- You enjoy occupations that involve gathering, storing, recording, measuring, and distributing data or people.
- You are talented at arranging, scheduling, establishing order, and creating organizations.
- You have an affinity to other guardians such as George Washington, Colin Powell, Mother Teresa, Harry Truman, and J.P. Morgan.
- You would probably enjoy a career as a businessperson, librarian, doctor, nurse, military officer, salesperson, coach, or social worker.

Idealist

- You seek a unique identity, hunger for deep and meaningful relationships, and aspire to profundity.
- You are enthusiastic, have insight into people, and are good at influencing others and helping them reach their full potential.
- You are talented at teaching, counseling, interviewing, and tutoring people.
- You have an affinity to other idealists such as Emily Brontë, Sidney Poitier, Mohandas Gandhi, Eleanor Roosevelt, Sandra Day O'Connor, and Oprah Winfrey.
- You would probably enjoy a career as a teacher or trainer, employee recruiter, counselor, or human services worker.

Rational

- You seek knowledge, trust in reason, and hunger for achievement.
- You are interested in complexity and are good at understanding it.
- You are interested in complex machines, such as airplanes, or in complex biological organisms, such as humans, plants, and animals.
- You have an affinity to other rationals such as Albert Einstein, Marie Curie, Booker T. Washington, Charles Darwin, Thomas Edison, and Bill Gates.
- You would probably enjoy a career as a scientist, architect, engineer, military strategist, inventor, or executive.

Chapter 3 Quotes

"**W**hoever wants to reach a distant goal must take small steps."

SAUL BELLOW, NOVELIST

"**M**an is a goal-seeking animal. His life only has meaning if he is reaching out and striving for his goals."

ARISTOTLE, PHILOSOPHER

"**S**tress is an ignorant state. It believes that everything is an emergency. Nothing is that important. Just lie down."

NATALIE GOLDBERG
WRITER, PAINTER, AND TEACHER

"**A** journey of a thousand miles begins with a single step."

CHINESE PROVERB

"**S**tart by doing what's necessary, then what's possible, and suddenly you are doing the impossible."

ST. FRANCIS OF ASSISI, MONK

"**I** cannot give you the formula for success, but I can give you the formula for failure which is: Try to please everybody."

HERBERT BAYARD SWOPE, JOURNALIST

"**T**here are two ways of meeting difficulties: You alter the difficulties or you alter yourself to meet them."

PHYLLIS BOTTOME, NOVELIST

"**O**bstacles don't have to stop you. If you run into a wall, don't turn around and give up. Figure out how to climb it, go through it, or work around it."

MICHAEL JORDAN, ATHLETE

Chapter 3 Keys to Success

Be proactive about your goals—only you can make them happen. (p. 90)

Be specific when setting your goals. (p. 91)

Short-term goals and long-term goals are equally important. (p. 94)

Keep reminding yourself to stick to your goals. (p. 97)

Once you have achieved one goal, move on to the next. (p. 97)

Choose your goals to please yourself, not others. (p. 99)

Don't hesitate to ask for support when you need it. (p. 100)

You will need to adapt to change throughout your life. (p. 101)

It's normal to feel stress when faced with change. (p. 105)

Look for uplifts to offset the stresses of life. (p. 106)

Fatigue and irritability can be signs of stress overload. (p. 106)

Learn to recognize situations that cause you stress. (p. 109)

Make time for relaxation every day. (p. 110)

Regular exercise keeps your mind and body fit. (p. 110)

Practice a technique for clearing your mind of worries and distracting thoughts. (p. 111)

Establish a support network. (p. 112)

Make time for refreshing, entertaining activities. (p. 112)

Remember to keep your sense of humor. (p. 113)

Anger harms your physical and mental health. (p. 117)

Figure out what makes you angry—and why. (p. 119)

Focus on staying calm. (p. 121)

Change what you can, and accept what you can't. (p. 121)

Your thoughts and feelings are valid, and you have a right to assert them. (p. 122)

SMART Goals

FIGURE 3.1

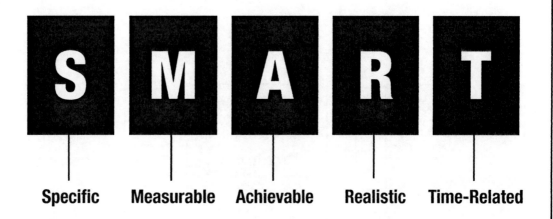

S **M** **A** **R** **T**

Specific   Measurable   Achievable   Realistic   Time-Related

Look Before You Leap The more time and thought you invest in formulating your goals, the more likely you'll be to achieve them. *Why do you think that many experts advise putting goals down in writing?*

The ABC Model

FIGURE 3.2

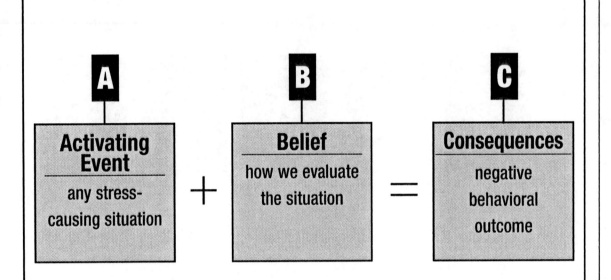

A **Activating Event** any stress-causing situation

+

B **Belief** how we evaluate the situation

=

C **Consequences** negative behavioral outcome

Taking Control The ABC formula demonstrates how negative, irrational beliefs can create stress and lead to unwanted consequences. *How can becoming more aware of your personal stressors help you control stress?*

Passive-Aggression Questionnaire

How often do you think or act in the following ways?

	Never	Sometimes	Often
1. When you want to avoid an obligation, you make an excuse instead of telling the truth.			
2. You suppress your anger rather than express it.			
3. You get into trouble for not keeping promises.			
4. You feel unappreciated.			
5. You get angry when people give you suggestions or "constructive" criticism.			
6. You feel that people don't understand you or your feelings.			
7. You feel that your misfortune is greater than other people's misfortune.			
8. Even when things are going well for you, life seems gloomy.			
9. You make sarcastic jokes about other people.			
10. You blame other people for your setbacks and failures.			
11. You agree with someone, but then side with others against that person.			
12. If you don't like a certain task, you do it so inefficiently that people just give up asking you to do it.			
13. You feel that people don't give you enough credit for the good job you do at work.			
14. You have problems with authority figures.			
15. You promise other people you'll do certain things, but you don't get around to doing them.			

Scoring: Assign zero points for every **Never**, one point for every **Sometimes**, and two points for every **Often**.

1–9 You generally deal with your negative emotions well.

10–19 You show occasional passive-aggressive behavior, which is probably harming you and others.

20–30 You have many passive-aggressive habits that need changing. These habits are sabotaging you and creating large problems for others.

Stressful Life Events

Life Event	Stress Value
1. Death of spouse	100
2. Divorce	73
3. Marital separation	65
4. Detention/imprisonment	63
5. Death of a close family member	63
6. Major personal injury or illness	53
7. Marriage	50
8. Dismissal from work	47
9. Marital reconciliation	45
10. Retirement from work	45
11. Major change in the health or behavior of a family member	44
12. Pregnancy	40
13. Sexual difficulties	39
14. Gaining a new family member	39
15. Major business readjustment, such as reorganization or bankruptcy	39
16. Major change in financial state—worse or better	38
17. Death of a close friend	37
18. Changing to a different line of work	36
19. Major change in the number of arguments with partner	35
20. Taking out a mortgage or loan for a major purchase	31
21. Foreclosure on a mortgage or loan	30
22. Major change in responsibilities at work/school	29
23. Son or daughter leaving home, marrying, or attending college	29
24. Trouble with in-laws	29
25. Outstanding personal achievement	28
26. Partner beginning or ceasing work outside the home	26
27. Beginning or ceasing formal schooling	26
28. Major change in living conditions	25
29. Change of personal habits such as dress or social circle	24
30. Trouble with boss	23
31. Major change in working hours or conditions	20
32. Change in residence	20
33. Changing to a new school	20
34. Major change in usual type and/or amount of recreation	19
35. Major change in religious activities	19
36. Major change in social activities such as time with friends	18
37. Taking out a mortgage or loan for a lesser purchase	17
38. Major change in sleeping habits	16
39. Major change in number of family get-togethers	15
40. Major change in eating habits	15
41. Vacation	13
42. End-of-year holidays	12
43. Minor violations of the law such as traffic tickets	11

SOURCE: ADAPTED FROM T. H. HOLMES AND R. H. RAHE, "THE SOCIAL READJUSTMENT RATING SCALE," *JOURNAL OF PSYCHOSOMATIC RESEARCH* 11 (1967), 213-18.

The Most Stressful Jobs

Inner City High School Teacher
Police Officer
Firefighter
Race Car Driver
NFL Player
Miner
Taxi Driver
Air Traffic Controller
Medical Intern
Stockbroker
Senior Corporate Executive
Journalist
Customer Service/Complaint Worker
Secretary
Waiter
President of the United States

Comparable Work Environments and Salaries

Least stressful work environments

Statistician
Mathematician
Computer systems analyst
Hospital administrator
Historian

Stressful work environments

Taxi driver
NFL player
Race car driver
Firefighter
President of the United States

Highest salaries

NBA player ($4,637,825)
Major League Baseball player ($1,954,400)
NFL player ($1,836,460)
Race car driver ($508,569)
President of the United States ($400,000)

Lowest salaries

Child care worker ($17,077)
Maid ($17,077)
Waiter/Waitress ($16,083)
Catholic priest ($16,079)
Dishwasher ($16,046)

SOURCE: LES KRANTZ, JOBS RATED ALMANAC (BARRICADE BOOKS, 2002).

Chapter 4 Quotes

"*Allow yourself to fail and you will be more likely to succeed.*"

EDWARD DECI
PSYCHOLOGIST

"*If I could wish for my life to be perfect, it would be tempting but I would have to decline, for life would no longer teach me anything.*"

ALLYSON JONES
AUTHOR

"*Our deepest fear is not that we are inadequate. Our deepest fear is that we are powerful beyond measure. It is our light that most frightens us. We ask ourselves, 'Who am I to be brilliant, gorgeous, talented, fabulous?' Actually, who are you not to be?*"

MARIANNE WILLIAMSON
AUTHOR

"*Self-respect cannot be hunted. It cannot be purchased. It is never for sale. It cannot be fabricated out of public relations. It comes to us when we are alone, in quiet moments, in quiet places, when we suddenly realize that, knowing the good, we have done it; knowing the beautiful, we have served it; knowing the truth, we have spoken it.*"

NOËL COWARD
PLAYWRIGHT

"*I began to understand that self-esteem isn't everything; it's just that there's nothing without it.*"

GLORIA STEINEM
AUTHOR AND ACTIVIST

"*The worst loneliness is not to be comfortable with yourself.*"

MARK TWAIN
AUTHOR

Chapter 4 Keys to Success

Self-esteem motivates you to work hard and succeed. (p. 128)

When you feel good about yourself, you have the confidence to try new things. (p. 129)

Having healthy self-esteem lets you feel good about your accomplishments, big or small. (p. 135)

Remind yourself that there are people who love and appreciate you. (p. 137)

Supportive, nurturing relationships help guard against loneliness and low self-esteem. (p. 140)

No matter what your age, you can learn to value yourself. (p. 140)

It's not what you can't do that holds you back—it's what you *think* you can't do. (p. 141)

To boost your self-expectancy, work to accomplish a series of increasingly difficult goals. (p. 143)

When you face your problems head-on, your self-esteem grows. (p. 147)

Your skills and personal qualities are unlike anyone else's. (p. 148)

For self-acceptance, you need an accurate view of your strengths and weaknesses. (p. 150)

Think of yourself as your body's friend, not its enemy. (p. 155)

Measure your progress according to your goals, not someone else's. (p. 156)

Remember the difference between fantasy and reality. (p. 158)

Your inner critic hurts your self-esteem by repeating negative messages from your past. (p. 160)

Learn to stop the inner critic in its tracks. (p. 161)

Turn your negative self-statements into positive affirmations. (p. 164)

Criticism often stems from a simple difference of opinion. (p. 165)

Constructive criticism helps you improve yourself. (p. 166)

Listen to constructive criticism, restate it, then ask for suggestions. (p. 167)

Acknowledge destructive criticism, then correct any errors. (p. 168)

Before you respond to a vague criticism, probe for specifics. (p. 170)

You have the right to be treated with respect. (p. 174)

Childhood Origins of Self-Esteem

FIGURE 4.1

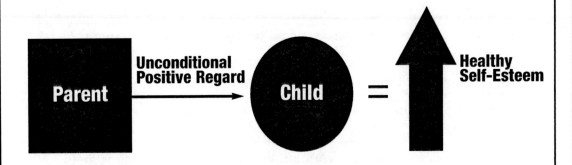

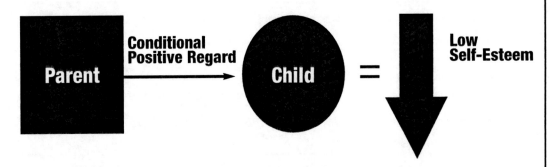

Positive Regard Your self-esteem is developed and established early on in your life. Studies show that parents' style of child-rearing during the first three or four years greatly affects children's self-esteem. *Besides parents, what other important adults might influence a child's self-esteem?*

You and Your Ideal

FIGURE 4.2

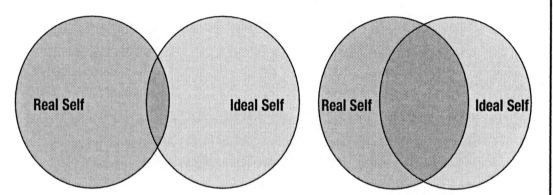

Low Self-Esteem   High Self-Esteem

Striving for Perfection The further away our ideal self is from our real self, the more our self-esteem suffers. *How can you control the gap between your real and ideal self?*

Responding to Constructive Criticism

FIGURE 4.3

Constructive Criticism

↓

Listen carefully.
Check for understanding.

↓

Restate the criticism.

↓

Ask for suggestions.

To Your Advantage Constructive criticism is a source of valuable information. Asking for suggestions helps you find creative solutions to the problem behind the criticism. *If you were a manager, would you feel comfortable giving your employees constructive criticism? Why or why not?*

Responding to Destructive Criticism

FIGURE 4.4

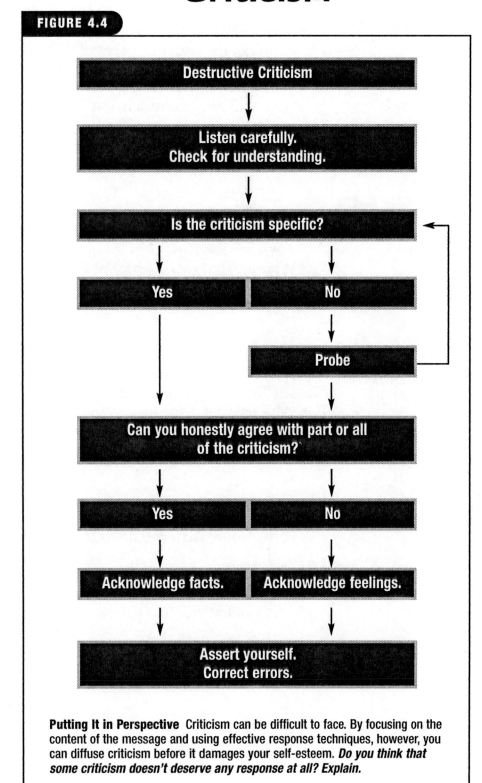

Putting It in Perspective Criticism can be difficult to face. By focusing on the content of the message and using effective response techniques, however, you can diffuse criticism before it damages your self-esteem. *Do you think that some criticism doesn't deserve any response at all? Explain.*

History of Your Self-Esteem

Elementary School

- How did you feel about yourself when you were a student in elementary school? Was your self-image positive or negative? Explain.
- Who or what was the biggest influence on your self-image and self-esteem at this time? Why?

High School

- How did you feel about yourself during high school? Was your self-image positive or negative? Explain.
- Who or what was the biggest influence on your self-image and self-esteem at this time? Why?

Today

- How do you feel about yourself today? Is your self-image positive or negative? Explain.
- Who or what is the biggest influence on your self-image and self-esteem today? Why?

The Future

- Do you think you will feel better about yourself in the future than you do today? Why or why not?
- What do you think the biggest influence on your self-image and self-esteem will be in five years? In ten years? Why?

Rosenberg Self-Esteem Scale

Read the statements below and indicate how true each one is for you by putting a check mark in the appropriate box.

	Strongly Agree	Agree	Disagree	Strongly Disagree
1. I feel that I'm a person of worth, at least on an equal plane with others.				
2. I feel that I have a number of good qualities.				
3. All in all, I am inclined to feel that I am a failure.				
4. I am able to do things as well as most other people.				
5. I feel I do not have much to be proud of.				
6. I take a positive attitude toward myself.				
7. On the whole, I am satisfied with myself.				
8. I wish I could have more respect for myself.				
9. I certainly feel useless at times.				
10. At times I think I am no good at all.				

Scoring: For items 1, 2, 4, 6, and 7, assign yourself three points for every **Strongly Agree**, two points for every **Agree**, one point for every **Disagree**, and zero points for every **Strongly Disagree**. For items 3, 5, 8, 9, and 10, assign yourself zero points for every **Strongly Agree**, one point for every **Agree**, two points for every **Disagree**, and three points for every **Strongly Disagree**.

What is your total?_____

The higher your total, the stronger your self-esteem.

0–10 Low self-esteem

11–20 Moderate self-esteem

21–30 High self-esteem

Chapter 5 Quotes

"**H**ope is not a dream, but a way of making dreams become reality."

LEO SUENENS
RELIGIOUS LEADER

"**S**uccess is a process, a quality of mind and way of being, an outgoing affirmation of life."

ALEX NOBLE
AUTHOR

"**A**bility is what you're capable of doing. Motivation determines what you do. Attitude determines how well you do it."

RAYMOND CHANDLER
WRITER AND POET

"**A**ttitude is more important than the past, than education, than money, than circumstances, than what people do or say. It is more important than appearance, giftedness, or skill."

W.C. FIELDS
COMEDIAN AND ACTOR

"**I**t is important to live each day with a positive perspective. It is not wise to pretend problems do not exist, but it is wise to look beyond the problem to the possibilities that are in it. When Goliath came against the Israelites, the soldiers all thought, 'He's so big, we can never kill him.' But David looked at the same giant and thought, 'He's so big, I can't miss him.'"

DALE TURNER
AUTHOR AND MOTIVATIONAL SPEAKER

Chapter 5 Keys to Success

Positive thinking gives you the drive to make good things happen for yourself. (p. 180)

Positive thoughts lead to positive feelings and positive actions. (p. 183)

Look for things to be grateful for. (p. 186)

Use positive words and choose positive friends. (p. 186)

Taking constructive action feels better than complaining. (p. 188)

Focus on finding solutions, not bracing for the worst. (p. 190)

Worrying prevents you from taking risks. (p. 191)

Thinking well can make you well. (p. 194)

Following a healthy lifestyle is one of the most positive things you can do for yourself. (p. 195)

Eat for health and energy. (p. 199)

Look at exercise as fun time for you, not as a chore. (p. 199)

Self-defeating attitudes trick you into believing you can't succeed. (p. 201)

Negative attitudes produce negative results. (p. 202)

Learn to recognize your self-defeating attitudes and turn them around with positive self-talk. (p. 203)

Life's setbacks and frustrations can't defeat you, but a negative attitude toward them can. (p. 204)

Examine your thinking for distortions and exaggerations. (p. 209)

Try to think in realistic terms, not absolutes. (p. 211)

Negative thoughts lead to unpleasant emotions and self-defeating actions. (p. 212)

Separate your emotional reaction from the reality of your situation. (p. 215)

Positive Habits

The Power of Positive Thoughts

FIGURE 5.1

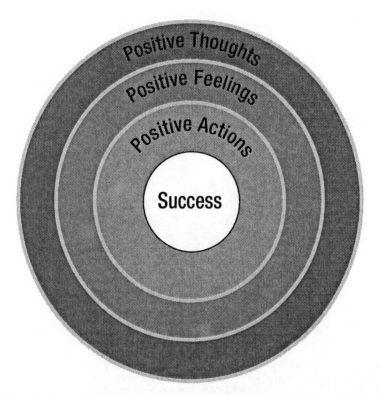

On Target Thoughts, feelings, and actions go hand in hand. When you have positive thoughts, you experience positive feelings and have the energy and drive to take positive actions. *Do you believe that you can change your way of thinking by choosing to do so? Why or why not?*

The Food Guide Pyramid

FIGURE 5.2

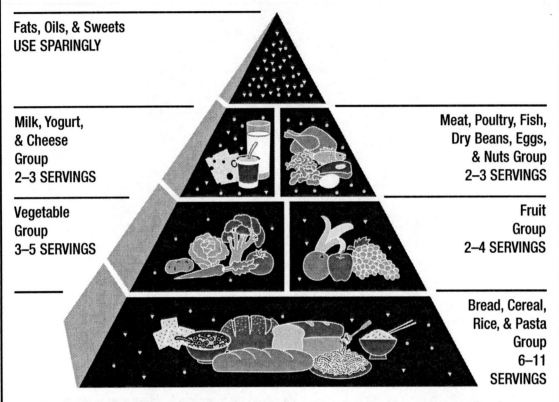

Fats, Oils, & Sweets
USE SPARINGLY

Milk, Yogurt,
& Cheese
Group
2–3 SERVINGS

Meat, Poultry, Fish,
Dry Beans, Eggs,
& Nuts Group
2–3 SERVINGS

Vegetable
Group
3–5 SERVINGS

Fruit
Group
2–4 SERVINGS

Bread, Cereal,
Rice, & Pasta
Group
6–11
SERVINGS

Source: U.S. Department of Agriculture/U.S. Department of Health and Human Services

Body and Mind It takes effort and planning to eat right. Processed foods, such as sugary snacks and greasy fast foods, are usually easier to find, as well as cheaper and faster, than healthful foods. *What obstacles do you think prevent people from eating more healthfully? Why?*

Self-Defeating Attitudes: A Vicious Cycle

FIGURE 5.3

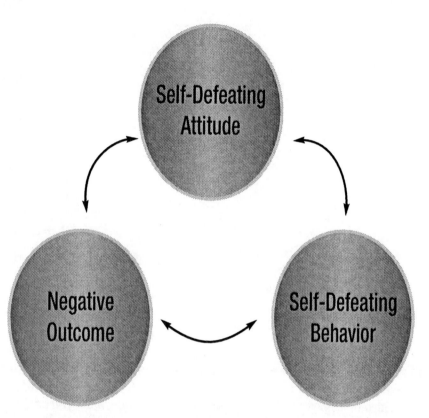

Stop the Cycle When we have negative attitudes, we tend to act in ways that make our negative predictions about events come true. *How can you break this vicious cycle?*

The ABCDE Method

FIGURE 5.4

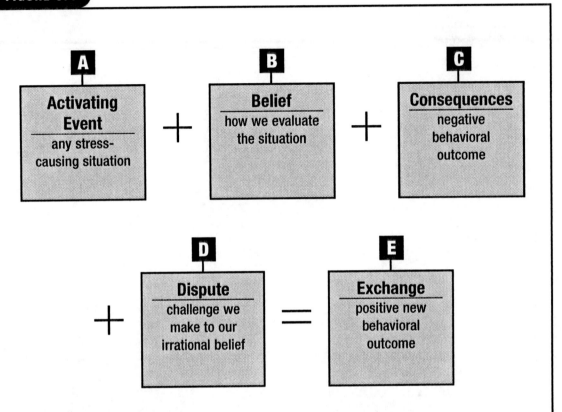

A Activating Event — any stress-causing situation

+

B Belief — how we evaluate the situation

+

C Consequences — negative behavioral outcome

+

D Dispute — challenge we make to our irrational belief

=

E Exchange — positive new behavioral outcome

Turning Beliefs Around Once we are aware of the irrational beliefs that are distorting our thinking and making us unhappy, we can use effective disputes to create healthier, more positive outcomes for ourselves. *What are some questions you can ask yourself to help dispute an irrational belief?*

Do Negatives Outweigh Positives?

Negative qualities often command more attention and seem more important than positive qualities:

- As people think over upcoming decisions, potential losses are often given greater weight than potential gains.

- In the social sphere, one negative personal characteristic influences people's feelings about an individual more than a host of positive characteristics.

- Negative experiences color marital satisfaction; they have more impact than do positive experiences.

- People are more likely to find an unusual face in a crowd and quickly if the face looks angry than if it looks happy.

- Subjects who examine a description of a person that uses equal numbers of positive and negative adjectives are likely to subsequently recall more negative adjectives than positive ones.

- Humans are "prepared" to learn to react with negative emotions and to quickly learn to avoid certain stimuli, such as snakes, spiders, and angry faces, that may have posed a threat to early ancestors. Although people are able to learn to avoid other stimuli, such as flowers or happy faces, that did not threaten their ancestors, they do so with greater difficulty.

Being particularly attuned to objects that could potentially be dangerous makes evolutionary sense; in past epochs, such stimuli probably threatened survival. In the contemporary world, this bias to fear such possibly dangerous stimuli can be the source of phobias. Moreover, these negative biases can erode the quality of life, the wisdom of choices, and the longevity of relationships. Knowing that these biases exist may stimulate the development of methods to counteract their potentially destructive effects on social and emotional life.

SOURCE: NATIONAL INSTITUTE OF MENTAL HEALTH, "A NATIONAL INVESTMENT." A REPORT OF THE NATIONAL ADVISORY MENTAL HEALTH COUNCIL, 1995, NIH PUBLICATION NO. 96-3682.

Murphy's Laws

- If anything can go wrong, it will go wrong.

- If everything seems to be going well, you must have overlooked something.

- Everything goes wrong at once.

- Every solution breeds new problems.

- Everything takes longer than it takes.

- Toast always falls with the buttered side down.

- As soon as you mention something good, it goes away.

- As soon as you mention something bad, it happens.

- No good deed goes unpunished.

- If you want something bad enough, chances are you won't get it.

- The light at the end of the tunnel is a train.

- Whatever you can have, you don't want.

- If this was worth doing, someone would have already done it.

- Behind every minor problem is a major problem.

- If you work hard, someone else will get the credit.

- If you make a fool of yourself, someone is always there to notice it.

False Memory Test

1. bed, rest, awake, tired, dream, wake, snooze, blanket, doze, slumber, snore, nap, peace, yawn, drowsy

sleep

2. nurse, sick, lawyer, medicine, health, hospital, dentist, physician, ill, patient, office, stethoscope, surgeon, clinic, cure

doctor

3. thread, pin, eye, sewing, sharp, point, prick, thimble, haystack, thorn, hurt, injection, syringe, cloth, knitting

needle

4. hot, snow, warm, winter, ice, wet, frigid, chilly, heat, weather, freeze, air, shiver, Arctic, frost

cold

5. apple, vegetable, orange, kiwi, citrus, ripe, pear, banana, berry, cherry, basket, juice, salad, bowl, cocktail

fruit

6. hill, valley, climb, summit, top, molehill, plain, peak, glacier, goat, bike, climber, range, steep, ski

mountain

Chapter 6 Quotes

"**N**ot everything that is faced can be changed, but nothing can be changed until it is faced."

JAMES BALDWIN

AUTHOR

"**O**pportunities are usually disguised as hard work. So no one recognizes them."

ANN LANDERS

ADVICE COLUMNIST

"**I** cannot say whether things will get better if we change; what I can say is they must change if they are to get better."

G. C. LICHTENBERG

PHILOSOPHER

"**I**nsanity is continuing to do the same thing over and over and expecting different results."

ALBERT EINSTEIN

PHYSICIST

"**A**s long as we are persistent in our pursuit of our deepest destiny, we will continue to grow. We cannot choose the day or time when we will fully bloom. It happens in its own time."

DENIS WAITLEY

(FROM *SEEDS OF GREATNESS*)

Chapter 6 Keys to Success

All successful people rely on self-discipline. (p. 224)

Success doesn't always come on the first or second try. (p. 226)

Don't wait for someone else to do something—take action! (p. 228)

Before you act on impulse, stop, think, and decide. (p. 231)

Self-improvement requires the willingness to change. (p. 233)

It takes courage to try something new. (p. 233)

Your self-esteem rises when you make positive changes. (p. 236)

Almost everything in life is a choice. (p. 239)

When your habits have negative consequences, it's time to change them. (p. 239)

It takes effort to commit to changing. (p. 240)

Before you can change a habit, you need to understand it. (p. 240)

Are your habits stubborn? Be more stubborn! (p. 243)

Use positive self-talk to create a mental image of the new you. (p. 243)

Positive self-talk helps you change for good. (p. 245)

Critical thinking helps you solve problems and overcome obstacles. (p. 246)

Think and communicate with a clear purpose. (p. 251)

Learn to distinguish facts from opinions. (p. 252)

Learn to separate the relevant from the irrelevant. (p. 253)

Remember that your point of view is only one of many. (p. 254)

Look at critical thinking as a learning process. (p. 255)

When you make a major decision, you are creating a new future for yourself. (p. 258)

Consider every possible option. (p. 260)

Use your values and goals to guide your choices. (p. 261)

The results of your decisions can teach you a great deal. (p. 263)

Standards of Critical Thinking

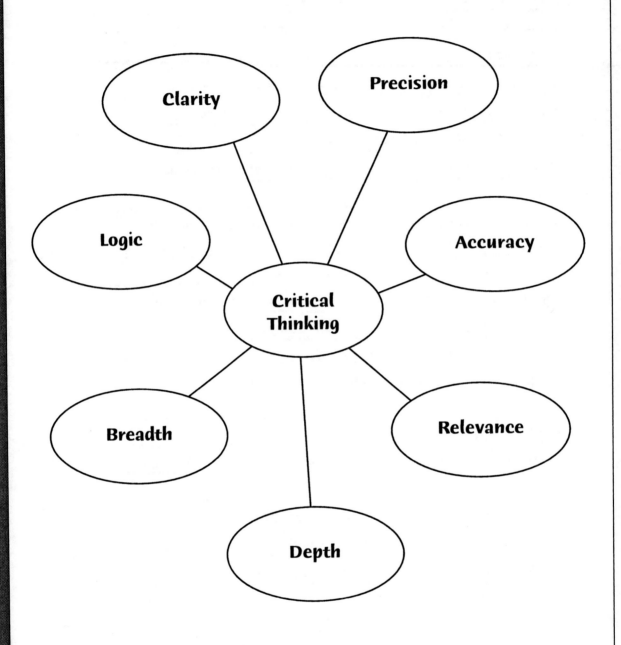

Characteristics of Critical Thinkers

Critical thinkers...

take their time when making important decisions

don't need to be right about everything

examine their own beliefs

are concerned with being fair and accurate

are willing to criticize a popular belief if it is the right thing to do

don't mind admitting that they don't know something

make sure that their beliefs are based on factual evidence

try to make sense of information, not just memorize it

make sure they understand something before they judge it

know that their point of view isn't the absolute truth

see things in shades of grey, not in black and white

give consideration to facts that contradict their beliefs

look for exceptions to generalizations

would rather find a solution that benefits everyone than get their own way

demand evidence before they will believe something

are willing to try any good idea, even if it's unpopular

know exactly why they believe or don't believe certain things

know that an idea can "feel right" but still be wrong

The Decision-Making Process

1. DEFINE THE DECISION
- Redefine problems as opportunities
- Frame the decision in several ways

2. LIST ALL POSSIBLE OPTIONS
- Brainstorm as many options as possible
- Keep an open mind
- Seek other points of view

3. GATHER INFORMATION
- Research the situation
- Seek advice from knowledgeable people

4. ASSESS THE CONSEQUENCES
- Weigh the pros and cons of each option
- Use your values and goals as standards
- Be prepared for uncertainty

5. CHOOSE ONE OPTION
- Focus on one central value or goal
- Be prepared for conflict
- Decide!

6. ACT
- Commit yourself through action
- Be prepared for regret

7. EVALUATE YOUR PROGRESS
- Learn from experience
- Prepare for new decisions down the road

Weighing Pros and Cons

Pros		
Option	Goal(s) it would support	Value(s) it would support
1.		
2.		

Cons		
Option	Goal(s) it would contradict	Value(s) it would contradict
1.		
2.		

Ingredients of Self-Discipline

FIGURE 6.1

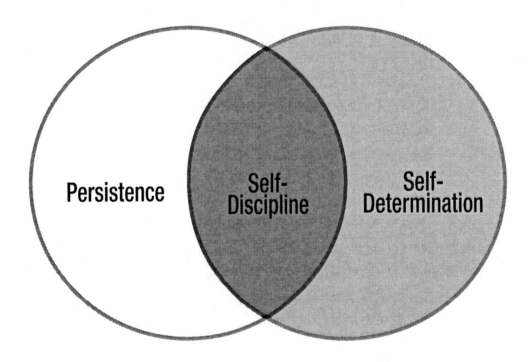

Taking Charge Self-discipline lets you control your life and make your plans and dreams a reality. *How could practicing self-discipline raise your self-esteem?*

Chapter 7 Quotes

"**T**o succeed, you need to find something to hold on to, something to motivate you, something to inspire you."

TONY DORSETT

ATHLETE

"**L**ife shrinks or expands in proportion to one's courage."

ANAÏS NIN

AUTHOR

"**Y**ou may be disappointed if you fail, but you are doomed if you don't try."

BEVERLY SILLS

SINGER

"**Y**ou gain strength, courage, and confidence by every experience in which you really stop to look fear in the face. You must do the thing which you think you cannot do."

ELEANOR ROOSEVELT

HUMANITARIAN

"**W**hatever we believe about ourselves and our ability comes true for us."

SUSAN L. TAYLOR

JOURNALIST

"**R**isk! Risk anything! Care no more for the opinion of others, for those voices. Do the hardest thing on earth for you. Act for yourself. Face the truth."

KATHERINE MANSFIELD

AUTHOR

Chapter 7 Keys to Success

Look for ways to motivate yourself. (p. 272)

Positive motivation brings you closer to your goals. (p. 273)

Lasting motivation comes from inside. (p. 275)

Aim for inner fulfillment, not outward achievements. (p. 275)

The motivation for self-improvement comes from inside. (p. 276)

Needs motivate much of human behavior. (p. 280)

Satisfying basic survival needs requires hard work. (p. 282)

We all need to feel secure in our environment. (p. 283)

Low self-esteem can crush motivation. (p. 284)

Desire and self-discipline keep you going along the tough road to your goals. (p. 289)

Fear of failure drains positive motivation. (p. 290)

You may fail, but you are never a failure. (p. 292)

Fear of success defeats your goals. (p. 295)

Having unrealistic expectations of yourself can drain your motivation. (p. 295)

Give yourself permission to make mistakes. (p. 296)

Use your success to inspire others. (p. 296)

Use visualization to harness the power of the subconscious mind. (p. 298)

Visualize yourself succeeding, and you will succeed. (p. 299)

Visualize yourself as the person you want to be. (p. 300)

Use positive self-talk again and again. (p. 300)

Intrinsic and Extrinsic Goals

Intrinsic Goals

Wealth

Fame

Physical Attractiveness

Extrinsic Goals

Satisfying Relationships

Personal Growth

Contribution to the Community

Positive and Negative Motivation

FIGURE 7.1

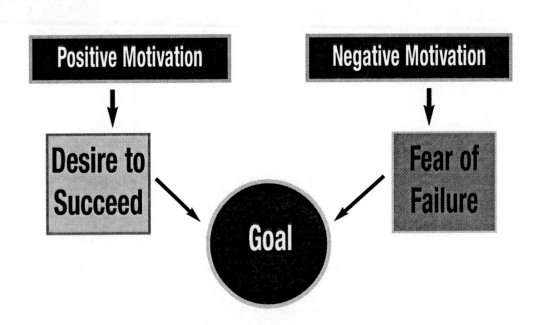

In the Right Direction Positive motivation harnesses the power of positive thoughts and feelings to move you closer to your goal. *Why do you think negative motivation is associated with low self-esteem?*

Hierarchy of Needs

FIGURE 7.2

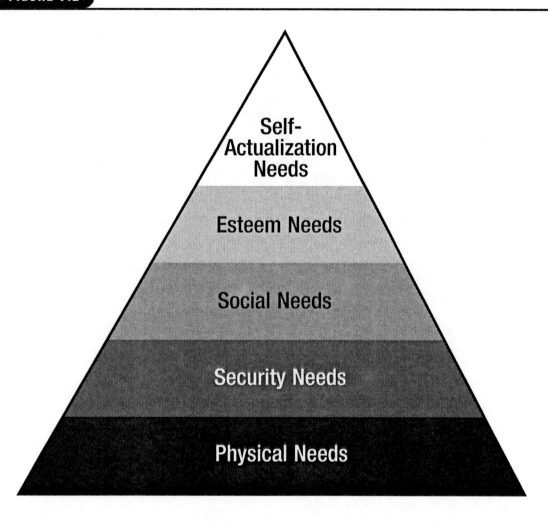

Self-
Actualization
Needs

Esteem Needs

Social Needs

Security Needs

Physical Needs

Needs as Motivators Needs motivate much of our behavior. If we are hungry, we seek food; if we are lonely, we seek companionship; if we are bored, we seek stimulation. *When might someone ignore a lower-level need in order to fulfill a higher-level need?*

Expanding the Comfort Zone

FIGURE 7.3

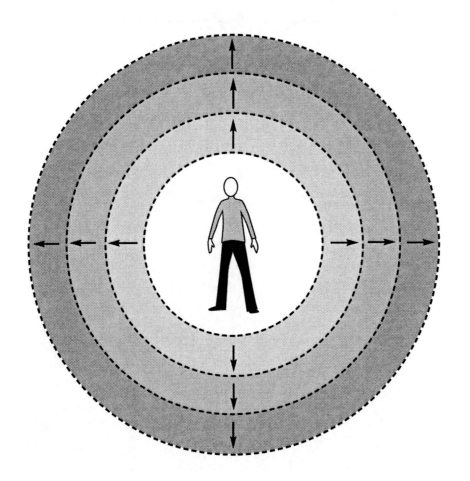

Step by Step Every time you try something new, you expand your comfort zone. *Why is it better to expand your comfort zone with small steps than with giant leaps?*

Work Motivation

Skill Variety

A job with skill variety calls on a wide range of your skills, abilities, and areas of knowledge. Instead of simply doing the same thing again and again all day, you take on different tasks and build new skills and interests.

Task Identity

Task identity refers to the degree to which a job requires completion of a whole, identifiable piece of work. A job with high task identity allows you to do a single project or task from beginning to end and to see the outcome of your work.

Task Significance

Task significance is your feeling that your work has meaning, that what you do has a positive impact on the world and on other people.

Job Feedback

Feedback is information about how well you are doing your job and how you can do better in the future. Workers are most motivated when feedback comes from the process of doing the job itself. Workers are less motivated to do a good job when all of their feedback comes from supervisors.

Autonomy

In a work context, autonomy means having freedom and decision-making power to schedule work and to determine how it will be carried out. Autonomy gives you the feeling that your supervisor respects your abilities and work ethic.

Recharging Motivation

Ellen

Ellen was a single mother of two girls, ages seven and nine. She attended night classes in accounting and worked full-time as an accounting clerk. Ellen had recently divorced, and her goal was to complete her associate degree as fast as possible so she could earn a higher salary and rent a nicer apartment with more room for her daughters. In her first semester, Ellen signed up for the maximum number of units because the courses didn't look that difficult. Since Ellen was away from home five nights a week, her daughters felt neglected and started acting out at school. Ellen was going to school for the sake of her daughters, but now they were angry at her. Ellen was intensely motivated at the beginning of the semester, but as soon as she realized how much work she would have to put in, she grew exhausted. After a few weeks she could barely force herself to crack open a textbook.

Luis

Luis had moved from Bolivia to California at the age of fourteen. In just a few short years, he had learned English and become one of his high school's top science students. With the encouragement of his career counselor, Luis decided to attend college and study computer science. The counselor helped him fill out applications and apply for loans and scholarships. But as the application deadline approached, Luis became more and more apprehensive. He still sometimes struggled with English, especially in social settings, and he wasn't fully comfortable with American culture. He pictured himself becoming socially isolated and falling behind the other students. Luis felt like giving up altogether.

Marcus

Marcus had been slightly overweight since childhood. He was accustomed to a high-fat diet and a sedentary lifestyle. Looking at himself in the mirror one day, he suddenly resolved to lose thirty pounds. Marcus pictured himself feeling fit and enjoying outdoor sports. He told himself that losing weight was just a matter of will power. Unfortunately, Marcus's kitchen was stocked with junk food, which made it practically impossible to avoid snacking. The cafeteria at work sold greasy food in enormous portions, which didn't help either. Since Marcus could barely boil water, he had no idea how to prepare healthy meals. He really wanted to reach his goal, but it seemed like food was out to get him at every turn.

Chapter 8 Quotes

"*You are good when you strive to give of yourself. Yet you are not evil when you seek gain for yourself.*"

KAHIL GIBRAN
AUTHOR

"*He who hesitates is last.*"

MAE WEST
ACTOR

"*A penny saved is a penny earned.*"

BENJAMIN FRANKLIN
AUTHOR, INVENTOR, AND POLITICIAN

"*Time is the substance from which I am made. Time is a river which carries me along, but I am the river; it is a tiger that devours me, but I am the tiger; it is a fire that consumes me, but I am the fire.*"

JORGE LUIS BORGES
AUTHOR

"*Tomorrow is often the busiest day of the week.*"

SPANISH PROVERB

"*Wealth consists not in having great possessions, but in having few wants.*"

EPICURUS
PHILOSOPHER

Chapter 8 Keys to Success

Plan ahead to spend your time doing what you value. (p. 308)

It's important to know where your time goes. (p. 309)

Make time for activities that relate to your goals. (p. 310)

Allow yourself at *least* seven hours of sleep. (p. 313)

Spend most of your time on things that are both urgent and important. (p. 313)

Spend 80 percent of your time and energy on your top priorities. (p. 315)

Make a to-do list, then stick to it. (p. 315)

Make sure you know how long each task will take. (p. 318)

Look over your schedule daily. (p. 319)

The longer you procrastinate, the larger a problem grows. (p. 322)

Divide your project into segments, then tackle just one. (p. 323)

Money helps us meet our basic needs, but it doesn't buy happiness. (p. 327)

Look at money as a tool to achieve your goals, not as a goal in itself. (p. 328)

Financial planning helps you achieve peace of mind. (p. 328)

The basic recipe for financial fitness is to spend less than you earn. (p. 329)

Lifestyle expenses add up fast. (p. 330)

Do you spend money on things that don't really matter to you? (p. 333)

Aim to save ten percent of your income. (p. 334)

Resist the temptation to overspend. (p. 338)

Shopping is an expensive hobby. (p. 339)

Devote every penny you can to paying off debt. (p. 341)

Money is a link between the present and the future. (p. 342)

Perfectionism: A Vicious Cycle

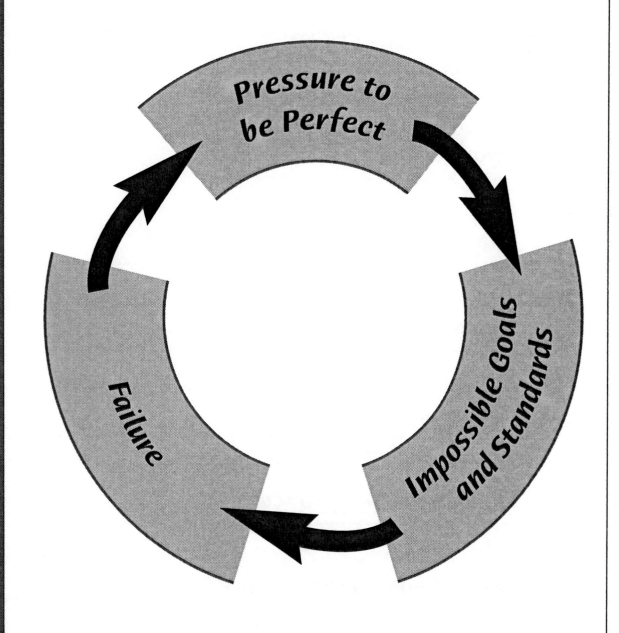

Procrastination Excuses

- *It's not due yet.*

- *I work better under pressure.*

- *I don't feel like it.*

- *It's too hard.*

- *It's boring.*

- *No one else has started yet.*

- *I don't know where to start.*

- *I don't know how.*

Where the Money Goes

FIGURE 8.1

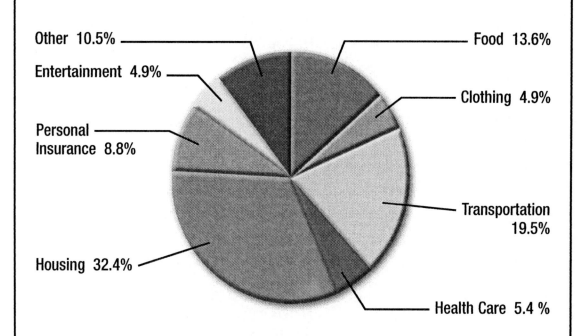

Other 10.5%

Entertainment 4.9%

Personal
Insurance 8.8%

Housing 32.4%

Food 13.6%

Clothing 4.9%

Transportation 19.5%

Health Care 5.4 %

SOURCE: Bureau of Labor Statistics, 2002.

Spending by Category Housing and transportation are Americans' biggest expenses. If you live in an area that lacks affordable housing, you may have to set aside 40 percent of your income to pay the rent or mortgage. *Why do you think that Americans' transportation costs are so high?*

Persuasive Words Used in Advertising

amazing

announcing

bargain

challenge

compare

discovery

easy

guarantee

health

hurry

improvement

introducing

love

magic

miracle

money

new

now

offer

proven

quick

remarkable

results

revolutionary

safety

save

sensational

startling

suddenly

wanted

you

Chapter 9 Quotes

"*The most important single ingredient in the formula of success is knowing how to get along with people.*"

THEODORE ROOSEVELT
POLITICIAN

"*How far you go in life depends on your being tender with the young, compassionate with the aged, sympathetic with the striving, and tolerant of the weak and strong. Because some day in your life, you will have been all of these.*"

GEORGE WASHINGTON CARVER
SCIENTIST

"*There is only one rule for being a good talker—learn to listen.*"

CHRISTOPHER MORLEY
AUTHOR

"*If you find it in your heart to care for somebody else, you will have succeeded.*"

MAYA ANGELOU
POET AND WRITER

"*To mature is in part to realize that while complete intimacy and omniscience and power cannot be had, self-transcendence, growth, and closeness to others are nevertheless within one's reach.*"

SISSELA BOK
PHILOSOPHER

"*Anger and intolerance are the twin enemies of correct understanding.*"

MAHATMA GANDHI
PHILOSOPHER AND ACTIVIST

Chapter 9 Keys to Success

Good communicators are self-aware. (p. 349)

Everyone interprets messages differently. (p. 352)

Good communication requires effort. (p. 353)

Emotional awareness helps you communicate well. (p. 353)

Words are expressions of thoughts—to speak clearly, think clearly. (p. 354)

Cultural differences affect communication. (p. 354)

Nonverbal signals often tell more than words. (p. 357)

Nonverbal cues often suggest what a person is thinking and feeling. (p. 358)

Pay attention to nonverbal cues in all five senses. (p. 358)

Our voices and bodies are powerful communication tools. (p. 360)

Men and women communicate differently. (p. 361)

Look for role models who are effective speakers. (p. 363)

Stay open to feedback of all kinds. (p. 364)

Take responsibility for your feelings. (p. 364)

Resist the urge to interrupt. (p. 366)

Think about how group norms affect your behavior. (p. 371)

When you are anxious to conform, you lose your real self. (p. 371)

Welcome diverse opinions. (p. 372)

Don't assume that the groups you belong to are better than others. (p. 374)

Positive stereotypes often mask negative feelings. (p. 374)

Be quick to empathize and slow to criticize. (p. 376)

Perform an empathy check-up on yourself. (p. 377)

Everyone is different because everyone is unique. (p. 377)

Intimacy requires time, trust, and emotional openness. (p. 378)

To build intimate relationships, you need to reveal your true self. (p. 382)

Self-awareness is crucial in relationships. (p. 383)

The more you invest in a relationship, the more you get back. (p. 383)

Conflict can strengthen a relationship. (p. 384)

Focus on solutions, not blame. (p. 386)

Elements of Communication

FIGURE 9.1

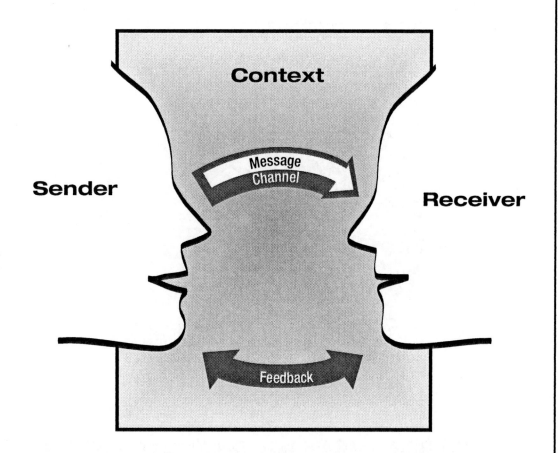

Sending and Receiving Every communication requires a sender, a message, a channel, a receiver, feedback, and a context. *Which channels of communication make it impossible for the receiver to provide feedback immediately?*

Influences on
Nonverbal Communication

FIGURE 9.2

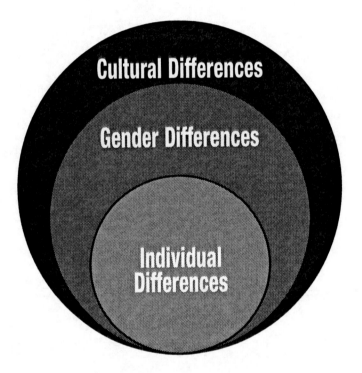

Putting It in Context Nonverbal signals are used in different ways by different cultural groups, by men and women, and by individuals. *What do you think explains the fact that women use submissive nonverbal signals more often than men do?*

The Johari Window

FIGURE 9.3

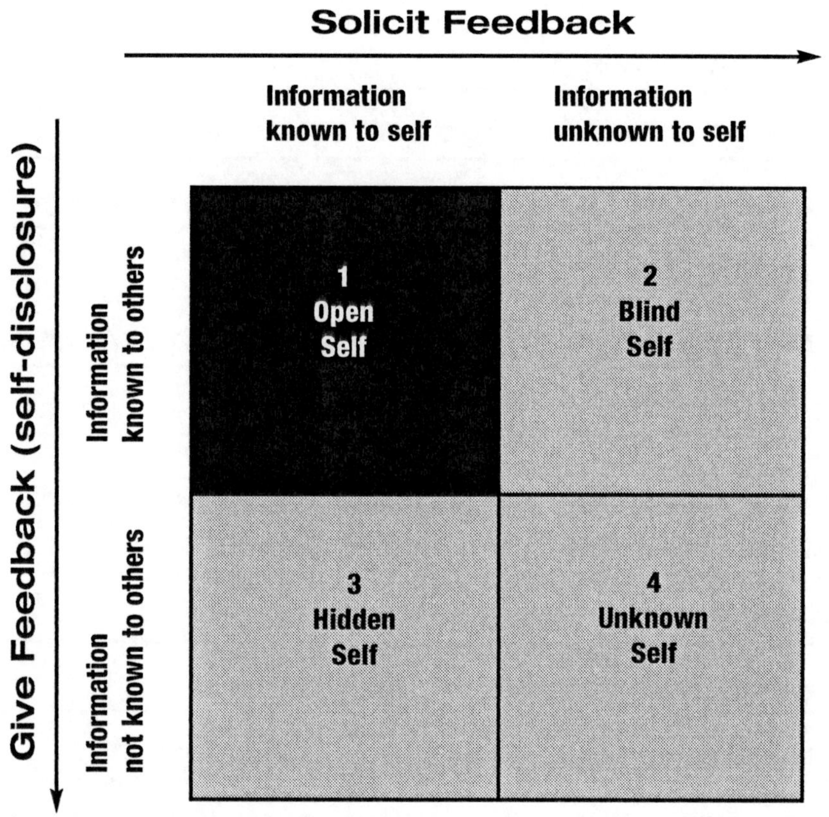

Solicit Feedback

	Information known to self	Information unknown to self
Information known to others	1 Open Self	2 Blind Self
Information not known to others	3 Hidden Self	4 Unknown Self

Give Feedback (self-disclosure)

To Disclose or Not to Disclose The Johari window shows how we understand ourselves and how we interact with others. *Which of these four selves do you think contains the most information about you? Explain.*

SOURCE: Joseph Luft, *Groups Process: Introduction to Groups Dynamics* (Palo Alto, CA: National Press, 1970).

Listening Do's and Don'ts

Which are do's and which are don'ts?

- **Giving the speaker your full attention**
  _____

- **Showing pity**
  _____

- **Leaning forward**
  _____

- **Saying "uh huh" or "go on"**
  _____

- **Restating the factual content of the message**
  _____

- **Listening for feelings, not facts**
  _____

- **Restating the emotional content of the message**
  _____

- **Restating the errors in the message**
  _____

- **Tuning out**
  _____

- **Putting yourself in the speaker's shoes**
  _____

- **Leaning back**
  _____

- **Looking the speaker in the eye**
  _____

- **Rehearsing what you are going to say**
  _____

- **Reassuring the speaker that everything will work out fine**
  _____

- **Internally relating the speaker's words to something in your experience**
  _____

- **Using "I" statements**
  _____

- **Making sure you get to speak at least half the time**
  _____

- **Listening for facts and feelings**
  _____

- **Showing empathy**
  _____

- **Using "you" statements**
  _____

- **Changing the subject to something more interesting**
  _____

Listening Do's and Don'ts
(answer key)

Listening Do's	Listening Don'ts
Giving the speaker your full attention	Showing pity
Leaning forward	Listening for feelings, not facts
Saying "uh huh" or "go on"	Restating the errors in the message
Restating the factual content of the message	Tuning out
Restating the emotional content of the message	Leaning back
Putting yourself in the speaker's shoes	Rehearsing what you are going to say
Looking the speaker in the eye	Reassuring the speaker that everything will work out fine
Internally relating the speaker's words to something in your experience	Making sure you get to speak at least half the time
Using "I" statements	Using "you" statements
Listening for facts and feelings	Changing the subject to something more interesting
Showing empathy	

Communication and Interview Success

VERBAL COMMUNICATION

Positive	Negative
Asking questions about the job and company	Not asking questions about the job or company
Listening actively	Talking excessively
Providing specific, detailed answers; relating your strengths to the job	Giving short answers with very little detail
Showing respect and a positive attitude toward others	Criticizing past employers
Speaking articulately	Speaking inarticulately

NONVERBAL COMMUNICATION

Positive	Negative
Having a professional appearance	Having an unprofessional appearance
Using calm, self-confident body language	Using nervous mannerisms
Speaking at a comfortable volume	Speaking loudly or too quietly to be heard
Displaying enthusiasm through body language, posture, and tone of voice	Displaying lack of enthusiasm through body language, posture, and tone of voice
Maintaining eye contact	Avoiding eye contact

Improving Relationships Through Communication

Write some of the good things about your relationships with the people listed. Then write some ways each relationship could be improved, and how you could use communication skills to make that improvement.

My partner

What's good: _____

What could be better: _____

Communication solution: _____

My family

What's good: _____

What could be better: _____

Communication solution: _____

My friend(s)

What's good: _____

What could be better: _____

Communication solution: _____

My instructor(s)

What's good: _____

What could be better: _____

Communication solution: _____

My coworker(s)

What's good: _____

What could be better: _____

Communication solution: _____